PELIC

CHILDREN OF THE ASHES

ROBERT JUNGK

ROBERT JUNGK

Children of the Ashes

THE STORY OF A REBIRTH

Translated by
CONSTANTINE FITZGIBBON

Penguin Books

Penguin Books Ltd, Harmondsworth, Middlesex
AUSTRALIA: Penguin Books Pty Ltd, 762 Whitehorse Road,
Mitcham, Victoria

—

Strahlen aus der Asche first published in Germany 1959
This translation first published in Great Britain by Heinemann 1961
Published in Pelican Books 1963

—

Copyright © Alfred Scherz Verlag, Bern und Stuttgart, 1959
This translation copyright © William Heinemann Ltd, London, and
Harcourt, Brace and World, Inc., New York, 1961

—

Made and printed in Great Britain
by Cox and Wyman Ltd,
London, Reading, and Fakenham
Set in Monotype Times

CONTENTS

The persons who appear in this report are real and are referred to by their proper names; some of them have made personal contributions to what follows, by means of diaries, reminiscences, and verbal statements. None of the people or the events have been invented by the author.

To those individuals who still dare to be humanists.

'Il leur a fallu se forger un art de vivre par temps de cata-
strophe, pour naître une seconde fois, et lutter ensuite, à
visage découvert, contre l'instinct de mort à l'œuvre dans
notre histoire.'

'They had to fashion for themselves an art of living in
times of catastrophe, in order to be reborn, and then
fight openly against the death-instinct at work in our
history.'

ALBERT CAMUS

Speech of Acceptance upon the Award of the Nobel Prize for
Literature, 10 December 1957.

1

Void and Chaos
(1945)

THE BOOK

1

I WAS looking for Kazuo M. and my guide was the prison chaplain, Yoshiharu Tamai. His is a narrow-chested house, 33 Ichome Ohtemachi, located only a few yards from what was once the centre of the atomic explosion. It is there that he lives and there too, whenever his heavy duties permit, he holds religious services in a meticulously clean chapel, bleached white.

This man of God, living a life of self-chosen poverty, enjoys, by reason of his vocation, a reputation among his fellow-citizens which unlocks souls that are normally closed and silent. That is why my friend and interpreter, Willie Togashi, who had accompanied me on my quest to Hiroshima, was of the opinion that the Reverend Tamai would probably be able to answer a question which I had hitherto asked in vain – namely what traces the Hiroshima catastrophe had left in the minds and souls of the survivors.

We climbed the narrow stairs to the parson's workroom. No sooner had he heard from the interpreter the nature of my request than he began to hunt through a briefcase, from which he extracted a long, already yellowing manuscript, dated 1955. This he laid upon a 'table' made of white-lacquered packing-cases, and immediately started to thumb through it.

'This is a letter written in the town prison,' Tamai explained, 'but the writer did not want the fact to be immediately apparent. Therefore he didn't give the prison as his address, but only the street number of his "home".'

The beginning of the letter, in which the writer excused himself for not having written earlier and explained that like all his fellow-prisoners he had been suffering from a temporary eye infection, was rapidly translated by Togashi. But then he suddenly stopped.

'What is it, Willie?' I asked.

He laughed, with a certain embarrassment, and said:

'It's not very friendly, what he writes next . . .'

'Not very friendly to whom?'

'Well, to tell the truth, he has some nasty things to say about Mrs Roosevelt.'

'What has Mrs Roosevelt got to do with it?'

'She must have been visiting Hiroshima just before he wrote this letter. I myself remember that she went to considerable pains to explain to us precisely why the Americans had dropped the atom bomb.'

I insisted that Togashi continue to translate the letter, no matter how embarrassing it might be for him to do so. Like all 'Westerners' visiting Hiroshima I had been astonished by the speed with which the sorely stricken population of that town had overcome all feelings of hatred. But was this attitude genuine? Now at last I was offered a glimpse of what was going on behind the 'Curtain of Politeness'.

'Actually it's only a few poems,' Willie explained. He wished to diminish their unpleasant effect in advance. 'Kazuo M. – that's the writer's name – begins by asking the parson to explain what the meaning of the word "Trinity" is. And then, only then – ' my interpreter stopped to draw breath, ' – he goes on to quote a few poems for which he had won some sort of prize in a prison competition. If you permit, I shall now do my best to translate one of these:

> *The great mushroom cloud has swallowed me –*
> *Do not look away, Mrs Roosevelt:*
> *Within its darkness lie I all my life.*

Should I read on?'

'Yes, please.'

'In the next verse he speaks of a friend, Yasuji, who died on "that day" with curses on his lips. Then another four lines addressed to Mrs Roosevelt. He asks her sarcastically if the ruins of Hiroshima were intended to serve as signposts on the road to peace. And this . . . I believe that this is what you're really looking for:

> *Not on the skin alone*
> *Suppurate pustules.*
> *Deeper are the heart wounds.*
> *Will they ever heal?'*

'Yes,' remarked the Reverend Tamai, 'Kazuo often spoke to me about his "Cheloid of the Heart" – cheloids, as you doubtless know, are what they call the great, puffy burn scars that a few survivors still carry with them to this day. In his opinion had it not been for the deep spiritual wounds inflicted upon him on the day of the *Pikadon* and in the weeks that followed immediately after, he would never have become what he now is: a murderer, and worse than a murderer – for there is no point in beating about the bush – a common thief who murdered in order to steal.'

2

A few days later I found myself seated in the office of the Educational Director of Hiroshima Prison, a certain Mr Kawasaki. The man sitting opposite me, aged about thirty, was not at all my idea of a dangerous criminal, sentenced to life imprisonment. In his simple blue prison uniform, with his fine, shaven head slightly bowed, he was more like a monk who had sought and found refuge from an over-oppressive world behind his monastery walls.

As soon as the prisoner had entered the waiting-room with its western-style plush-upholstered furniture, I had been impressed by the intelligence and sensitivity of his facial expression. During the conversation that ensued I had ample opportunity to observe the mobility of his features, unusual among Japanese, for I could not understand the words he spoke and therefore tried, from mime and gesture, to understand something of what he was saying before the interpreter gave me the translation.

At this time Kazuo M. had already been living behind prison walls for close on seven years. It seemed to me as though he had waited all this time for the opportunity of finding somebody to whom he could pour out his heart, and since the chance had at last come to speak about the events which had led him ultimately to this gloomy building, he was visibly the prey to profound and strong emotions. But whenever the interpreter turned away from the convict, in order to tell me what he had just said and to await my next question, I could see how Kazuo M. made use of this brief respite to regain his self-control and master his feelings: his face might have been twisted with hatred, anger, disgust, or shame, but gradually he would force it to display, not quite convincingly, an expression of calm, of peace, of unconcern.

I have described the personal effect that he made upon me because this was the first occasion on which I saw what I was later to come upon again and again, and far more clearly, in reports, letters, diaries, and the written answers to my questionnaires: here was a man who was trying with all his might, indeed almost desperately, to achieve mastery over himself and what had happened to him. Again and again he would jump to his feet, walk rapidly up and down the room, become upset and stop, collapse into his chair, force himself to his feet again, think to overcome his emotions but instead be overcome by them, jump up once more. . . .

He frequently recalled to my mind that naked, hairless, and eyeless horse that so many of the survivors claimed to have seen in the ruined streets of Hiroshima during the first days after the disaster. Its long skull was encrusted with blood, for it was continually colliding with the few walls and ruined houses that were still standing; it would stumble on, wandering to the irregular rhythm of its hoofbeats, now with flaring, puffing nostrils, now with sunken head, now walking, now mournfully trotting, on and on through the city as it searched for a stable that was no longer there. Some said that the animal should be shot, lest in its blindness it tread upon one of the wounded lying by the roadside and kill him. But at that time no one had the strength to do so. It is not known what happened to the horse in the end, nor where it disappeared to.

3

Nine days after the destruction of Hiroshima, Kazuo M., who had only just escaped destruction himself, wilfully destroyed the sole remaining object in his possession that had survived.

He carried out this act calmly, deliberately, with almost ceremonial gestures, yet even then his handsome, oval face must have borne that expression of gloom and hatred which was henceforth

to be noticed, or so they said, by wellnigh anyone who ever met
Kazuo M.

The victim of this first premeditated 'murder' – for so was the
deed later referred to in retrospect – was a book. And a perfectly
ordinary book at that, a reader issued to the Middle Schools, a
book which at that time every boy in the Third Form throughout
the whole of Japan had to possess.

The fourteen-year-old boy had come upon the book a few days
after the great disaster, when digging in the rubble that had once
been his parents' home. When it fell out of a half-burned rucksack he had cried aloud for joy and had pressed it to his breast, as
though it were a school friend whom he had believed dead but
who had been miraculously saved. Kazuo M. knew entire poems,
proverbs, even whole passages of prose in the reader by heart.
During the last few, terrible hours he had recited some of these
aloud as if they were magic spells, but only now, when he saw
them in black and white within the sturdy, green, speckled covers
of this volume, did he feel reassured: now he knew that on the far
side of the desolate nightmare that was the present and the
immediate past there must indeed once have existed a world of
perfected form and pure civilization.

Books and pictures, writing brushes and painter's chalks, had
always been the boy's best friends and playmates. The sensitive,
introspective child had outgrown his contemporaries. Only
Yasuji, his sole friend, could in some ways glimpse and share the
delights that the other boy found in the shimmering world of the
poets and painters.

Kazuo was torn from this life among words and drawings when
the Japanese warlords, in a last and already hopeless effort, mobi-
lized the adolescents and drafted them to work in the munition
factories. He was sent to the book-keeping department of the
Mitsubishi shipyards, about one hour's travel by tram from his
parents' home.

Even at this distance, in the suburb of Furue, miles from the
centre of the explosion, the gigantic force of the blast had been felt
and within seconds had turned everything topsy-turvy that stood
in its way. Never would Kazuo forget the flash of piercing light,
which might have been reflected from the flat of some enormous,

polished, naked sword, nor the dull reverberation far away, *Do ... doo ...* which as it drew close was transformed into a sharp, painful, and finally screeching *Ju ... inn* that seemed to pierce through his eardrums, and which culminated in a sound like a thousand thunderclaps, *Gwann!*, that hurled him into a bottomless abyss. From this derives the Japanese word *Pikadon*, for *pika* means lightning and *don* thunder. Then, like an apparition in a dream, he had seen the paper-white face of Miss Sakata.

She was hurrying as usual, a businesslike little figure who had just emerged from the boss's office, an account-sheet in her hand, and was coming through the door into the big room where the clerks worked. She suddenly stopped, her expression turning to one of annoyance as if irritated by the scene of deplorable disorder that met her eyes: the white pieces of paper whirling across the room, the telephones jolted from their cradles, the trickles of black and red Indian ink. She seemed to be on the point of turning on her heels when, with a scream of pain she could no longer control, her twisted body fell quickly forwards: a great splinter of glass, shaped like a fishtail, had pierced her back and now pinned her to the ground; it continued to vibrate, with a curious, high, and extraordinarily delicate note.

The speed with which the pool of blood spread about her; the way her hands turned blue; the senseless running hither and thither of the other secretaries, with their black hair flying loose and their normally spotless white blouses stained with blood and filth; the helpless expression on the face of the chief clerk.

'Kacho-san, you must help her! Do something. Or she'll die.' Forgetting all the rules of politeness, Kazuo had shouted this at his superior: but this man, usually so filled with energy, had simply leaned motionless against his overturned desk. He could not grasp what had happened. He did not even try to stem the flow of blood trickling down his own face from the deep wound in his forehead.

The youth was still quite numb, but apparently uninjured. He jumped up and tried to draw out the cruel glass stiletto. He cut his hands and he could no longer grip it. So he wrapped a piece of cloth about the glass, that continued to vibrate, and tugged at it with all his strength.

The glass broke in his cut hands. At least a third of it remained in the wound. Miss Sakata's mauve lips opened and closed like gills as she gasped for breath. Then a tremor passed through her body, accompanied by a rattling sound. She was dead.

4

For many years Kazuo M. dared not summon up the memory of the horrors through which he had had to live on his way from the Mitsubishi Works through the panic-filled city. He had somehow managed at last to reach the quarter below Hijiyama Hill, where he lived. He had made it on foot and in his arms he was carrying the naked corpse of Sumiko, a girl with whom he had been to school. Mortally wounded, she had attached herself to him at some point during his passage through hell. Now he found the strength somehow to burn and bury her body. And somehow he survived the days that followed. His parents, too, and his younger sister Hideko had also been almost miraculously spared. They ate cold rice, pressed into balls and distributed by emergency mobile canteens. They slept in what had been an air-raid shelter, an unlit hole in the ground. This was a time of absent-minded handshakes, of wanderings as through a maze. Hair fell out, there was nausea and shivering fevers. And the most important thing was not to think deeply about the wounds being inflicted by the unspeakable events all about. To sleep, to sleep, to sleep!

Haruo Hiyoshi was a cameraman employed by the leading Hiroshima newspaper *Chugoku Shimbun*. During those days he walked back and forth through the ruins of the desolate city, carrying his camera, but he took only a few photographs. As he explained to me later: 'I was ashamed to give permanence on film to what my eyes were then forced to see.'

If only he had mastered his honourable repugnance! Posterity would then have been given a far more adequate picture of the 'new weapon's' effect than is to be derived from those much-reproduced photographs which usually depict Hiroshima after the disaster as a desert of ruins, without human beings. For it was no quick and total death, no heart attack of a whole city, no sudden, agonizing ending that struck Hiroshima. A mercifully quick release, such as is granted even to the vilest criminals, was denied to the men, women, and children of Hiroshima. They were condemned to long-drawn-out agonies, to mutilation, to endless sickness. No, neither during the first hours nor in the days that followed was Hiroshima a silent 'graveyard', filled solely with the mute protest of the ruins, as the misleading photographs imply; rather was it the site of movements repeated a hundred thousand times, of a million agonies that filled morning, noon, and night with groans, screams, whimperings, and of crowds of cripples. All who could still run, walk, hobble, or even drag themselves along the ground were searching for something, for a few drops of water, for food, for medicine, for a doctor, for the pitiful relics of their possessions, for shelter. Or searching for the uncountable thousands who need no longer suffer, for the dead.

Even in the unending nights, beneath the bluish glow reflected from the piles of corpses that the clearance squads had stacked with military precision, this whimpering, helpless hurrying hither-and-thither never stopped.

5

On the morning of 15 August 'Announcement Teams' of military policemen drove through the vast field of ruins and broadcast the following statement: 'Attention everyone, attention. Today at twelve noon the Emperor in person will make an important announcement over the radio. All who are capable of moving should make their way to the railway station, where the Emperor's speech will be relayed over the loudspeaker system.'

It is true that Kazuo M. was extremely weak. Nevertheless, he dragged himself to the station, in order to hear what the announcement might be. For like many others he thought that the 'Tenno' was going to announce final victory. A few hundred persons, in rags, wounded, sick, leaning on sticks or crutches, were gathered on the square facing the ruined station.

From the loudspeaker there came first of all a confused medley of strange and meaningless noises. When at last the Emperor's clear, light voice became audible, it seemed to tremble, almost as though he were on the verge of tears: 'Prepare to endure the unendurable. . . .'

What had he meant? None of the audience had understood exactly what it was that he had actually said. Perhaps the faulty transmission was to blame, or the fact that the language of the court was hard for the ordinary man in the street to follow? Or perhaps it was simply impossible for their senses to grasp the meaning of a statement that they had hitherto held to be an impossibility?

The man who subsequently became Mayor of Hiroshima, Shinzo Hamai, had listened to the speech in the ruins of the Town Hall, and he recalls: 'Maybe something had gone wrong with the batteries, or with the loudspeaker itself, but in any event the broadcast was completely incomprehensible. I asked an official afterwards what it had actually been about. He answered without any apparent interest: "It seems we've lost the war." I was simply unable to believe this.'

Those who had listened to it in the square opposite the station quickly ceased to doubt. Part of the crowd broke into a storage shed in the depot where they got drunk on the stocks of rice wine that they found there. Others burst into tears, and many beat the singed ground, in despair, with their burned fists. The majority however simply slipped silently away, resigned to their fate.

Kazuo M. was one of those for whom the horrors of the immediate past only became the reality when he had heard those words. For nine days he had found consolation in the thought that the nightmare must end. Only now did his heart and mind grasp the full meaning of what his eyes had long been telling him: the world of yesterday, the world that had existed between the covers of his reader, was no more. This was the moment at which he became filled with an overwhelmingly strong compulsion: he must 'execute' that book. Not a single line of writing should be allowed to 'escape punishment'. He was determined to tear each and every one of its pages into such tiny shreds that nothing should remain legible. When anything even resembling what had happened to him on 'that day' could occur – could be allowed to occur – then all the words in his beloved reader were nothing but lies. After that, what value could be attached to thought, to knowledge? What did he care henceforth for morality, social position, the law? At the top of his voice he yelled into the vast emptiness that now surrounded him: '*Otonawa-baku!* All men are fools!'

Hundreds and hundreds of printed lines. How is it possible to press so many into so small a book? For a moment Kazuo let his hands drop to his sides, suddenly overcome by the senselessness, the pointlessness, of what he intended to do. Then from a nearby cave-dwelling in the side of Hijiyama Hill he heard the shrill and helpless cry of a little girl: '*Itai, itai!* It hurts, it hurts!' and he remembered little Sumiko, whom he had carried through the burning town.

Death to all words! To hell with them all! The tiny white scraps of paper fluttered like snowflakes to the scorched earth, a miniature blizzard that had blown weirdly into this burning August. The boy jumped to his feet and began to chase them. As he did so, he yelled crazily.

THE ATOMIC DESERT

1

THERE are deserts of sand, deserts of stone, deserts of ice. But since August 1945, Hiroshima – or more exactly the spot where Hiroshima once stood – has constituted a new, peculiar, and original sort of wilderness: an atomic desert, the handiwork of *homo sapiens*, and beneath its grey-black surface there still remain the traces of his activity and the pitiful remnants of his fellow-men.

The survivors, and the tens of thousands who lived elsewhere who had come to dig among the ruins for relatives and friends, gradually moved outwards in their search, away from the inner 'Circle of Death' until they were digging one, two, and even three miles away from the point of maximum destruction. And the Circle of Death, this evil, harrowed, desolate expanse, now lay lifeless, enclosed within the green waters of the many-mouthed River Ohta, upon whose surface, with each ebb and flow of the tide, corpses, like autumn leaves, floated now upstream, now down: strangely enough the male corpses all floated upon their backs, the female ones upon their bellies.

Only a handful of foolhardy men now ventured into this no-man's-land. They dug in the ruins, searching for any buried object that might be sold for money.

It was in little groups of three or four people that they thus searched for loot, and they soon acquired a remarkable knowledge of the terrain. They were particularly on the look-out for metals, since any form of scrap possessed a rarity value after all the years of collecting and commandeering for the metal-hungry forces of Japan. What they seached for with especial thoroughness beneath the ashes and charred beams were old bathrooms. For many a household had managed throughout all the war years to preserve its *goemon-buro*, or deep, copper hip-bath, and these were now worth almost their weight in gold.

Another explorer of this wilderness was a slender man with

moustache and spectacles who wore a white laboratory coat that did not at all go with his military cape and puttees. He too collected busily and went home each evening to his family in the fishing village of Kuba with a full rucksack and bulging haversack. But when he emptied his loot on to the *tatami* at home, it contained almost nothing that could be sold. For what he collected was simply stones, of all sorts and sizes.

Professor Shogo Nagaoka was a well-known geologist attached to Hiroshima University, and it is thus scarcely a matter of surprise that it was his custom, with pick and shovel, to search for fossils, minerals, and petrifactions. Only nowadays it was not some patch of virgin soil that he dug, but rather did he pick busily away at a place where, only a few days before, the centre of a great city had stood.

When the treasure-hunters met the scholar they always asked him the same question. Seriously meant to begin with, it had become a sort of standard joke between them. 'Why don't you join in with us, Professor? You know all this area by now like the back of your hand. Just tell us when you find metal. There'd be a fortune in it for you.'

To which Nagaoka would reply: 'Come over here, and I'll te you where I've seen some.'

Naturally it never occurred to the scholar to take the cut in the profits that they offered him. But he did ask for something in return. This was that they should hand over to him any well-preserved shadows. For that was what he was looking for above all else in the atomic desert. It is well known that the exceptionally brilliant light cast by the *Pikadon* had bleached everything it touched. Thus whenever a plant, an animal, or a human being happened to be in front of a flat surface a 'shadow' would be cast, often as clear cut as a silhouette, an unbleached area upon a whitened background. When the metal-seekers came upon the outline of a leaf, a hand, a head, on a piece of rubble they would bring it to the scholar, or would lead him to the spot. In exchange he would give them information that was of value, as for example: 'Over there, the mound of rubble beside the third tree-stump, you'll find a saucepan,' or: 'It'd be worth your while to dig in the second rubble heap on the left beyond the next cross-roads.'

2

Apart from such shadows of living creatures and of objects turned
to charcoal by the heat of the atomic flash, the professor also
collected hundreds of other specimens – materials which had not
been destroyed, but only transmuted or changed in the huge blast
furnace that had been the explosion. These included weirdly coloured earthenware tiles, bottles twisted into extraordinary shapes,
singed fragments of cloth, and an ever increasing quantity of
stones. And what stones! Stones such as existed nowhere else on
earth. In the uniquely high temperature produced by the atom
bomb they had begun to 'weep' or to 'bleed'. This was clearly
apparent when one of these stones was dissected. The deep black
centre remained intact, but part of this core had forced its way
through the light grey surface to emerge as boils or sores. It was
as if the very stones had contracted mange or leprosy. The geologist's attention had first been drawn to these abnormal mutations on the day after the disaster, when he walked through the
still burning city preoccupied only with the fate of his students
and of his collection of minerals that had been in the university.
To be precise – and I am now quoting Nagaoka, who says this
with a self-deprecatory smile – he had not at first seen the novel,
amazing, unprecedented change that had come over the stones of
Hiroshima, but rather had he felt their strange alteration.

For when he decided to collapse, exhausted, upon the base of
an old stone lantern near the ruins of the Gokoku shrine, he was
forced to jump up again at once. It was as though he had sat upon
a pin-cushion.

What he now saw was so remarkable, so unexpected, that he
automatically gave a loud cry of astonishment: the normally
smooth granite had thrust out countless tiny needles of stone. The
overpowering heat had, apparently, caused it momentarily to
melt and a wave-pattern remained, revealing the directions in
which the liquefied stone had begun to run away.

The scholar recognized at that moment, and before he knew
anything concerning the nature of the bomb that had been dropped on Hiroshima, that he was here confronted with something

absolutely new, that something must have happened which was, quite literally, astonishing, and that it was his duty to begin forthwith the study of these unusual phenomena.

Nagaoka's normal equipment consisted of a small pickaxe, such as geologists and mineralogists carry on field trips, a simple camera, and a 'dip', which is a sort of carpenter's plumb-line, with which he could measure the degree of inclination of wall remnants, gravestones, posts, and trees. This searcher among ruins also carried a few pieces of cloth or of paper in which he carefully wrapped those specimens he was taking home.

In a work* that contains hundreds of precise drawings and photographs this man of science later proved his statement that he had collected no less than 6,542 fragments of rubble within the thousand-yard-wide area beneath the epicentrum: these he described, and their places of origin were marked upon his map. Eight hundred and twenty-nine of these specimens were then subjected to a more detailed examination. The professor was thus enabled not only to describe exactly the varying degrees of liquefaction and surface mutation suffered by numerous types of stone, but also, with the help of the shadows preserved upon the stones and the use of trigonometry, to ascertain the precise height at which the bomb had exploded – something which the Americans had kept strictly secret. Stone objects such as temple walls and gravestones, already worked by the hands of men, were tossed backwards within a fraction of a second by the new weapon into the conditions that had prevailed upon earth in geological epochs long ago. Or was what he here saw and noted merely a forecast of a future in which mankind would have transformed this world into a ball of fire?

The scope of his researches was soon widened. Professor Nagaoka now began to collate everything that had any connexion with 'that day'. The geologist became an historian, or perhaps archaeologist would be a more accurate word. For he now disinterred, with the utmost care, the skeletons of the dead; like the first excavators of that ashen cemetery that had once been Pompeii, he found the dead sometimes in the posture of flight, sometimes

* Shogo Nagaoka; *The Measurement of the Hypocentre and the Landsite of the Hypocentre by the Atomic Bomb dropped on Hiroshima.*

intertwined in a last and desperate embrace. He collected clocks whose hands had stopped forever at the precise moment of the disaster, banknotes and the leaves of books carried by the fire-storm miles out into the encircling countryside. He devoted particular attention to those tiles which bore family emblems, for these were often the sole trace that such a family had ever existed. In his home the piles of fragments and remnants grew taller, memorials to a technological civilization entering the suicidal phase: ulcerated gas-cookers, bicycles turned to corkscrews, a section of a motor-car engine into which was horribly fused the skeleton hand of the mechanic who had been tinkering with it, Demiurge, surprised and turned to coke. It was a wretched heap, quite devoid of the dignity that we associate with the ruins of antiquity, grotesque memorials of perishable materials, dead and done with.

The professor came upon some forty corpses to whom he gave the last rites. He also found the first clear signs of renascent life: a thick covering of that 'railway grass' which had been imported from the U.S.A. in the previous century to cover and bind railway embankments, and seeds that were sprouting, and live pollen, and certain trumpet-shaped, red, mountain flowers such as had never before been seen in the lowlands around Hiroshima. These were growing from the mountain clay which had once been brick walls. Many years ago the seeds had been baked hard in the reddish earth that had been brought down from the mountains. Now the explosion had liberated them, while the heat and the rays had caused them to flower. Even in the pond of the destroyed castle fresh lotus flowers had sprung from the rusty-black, parched leaves.

When, as was usually the case, the professor took his family with him on these expeditions, it was their habit to stop at a place which had previously been one of the most frequented squares of the city near the tramway stop Kamiyacho. There they would build a little fire and roast the sweet potatoes of which the professor had discovered a store, each as big as a man's thumb, at the foot of a memorial commemorating the dead of the Russo-Japanese War. He could even find his sweet potatoes after dark, for nearby and for weeks on end there burned a gigantic cedar tree, a powerful beacon above the sea of ruins.

3

When Shogo Nagaoka stood at the centre of that 'Place of Suffering' whose bourns lay beyond the horizon, alone and abandoned as if he were the single, solitary survivor in a devastated world, he experienced for the first time that sentiment of being unutterably lost that the Japanese calls *sabishia*. But then he felt – as he says today – another emotion which seemed to arise from the depths of his being and which amazed him, a feeling of elation and enthusiasm, for which the Japanese word is *kangeki*. Often distressed almost to the point of despair by the horrifying incidents and details that met his eye each day, by these fragments of a man-made catastrophe, the effect upon him was equally strong when, in the course of his daily peregrinations, he came upon little examples of decency, of attempts to behave properly and according to the moral code. It might seem at first glance senseless and even comical in a gruesome sort of way, when solitary survivors or the relatives of the dead bowed low and with dignity before some empty piece of ground in honour of those who had died there, or when, as he once saw, a mourning mother searching for her daughter's remains decided at last that one mound of ash, indistinguishable from the ash all about, was what she was looking for, and ceremoniously collected this, and was satisfied. But such ceremony showed a clear intention of opposing an ethic to utterly senseless devastation, an order to a chaos.

The originality and novelty of his new activities were also a source of *kangeki* to Nagaoka, of fresh inspiration. It was as though he felt himself, here in the solitude of the atomic desert, to be cast in the role of delegate for the spirit of humanity that remembers and mourns its past while yet preparing for, and thinking out, its future. Others might mock him for his preoccupation with 'worthless old junk' when he might be hunting for valuables that he could sell and thus transform into food. Yet somebody must attempt to transmit to posterity a comprehensible vision of Hiroshima's sacrifice: one man at least must preserve this nadir of human history in such a form that it could act as a warning to those devoid of conscience or deficient in imagination.

Professor Nagaoka's house became daily more encumbered with the objects that he collected. His wife observed with distress that her clean and tidy rooms were being gradually transformed into a museum filled with rubbish that stank of burning and decay.

When, late in August, rumours that the rubble of Hiroshima was 'poisoned' grew stronger, and when the professor himself first began to show the symptoms of the radiation sickness (even though on 6 August he had been quite far away from the explosion, at Kami no siki), his wife and their eldest son insisted that the 'dangerous and infectious rubbish' be moved out of the house, at once.

There was an unusually violent difference of opinion within the Nagaoka household, and in the heat of the argument the professor went so far as to shout at his family: 'In the long run these things are more important and more valuable than you are.'

But finally he gave in, and shifted his collection out into the garden. 'I am the oppressed minority in the Nagaoka family,' he says today, with a laugh.

If the truth were told, it was something quite different that had persuaded the collector to take this step, a suspicion that there was probably an element of truth in the rumours concerning the 'poison' that lurked among the rubble. For when, on one of the first rainy days, Professor Nagaoka decided that he would develop the many photographs he had taken, he found that of twenty rolls of film only four remained intact. Radioactive rays emanating from the ash and rubble had penetrated the other sixteen, making them completely worthless.

4

Towards the end of August 1945, Kazuo M. noted in his diary: 'Many rumours current in Hiroshima. For example, that the bomb contained poison. Anybody who breathed any of this in must die within one month. All grass and all flowers will wither away.'

These rumours were almost universally believed, because many survivors who had been only slightly wounded by the *Pikadon*, or in many cases had not been hurt at all, became invalids on or about 20 August. Some of these rapidly developed the symptoms of what is today called 'radiation sickness' (when the whole body has been subjected to a massive dose of radioactivity), and died.*

Even persons who had only arrived in the city after the disaster, in order to evacuate the wounded or to search for relatives among the rubble, became seriously ill. Hence the origin of the rumour that the bomb had contained a new sort of 'poison gas'. And Dr Hachiya, the director of the Hospital for Postal Employees, has stated that there were even people who maintained that when the bomb fell they saw with their own eyes a fine white mist that moved outwards just above ground level. Another Japanese doctor, Kusano by name, later attempted to account for this phenomenon. He wrote that below and close to the epicentre, immediately after the explosion, a fantastic quantity of radio-active dust was stirred up which, in combination with the ionized air, did in fact produce an effect similar to that of poison gas. The scientists Shohno and Sakuma have pointed out that many persons engaged in rescue work must have breathed in such radia-tion-infected dust. The result was cases of suffocation, diarrhoea, vomiting, and bleeding. Thousands of people lost their hair and even their eyebrows.

* The Japanese radiation expert, Tsuzuki, observed in Hiroshima the following four stages of the 'atom-bomb sickness':

Period	Time	Symptoms	Date
Early period	Immediately after explosion and for ensuing two weeks	Acute	6–19 August (approx.)
Middle period	Third to ninth week	Subacute complications	Approx. 20 Aug.–10 Sept.
Late period	Third and fourth month	Recuperation (often only temporary)	Early Oct.– early Dec.
Subsequent period	Fifth month and later	Damage to organism	After 5 Dec. 1945

As early as the third day after the disaster a systematic study of the new sickness was begun by certain Japanese. Dr Chuta Tamagawa was a pathologist, a professor at Okayama University who also had a professorial chair in the medical faculty of Hiroshima University, which at the time in question had moved to Kotachi. As soon as he saw the first cases of this sickness, he realized that he was confronted with symptoms that had nothing in common with those of the diseases described in the medical textbooks. Post-mortem examination of persons who had died after the explosion made him more than ever convinced that this was so. Therefore as soon as he had returned to the ruined city, on 9 August, he went to see his old school friend, now head of the Health Department, and asked permission to dissect a few of the victims. It is true that at this period thousands of unburied corpses still lay among the smoking ruins; yet even relatives required a special permit before such a corpse might be cremated. Any man who did not rely on his own initiative, but instead attempted to acquire such a permit through the 'normal channels', soon found himself lost in a labyrinth of bureaucratic formality. For the few available officials who had themselves survived the disaster insisted upon the normal production of papers and proofs of identity: in the circumstances that prevailed at this time, most people were naturally quite unable to produce these documents.

So it is not hard to imagine how difficult it must have then been to acquire permission for the autopsy of unidentified corpses. Professor Tamagawa, a particularly highly-strung and short-tempered man, soon gave up the struggle and left this frustrating city where he could achieve nothing. His colleague, Dr Seishi Ohashi, was luckier. Together with the famous Japanese nuclear physicist, Yoshio Nishina, he had been flown to Hiroshima from Tokyo as early as 8 August on the orders of the War Ministry. On 21 August he submitted to his military superiors the very first medical report (based on autopsies carried out on twelve atomic victims) dealing with the 'radiation sickness'. In this he laid particular stress on the damage to the bone marrow and to the lymphatic glands caused by gamma and beta rays.

But despite the fact that 'Tenno' had already announced, days before, Japan's readiness to surrender and thus had officially declared that the war was lost, the military authorities continued to treat Dr Ohashi's highly important report as 'top secret'. The result of this was that the doctors in Hiroshima, struggling as best they could to save the lives of thousands of sick people, were compelled to rely on guesswork. Since the real nature of the radiation symptoms was unknown to them – for neither friend nor foe saw fit to instruct them concerning the biological secondary effects of the 'new bomb' – they gave their patients treatment that was quite incorrect.

Professor Imahori, a historian at Hiroshima University, sums up the situation as it then existed in the following words: 'It must unfortunately be admitted that one error after another was made in the diagnosis of the atom bomb sickness. The fact was that, from approximately 10 August on, thousands of patients were suffering from fever and the passage of blood. They were all classified as dysentery cases. The Hospital for Postal Employees set up isolation wards, in order to prevent the spread of the infection, but the number of "dysentery" cases continued to grow. The basements of the Fukuya warehouse in the centre of Hiroshima were temporarily requisitioned and designated an "Infirmary for Infectious Diseases". Each day hundreds of persons, described as dysentery cases, were transferred to this infirmary, whether they wished so or not . . . and they were isolated. By the end of August it was established that those patients were in no case infected with dysentery bacilli. . . . From then on, the medical treatment was altered, but by this time it was already too late for a very large number of them. They had died because, as the result of a false diagnosis, they had been moved from their first sick beds and, in disgusting conditions, had been locked up in this infirmary. . . .'

Meanwhile, Professor Tamagawa, originally routed by the bureaucrats, learned of a new outbreak of the strange illness on or about 20 August. He decided to return to Hiroshima. But this time he was determined that no obstructionism on the part of the officials would prevent him from getting to the root of the problem. Late on the night of 27 August he awoke his old friend and colleague (they had been students together) and told the sleepy Dr Hachiya in loud terms that brooked of no denial that he planned to carry out post-mortems, and that he proposed to do just that, whether or not the 'idiots in the local administration' gave him permission. In the course of the last few days Hachiya had formed a theory of the 'new sickness', which, however, was in some respects self-contradictory. He was therefore delighted that such assistance would be forthcoming.

'For God's sake, though, speak more softly,' he interjected. 'I thank heaven that you have come back here. There is nobody I'd be more pleased to have here at this time than yourself.'

5

A decisive though purely passive role in the gradual illumination of the obscurity surrounding the 'new sickness' was played by Midori Naka, one of the most beautiful and distinguished actresses in all Japan, famous above all for her unique performances as *La Dame aux camélias*. She was the leading lady of the well-known *Sakura tai* (Cherryblossom Company), which had been having a season in Hiroshima since the beginning of June 1945. Unfortunately, the members of the company had been living in a house that was located some seven hundred yards from the explosion centre. Thirteen of them, out of a total of seventeen, were killed there on 6 August. Four remained alive, briefly. Among these was Miss Naka.

'When it happened I was in the kitchen, since it was my turn to make breakfast for the company that morning.' Thus did she later describe what she had seen. 'I was wearing a light housecoat, coloured red and white, and had a scarf tied about my head. When a sudden white light filled the room, my first reaction was that the hot water boiler must have exploded. I immediately lost consciousness. When I came to, I was in darkness, and I gradually became aware that I was pinned beneath the ruins of the house. When I tried to work my way free, I realized that apart from my small panties I was entirely naked. I ran my hands over my face and back: I was uninjured! Only my hands and legs were slightly scratched. I ran just as I was to the river, where everything was in flames. I jumped into the water and floated downstream. After a few hundred yards some soldiers fished me out.'

Up to this point the actress's story differs only in detail from that of countless others. Its significance lies in the fact that Midori Naka, though she felt very ill, was determined to get back to Tokyo just as soon as possible. Since she was a 'public figure', a seat was found for her in one of the rare trains that were then travelling to the capital; and, again because she was so famous, the very best doctors saw her at once. As it happened, one such doctor was Masao Tsuzuki, perhaps the greatest radiation expert in Japan. Handling the case of the beautiful Midori, he was thus enabled to study for the first time the 'new sickness' from Hiroshima. Of all the Japanese doctors, he was the only one for whom this sickness was not, in fact, quite so 'new'. For, almost twenty years before, he had carried out research on the effect that 'hard Roentgen rays' produced in rabbits: and he had then observed in his laboratory animals almost all the symptoms that the Hiroshima doctors were now encountering among the many survivors of the atomic explosion.*

A report on the last days of the actress Midori Naka runs as follows:

On 16 August she entered the hospital of Tokyo University. Almost nothing remained of that facial beauty and elegance of deportment which had made her famous. In the days that followed, her black hair began to fall out, and her white corpuscle count sank to between 300 and 400 (normal count: 8,000 approx.). In the hospital everything possible was done to save this marvellous woman. She was given one blood transfusion after another. At the beginning her temperature was 37·8 centigrade and her pulse eighty. But by 21 August her temperature had risen to forty-one, and on 23 August purple patches, each as big as a pigeon's egg, appeared upon her body, to the number of twelve or thirteen. On the following day her pulse had risen to 158. Midori maintained that she felt better that morning, but a few hours later she was dead. Only a few tiny hairs still adhered to her skull. When she was lifted off her bed, even these fell out, and floated slowly to the ground. . . .

* At the annual meeting of the American Roentgen Society in May 1926 Tsuzuki gave an address, which caused a considerable stir, on the subject. It was later published in the *American Journal of Roentgenology and Radium Therapy*, with the title: 'Experimental Studies on the Biological Action of Hard Roentgen Rays.'

6

It is probable that many of the sick in Hiroshima and Nagasaki who managed to survive owed this to the fact that Midori Naka was not an unknown person and therefore did not spend her last and agonizing days as an anonymous woman in some overcrowded isolation ward at Hiroshima, but rather was under the constant supervision of the radiation expert, Masao Tsuzuki, and of the blood specialist whom he had selected to handle her case, Jui Miyake. For the course that the sickness took, and the subsequent autopsy of the actress's body, now crumpled and light as a feather, enabled Tsuzuki, who had hitherto had only second- or third-hand reports of the sufferings of the survivors in the two atom-bombed cities, to establish beyond doubt the true nature of the sickness. He immediately used all his influence to ensure that the real diagnosis and the most promising method of treating the radiation sickness be made known with all speed to the doctors in the two cities devastated by the *Pikadon*.

Tsuzuki's first action was to visit those military authorities who had carefully locked away Dr Ohashi's report in their steel safes. The infuriated doctor made it quite plain to the soldiers that this was not at all the sort of report that should be treated as a military secret. On the contrary, it was essential that everything be done so that he and his colleagues could travel to Hiroshima and there tell the truth about the sickness. As a former admiral in the Imperial Navy he was listened to with the respect due to his rank.

On 29 August Tsuzuki and the group he was taking with him boarded an overcrowded train which deposited them on the following morning in Hiroshima. A few biologists who belonged to this team had shown a certain reluctance to undertake this journey, for they were more aware than were their companions of the danger that the radiation-infected ruins of Hiroshima could still constitute to human life. Nevertheless, they had finally overcome their personal fears, and fully conscious of the risks they were running, had gone along with the others.

On 3 September 1945, at 2 p.m., on the first floor of a ruined bank, Dr Tsuzuki gave his first address to his medical colleagues practising in Hiroshima. His subject was the 'radiation sickness'.

Dr Hachiya, who had attended this meeting, has stated: 'I was surprised to find such a small audience in the lecture room. Some, it is true, had been prevented from coming by the rain, but the real explanation was that there were so few doctors in Hiroshima that their number was not enough even to half-fill the room. . . .'*

'After a few introductory remarks, Professor Tsuzuki mounted the lecture stand. The fire-blackened walls of the room provided an apposite background for his talk on the atom bomb. He began by giving his theory concerning the development of the bomb, and then went on to discuss its powers of annihilation and the nature of the injuries it could inflict. He devoted particular attention to its explosive potential, to wounds caused by the extreme heat it generated, and to the internal effects that could be attributed to its rays. Finally he spoke of the danger that these rays implied for the human body. After Dr Tsuzuki had finished his speech, Dr Miyake took the floor and made a report concerning the results achieved in autopsies carried out on patients who had died of the radiation sickness.† What he had to say corresponded almost exactly with what we had observed in our daily practice. For a while I was irritated by the thought that he should be the first to make these observations publicly. But when he described the difficulty he had had in coming to the correct conclusions, I felt that this was a friendly bond between us and him, for he had had to overcome the same difficulties that had faced us.'

In his Diary, which has subsequently become famous, Dr Hachiya does not, however, report that part of the two speeches which was perhaps of the greatest practical importance, namely advice as to how to treat the radiation sickness.

Dr Miyake announced that the patients needed an unusual degree and amount of physical rest as well as a diet rich in protein, vitamins, salt, and calcium. He made one statement which, objectively quite correct, nevertheless struck his listeners as excep-

---

* Of the 190 Hiroshima doctors, 72 were reported missing or killed after the bomb had fallen.

† As soon as he arrived in Hiroshima Dr Miyake performed a number of post-mortem examinations. From 30 August to 6 September he went almost entirely without sleep and during this period he dissected twenty-six corpses.

tionally and shockingly callous: namely that there was no purpose in attempting to cure patients whose corpuscle count had sunk beneath a certain figure, since they must die in any event. The doctors were advised to concentrate on those cases that might yet be saved.

Dr Tsuzuki laid stress on the importance of stimulating the blood-building organs and emphasized the importance of heavy dosing with vitamin C. Remarkably enough, he also recommended the burning of aromatic incense sticks. In order to explain to the doctors the effect that ionizing rays produce upon the internal organs, he compared this with the effect of the so-called poison gases. This analogy, factually inadequate and intended indeed only as a vulgar comparison, was later held against the doctor by the Occupation Authorities and contributed in no small measure to his subsequent 'dismissal' in 1947.

Accompanying the doctors through the ruins of Hiroshima was a reporter named Katashima who worked for the Japanese news agency Domei. He had lost his parents in the *Pikadon*, and, since he had found neither the time nor a place in which properly to inter the pitiful remnants of his mother and father that he had collected among the ashes, he carried these with him everywhere.

'When he hurried through the town collecting material for his newspaper reports, the bones rattled in a metal box upon his hip,' a witness has stated. This reporter now wished to cable the contents of Tsuzuki's and Miyake's lectures immediately to the Domei representative in Lisbon. For though Japan had surrendered, radio links between the Japanese press and their offices in neutral countries were still functioning. As Katashima did not feel that he was competent to draft such a report alone and without the assistance of a medical expert who possessed the requisite special knowledge, he turned to Professor Tamagawa for help. The professor, however, had reservations concerning the absolute correctness of what his colleagues had said, and thus the report remained unwritten.

'In retrospect this seems particularly regrettable,' is the opinion of the historian Imahori. 'For only a few days later further activity on the part of the Domei News Agency was forbidden by Allied Headquarters, and in October the Agency was dissolved.

From then on, the voice of Japan – and with it the results of research into the effects of the atomic bomb – was silenced, so that for five years no word of all this reached the outside world. Had this report appeared in early September 1945 . . . the whole world would have known, with horror, what hitherto unexpected consequences the atomic bomb had brought in its train. . . . Perhaps the further manufacture of such weapons would have been forbidden even then. . . . In any event an important chance was missed of influencing the global situation in a decisive manner.'

7

The M. family also began to show the painful symptoms that revealed the radiation sickness. Setsuo M. complained that his eyesight had suddenly deteriorated, his wife began to lose her hair, while little Hideko vomited several times a day. Kazuo sat for hours each day in front of the entrance that led down to the air-raid shelter and stared out over the vast field of rubble. Later he attempted to recapture his mood, as it had then been, in a poem that he sent me:

> It rains and rains,
> In the slanting rain I sit,
> It drums upon my naked skull,
> It drips across my singed eyebrows,
> It runs into that bleeding hole, my mouth.
>
> Rain on my wounded shoulders,
> Rain in my lacerated heart.
> Rain, rain, rain,
> Wherefore do I live on?

Doctors practising in Hiroshima at the time have recorded that a second phase now set in, after the first period of desperate and confused activity that followed immediately upon the *Pikadon*; many survivors now gave an impression of utter apathy and showed no wish to go on living. This symptom they called

Muyoku-ganbo, and when they noted in a very sick patient's face an expression of listlessness increasing with each passing day, then they knew that there was no longer any hope of saving this particular life.

An eyewitness, the poetess Yoko Ohta, has described this condition: 'Each of us had for a time done everything possible, without knowing for sure what exactly it was that we were doing. Then we awoke, and now we wished to speak no more. Even the sheepdogs that roamed about ceased to bark. The trees, the plants, all that lived, seemed numb, without movement or colour. Hiroshima did not somehow resemble a city destroyed by war, but rather a fragment of a world that was ending. Mankind had destroyed itself, and the survivors now felt as though they were suicides who had failed. Thus the "expression of wanting nothing more" came to be seen upon our faces.'

A stubborn rumour continued to circulate: owing to the presence of 'poison gas' the soil on which Hiroshima had stood would remain uninhabitable for one or two generations. It was said that neither fauna nor flora could live here in the immediate future. True, since the *Pikadon* countless wild flowers had bloomed with a luxuriance never known before, while grasses and weeds were springing up everywhere, but this unbridled outburst of fertility was regarded by the populace as merely the last and final expression of the will to live, as a sort of euphoria on the part of nature. When early in September American newspapermen first arrived in Hiroshima, they were asked over and over again whether this 'poison gas' story was true. Unfortunately, since they lacked the technical knowledge, they were unable to deny it categorically, and thus the rumour gained renewed currency.

One of the few people who refused to believe that Hiroshima's soil had been 'poisoned' for at least seventy-five years was Kazuo's father, Setsuo M.

This proud and wiry little man had long suffered from the fact that the army had categorized him as medically unfit because he was so small and so short-sighted. Now he saw his chance of showing his fellow-citizens what sort of a man he really was, one of the few who would never accept defeat. To all who would listen, and to those who wouldn't as well, Setsuo M. announced in a loud voice: 'Even if all the world maintains that our town has become uninhabitable, my family and I intend to see it out here.' Or, in more flowery language: 'We shall put fear to flight, and transform the City of Death into a City of Life.'

The reserved Kazuo had little time for such flamboyant turns of phrase, yet he could not help feeling a certain admiration for his stubborn father. Now for the first time he understood what the neighbours had meant when they described M. senior as 'a fanatical fool'. Did this description not carry with it the implication that they themselves lacked his complete readiness for self-sacrifice and total commitment, and that they were aware of this?

Certainly Setsuo M. had never tried to 'fix' matters to his own advantage. When he had to close up his little business, because one of the countless war economy decrees declared that the sale and repair of gramophones was a 'luxury' enterprise and as such no longer permitted, he had not only accepted this order, which spelled the ruin of his professional existence, without the slightest murmur, but even appeared to be delighted by the news. For thenceforth this passionate patriot was able to devote his entire time and energy to an activity which had at least a distant resemblance to soldiering: he was an air-raid warden.

And he carried out his duties as such so enthusiastically that he had no time for anything else. As a result, the family M., after having exhausted their slender savings, sank into the most dire poverty. 'Father often quite forgot to provide any housekeeping money at all. Then Mother had to remind him, with tears in her eyes, that he had certain responsibilities towards his family which he ought also to fulfil.' Thus speaks Kazuo.

But, as is well known, Hiroshima, that sector of the 'internal front' where the keen and enthusiastic air-raid warden Setsuo M. stood guard, was for a long time spared the impact of war. While the United States Air Force was reducing one Japanese town after another to cinders and ashes, Hiroshima, for reasons that then seemed incomprehensible, remained untouched. The inhabitants hoped that the many emigrants from their city who now lived in Hawaii and the U.S.A. had somehow arranged that the city of their origin should be spared.

The first time that Setsuo M. saw 'action' on a large scale was less than two weeks before the atomic attack. For on 25 July, in view of experience gained from the holocausts when other cities had been plastered with napalm, it was decided to cut broad fire-breaks across the middle of Hiroshima, which involved the demolition of many hundreds of houses. Warden M. was ordered to clear in the most thorough fashion, the area about the Army Supply Depot. One of the hundred-odd houses that fell victim to this order was his own – a fact, however, that seemed to fill Kazuo's father with delight rather than distress, since this enabled him at last to make a visible sacrifice in his country's cause.

The family M. had thenceforth found lodgings in the house of another air-raid warden, a change, as Kazuo recalls, that filled his mother with anxious forebodings. There is a Japanese proverb which says: 'When three houses stand together, live not in the middle.' Yet what happened subsequently quite disproved this saying. The two neighbouring houses were smashed by the atom bomb into wooden splinters, while the one in the centre was to a certain extent sheltered by the other two and was only crushed and twisted 'like a sweet pretzel [*tankiri*]'. No member of the family M. was buried beneath the rubble. The worst they suffered were minor abrasions.

According to Japanese popular wisdom there are three con-ditions that man must fear above all else: the anger of the earth (earthquakes), the anger of the sky (thunder and lightning), and a father's anger. Setsuo M. was such a father, feared by his son Kazuo. Indeed he was if anything even more strict than was customary, owing to the fact that his son had been born on 11 February, which date is the most solemn festival of Imperial Japan. Two thousand five hundred and ninety years before Kazuo's birth the Emperor Jimmu had founded Japan, or so the history books said. The fact that the alleged birthday of his country and the actual birthday of his son fell on the same date filled Setsuo M. (who secretly regarded himself as a failure) with pride and high hopes. His sole male heir was expected to live up to the one and fulfil the other.

'High time you stopped mourning! Don't give in like this! Come on, help me build our new home!' With such exhortations, constantly repeated, Setsuo succeeded at last in making his son shake off the apathy and the longing for death that had weighed him down ever since the surrender. Reluctantly at first, but later with a sort of enthusiastic frenzy, Kazuo had obeyed his father's orders.

'They're mad!' passers-by would remark, as they observed father and son busily clearing their building site, while carefully laying aside charred beams that might yet be useful. They said the same when they saw the first, strong, wooden supports being driven into the ground. They were still saying it when Kazuo and his father were working on the roof of their new home. A note of triumph is detectable when Kazuo M. writes: 'As early as the thirty-second day our building stood, created from the materials that we had found on the charred ground. This was Hiroshima's "New Building No. 1".'

When the family first lay down to sleep under their new roof, Hideko whispered to her brother: 'Look, *Niisan* [elder brother], the stars are twinkling through the cracks in the roof.'

And Kazuo replied sarcastically: 'You've got the Americans to thank for your heavenly new house.'

8

When on the third day after the bombardment Dr Michihiko Hachiya looked through the holes in the wall that had once been the windows of his hospital, a sight met his eyes which he has described in the following words:

'Looking east, south, and west, was an unobstructed view of Hiroshima, and in Hiroshima Bay we could see the island Nino-shima. Near the centre of the city, some fifteen hundred metres distant, one could see the blackened ruins of the two largest buildings in Hiroshima, the Fukuya Department Store and the Chugoku Press Building. Hijiyama, the sacred and beautiful mountain in the eastern sector of the city, looked almost close enough to touch. To our north no buildings remained. For the first time, I could understand what my friends had meant when they said Hiroshima was destroyed.'

Any person who today should glance through the files of the principal local newspaper, the *Chugoku Shimbun*, must note with amazement the speed with which life began to pulsate again through those parts of the devastated city that surrounded the actual 'atomic desert'. Contrary to all the dictates of common sense, tens of thousands clung to the rubble-strewn patches of soil where once their homes had stood. Each day more and more people who had fled returned to the city; their number exceeded those who now moved away. The local newspaper itself provided the best example of this unqualified will that life must go on, a will that, to begin with, resided only in a handful of individuals. Already on 9 August, that is to say, three days after the catastrophe, the newspaper was again being delivered to its subscribers, wherever and whenever these could be found. It is true that this paper was in fact either the *Asahi* or the *Mainichi*, printed in neighbouring cities and brought to Hiroshima for distribution there: however, as a gesture of solidarity with, and help for, the stricken cities, these special editions were called (and bore the city of) the *Chugoku Shimbun*. Meanwhile, those members of that newspaper's staff who survived were struggling indefatigably in the shell of their almost totally burned-out building to bring out their own paper as soon as possible. Their first attempt to produce an emergency edition, using the presses of the small printing firm Sagawa, came to nothing owing to the intervention of the Provincial Chief of Staff, Major-General Matsumara, who assumed the role of local censor. Four members of the *Chugoku Shimbun* editorial staff therefore became for a while town-criers. Equipped with megaphones, they shouted the more important local news and announcements from the back of lorries.

Fortunately a gigantic rotary press had been carefully stored for safety in the little village of Nukushina, some three miles from Hiroshima. But neither the walls nor the windows of the old factory building in which it lay had withstood the distant blast effect of the *Pikadon*. The press was protected by three large army tents, with its most delicate elements wrapped in sacking. A major operation was now undertaken by the printers, electricians, mechanics, clerks, and editorial staff with the help of a number of casual labourers: first a printing house of a temporary nature was built; then electric current was provided over specially laid lines on rapidly constructed poles; when after many a fruitless attempt the cylinders of the press one evening gave their customary rumble and began slowly to tremble and to turn, the entire staff raised a glass of illegally brewed spirits ('*Suri*') and there and then, in the moonlight, drank a toast to the future of Hiroshima.

As early as 31 August, less than three weeks after the *Pikadon*, the first locally produced and locally printed post-war edition of the *Chugoku Shimbun* was on sale in the streets of Hiroshima. Thenceforth it appeared regularly, with advertisements and even, as in the old days, illustrations. 'Our darkroom was an air-raid shelter dug into the hillside,' one of the editors remembers, from the heroic days in Nukushina: 'but our type had to be cast in the open air, under the sunny sky. The final results of these two operations were remarkably similar: pictures and texts were scarcely to be told apart, for the whole page emerged from the press more or less black on black. On rainy days we had to go without our pictures. Before being used, the rolls of newsprint were beaten with wet bamboo sticks, and then dried over charcoal fires. . . .'

On 4 September 1945 the *Chugoku Shimbun* announced that the distribution of free, emergency rations was ending and that twenty-four temporary Food Offices were being set up.

On 7 September the newspaper reported for the first time the population figure for the municipal area of the city. It then stood at 130,000 compared with 390,000, inclusive of soldiers in garrison and evacuees, who had lived there before the catastrophe. Three days later the partial reintroduction of the electricity service was announced, and on 13 September it was stated that the city administration would provide building materials gratis to all whose houses had been totally demolished. And indeed the little municipal forest called Koganeyama was felled with all speed, the tree-trunks sawn up, and the planks distributed to all who asked for them – a vitally important and courageous measure, but one for which in years to come no official would accept the responsibility, for certain local politicians were later to complain that the wood had been distributed without 'any properly constituted authority' and therefore 'illegally'.

A powerful spur was given to this first phase of the rebuilding by the impending autumnal equinox, which usually sets in at the beginning of September in those regions with much rain and fierce storms. Sometimes this period of bad weather breaks even earlier, in the midst of summer. But August 1945 was a comparatively dry month, and the occasional gentle showers that fell were greeted by the people camping among the ruins as a relief, for they banished, at least for the time being, the great clouds of gnats and flies that settled alike on the living and on the corpses still rotting amidst the rubble and splinters.

In any event new and rapidly constructed huts began to arise, almost always at a respectful distance from the devastated city centre. While at the end of the year the population inhabiting the 'Circle of Hell' amounted to only 3·1 per cent of those who had lived there before, all the outlying districts were completely overcrowded. Up to two miles from the centre of the explosion the human density was 128·5 per cent of what it had been in the 'pre-atomic age'; beyond that distance the figure rose to 181·6 per cent, that is to say almost twice as many people were living in the suburbs as before.

In some of these outlying districts there had long lived thousands of persons regarded by their fellow citizens as 'unclean' for some reason or other, and therefore cut off from the rest of the population and banished to special areas. Hiroshima had an unusually large number of these ghettoes, known as *buraku*, because for hundreds of years this had been one of the high places of Buddhism: in this religious atmosphere, a great deal of the daily work was carried out by these unclean people called *eta* (literally 'filth'), since devout believers, following the letter of their law, refused to soil their hands by engaging in such tasks as the slaughter of beasts, the tanning of leather, or the removal and disposal of refuse. The horror inspired by these unfortunate 'unclean' persons was such that it was regarded as a defilement even to utter their name. Instead the four fingers of one hand were held erect, a gesture that identified the *eta* with four-legged creatures, thus reducing them to the status of animals.

It was a sort of compensating justice that these outcasts, huddled in their *burakus*, should have suffered less than the other inhabitants of Hiroshima from the *Pikadon*, simply owing to the fact that they had been banished as far as possible from the city centre. Overnight they had become a privileged class, for they at least still had a roof over their heads.

For the first time in centuries the walls of religiously inspired caste distinction trembled. In the nineteenth century the State had passed laws giving the *eta* complete civic equality; what had remained a dead letter now suddenly became the reality. Fugitives from Hiroshima found refuge in the *eta* ghettoes of Minami, Misasa, and Fukushima in the northern, central, and southern quarters. Meanwhile for the first time certain enterprising inhabitants of the *burakus* dared to venture into the devastated and temporarily deserted city centre, with the intention of making a living there.

Yet in exact proportion to the rise of Hiroshima from the ashes and the chaos that had prevailed during those first weeks, and to the recreation of a settled order of life, so the old walls of prejudice and contempt rose again about the *eta*. For a moment it had seemed as though this frightful new weapon had left one good legacy behind, in the emancipation of the *eta*. It had, it is true, caused the dividing wall to tremble, but it had not succeeded in knocking it down. Not even an atom bomb was strong enough for this.

9

With the onset of the colder weather, which began early in September, the local authorities of Hiroshima found themselves confronted with an urgent problem: how were they to clothe over one hundred thousand people who, with a few exceptions, had literally saved only their naked lives? During the hot weather they had got by with only a few rags and bare feet, but now to all the other problems there were added illnesses due to the cold. Many peoples were so weakened that a single chill was enough to carry them off in a few days.

A rumour circulated among the populace that, since Hiroshima had been a garrison town and also, during the war, the main port of embarkation for all troop transports bound for the South-East Asian fronts, there were huge stocks of military supplies of every sort hidden in the surrounding countryside. Enterprising persons had already discovered one or two small supply dumps. Many a man who had got a good tip from a supply officer, and who was able to organize the necessary transport with which to move the stock, laid at that time the foundation of a substantial post-war fortune. Thus for example what is now Hiroshima's leading shoe shop acquired its original stock (and with it a sort of monopoly that lasted for several months) from just such a treasure trove.

The task of taking over such stocks and depots as had not yet been looted, and ensuring their proper distribution among the populace, fell to Shinzo Hamai, a municipal official who had proved his abilities in the critical days that followed the dropping of the bomb. Catastrophes, like wars and revolutions, will suddenly thrust hitherto unknown men into high office and make them the leaders of their threatened society. Thus this open-faced, clean-shaven, broad-shouldered man in his thirties, of whom scarcely anyone outside official circles had heard before 6 August, became overnight the most important man in Hiroshima; this was due not only to the power inherent in his office, but also to his great energy and high ability.

The representatives of the regional authority and of the General Staff had either been killed or had fled in panic to the Tamonin Temple on the outskirts of the city, where they sat debating how best to overcome the unprecedented horror and chaos. Not so Hamai. Leaving them to their despair, he fought his way back into the city, which was still in flames, and reached the seat of government, in the Town Hall, where he installed himself in the only two remaining rooms that were not completely in ruins. From there for days on end he, and he alone, 'ruled' the city. On Hamai's initiative, emergency cookhouses were established overnight in the surrounding villages. Then he had set about at once arranging for new sources of supply. He was lucky. In the harbour he discovered a tanker entirely filled with vegetable oil: he found a gigantic refrigeration warehouse filled with edibles that were in danger of going bad as a result of the electricity breakdown, and after overcoming stubborn resistance on the part of the bureaucrats he 'liberated' its contents. He dashed hither and thither, an improvised and improvising field-marshal in the fight against hunger and thirst.

His keenest helpers were the officer cadets attending a tank school in the port area called Ujina. When first Hamai had asked them to help in the distribution of foodstuffs, their immediate answer had been that that was no concern of theirs. They were attending this school solely in order to learn the tactics of motorized warfare. The supply chief, however, refused to be fobbed off with this, and simply requisitioned the school and all its transport. The frustrated armoured corps heroes ended by taking to their new work with such enthusiasm that their joy at their supply 'victory' even seemed to have banished the sadness of the defeat itself. Their cry, 'Don't worry, we'll soon be back with more', brought immeasurable relief to the dying and the sick during those first chaotic days that followed the catastrophe, and sounded like a clarion call of encouragement in the ears of the others.

With his customary optimism Hamai now tackled his new task of clothing the 130,000 survivors of Hiroshima. He had no trouble in persuading the military authorities that they divulge to him where the hidden supply depots were located. But they also made plain to him, and at once, that this did not mean his difficulties were over.

'We've got underclothes, socks, boots, uniforms, and all the rest needed to clothe a soldier completely, enough indeed for a hundred thousand men, at no great distance from Saijo,' they told him. 'We should be delighted if you requisitioned it at once, since otherwise the Army of Occupation will only seize it as legitimate spoils of war. Just go and take it. Only how you plan to transport all that stuff into the city is another problem, your problem.'

In view of the extreme shortage of petrol, there could be no question of transporting such vast stocks to Hiroshima by road. So Hamai turned to the local railway administration. There they shook their heads: 'You'll need at least thirty goods trucks. We can't supply you with half that number.'

In the old days Hamai had avoided arguments. In the period after the disaster he had discovered that he possessed an unknown talent, the ability to convince others. By skilful argument or stubborn and deliberate silence he had hitherto always achieved his ends. And now, once again, he succeeded slowly in bringing the men responsible for the Saijo Railway round to his way of thinking. 'Right!' they said at last. 'Somehow or other we'll see to it that you get the trucks you need.'

They may have assumed that he would find it impossible to transport this huge mountain of clothing from the depot to the railway station within the time foreseen. For the dump where the clothing and much else as well were stored was a long way from the station, many miles inland, in the mountains, near a little village by the name of Kawakami.

'If I were you, I'd just give up,' said Lieutenant F., under whose administration that essential depot lay. He too was trying to frighten away the man from Hiroshima with his tiresome requests for help. 'How do you imagine you're going to set about it, young man? It took six hundred strong soldiers all of six months to transport that stuff up here. And you want to get it all moved down again in the brief period before the cold weather begins. It's unthinkable.' When Hamai showed absolutely no sign of being discouraged or indeed in any way moved by this argument, the officer lost his temper: 'Just in case it hasn't been drawn to your attention, I think I should tell you that we happen to have lost the war! What you are proposing to do is neither more or less than a pure waste of extremely valuable manpower.'

Then he turned sharply on his heel and with his back to his visitor proceeded to gaze out of the window. For him the conversation was over.

Hamai said not a word. He quoted the old proverb to himself: 'He who talks to one who is silent is soon stripped naked. . . .' and awaited the next outburst. With him waited the tens of thousands urgently in need of the clothes that would enable them to survive the coming winter.

The officer's next action was truly unexpected. With a stiff and awkward gesture he drew his revolver and released the safety catch. Hamai instinctively took a step backwards and quickly wondered where in this room he could take cover. But Lieutenant F. did not even turn towards him. Instead he began to fire his revolver wildly out of the window.

This conversation was taking place in the Administration Building of Saijo Agricultural College, most of which had been requisitioned by the army. Beneath the office in which the two men stood lay the open-air gymnasium. And when Hamai attempted to see what it was the excited soldier was firing at, he saw between the parallel bars and other gymnastic equipment huge piles of coats, trousers, greatcoats. It was into these that the lieutenant went on firing until he was out of ammunition.

Only then did he turn towards his visitor once again. His long, mongoloid face now bore an expression of despair rather than of anger: 'Don't you understand? I can't simply hand all this stuff over to you. Is it not possible that one of these days we might start to fight again? And you expect me to give up all this equipment without a word? Why, even the girls who work in the offices here have sworn that they want to continue the struggle to the bitter end.'

He was completely spent now. Unsure of himself, his mind apparently a blank, he stood there playing with his pistol. And when next he spoke, it was in a broken voice. He was close to tears. Even his last gesture of defiance at the defeat had come to nothing.

''We have done without so much, willingly, eagerly,' he murmured reluctantly. 'For years and years and years. And now we are told it was all in vain!' At last he tried to pull himself together. 'All right. At least something will have been achieved if we can help the people of Hiroshima. Maybe in years to come we shall once again need every Japanese. It will be a tremendous job, lugging all this stuff down to the railway. But you can rely on me, I shan't put any more obstacles in your way.'

Hamai very quickly found helpers for the transportation. Forestry students from Saijo soon moved the 'Treasure of Kawakami' down to the railway line, using for this purpose handcarts, peasants' wagons, bicycles, and even prams. So at least half the shirts, furs, caps, sandals, jackboots, coats, and blankets reached the freezing inhabitants of Hiroshima just before the bad weather set in. Meanwhile Hamai had found and 'liberated' – this time with no trouble – another supply dump; this one belonged to the

Navy, and its contents had been destined for the war in the South-West Pacific. He distributed them.

That is why strangers who visited Hiroshima at this time reported that the entire population was playing at soldiers. For not only the men but also the girls, the old people, the pregnant women, the children, and even the tiny tots were all wearing brand-new, often fantastically tailored but nevertheless practical and recognizable uniforms. Thus did the tragedy of Japanese militarism end inadvertently on this note of travesty, of fancy dress. Even cripples and those whose faces bore the sign of forthcoming atomic death were part of the masquerade.

Almost everywhere else in Japan anybody who had ever worn a uniform was busy getting rid of this compromising clothing, for fear lest he be imprisoned by the expected foreign Occupation Forces or be made to stand trial for crimes of violence committed against the enemy or the civilian population in formerly Japanese-occupied territories. But in Hiroshima the atom-bombed civilian had no fear of wearing the compromising khaki that yesterday had struck terror into the hearts of all Asians and was now a source of terror to its Japanese wearers themselves. It almost seemed as though the survivors of the *Pikadon* felt that by passing through its searing fire they had become purged of all guilt.

Particularly valuable were the high jackboots, themselves the quintessential symbol of an age that was over. For the autumnal rains had set in at full flood. The pathways between the huts and across the expanse of ruins were pitted with holes, and the ash everywhere was quickly transformed into blackish slime.

AFTER THE DELUGE

1

THE literal translation of Hiroshima is broad (*hiro*) island (*shima*). The centre of the city has always lain upon an island encircled by the two principal arms of the seven-mouthed River Ohta. The other city districts gradually came into existence upon land reclaimed from the river and the sea. Being so low-lying, these delta lands have always been liable to flooding when the river overflows its banks. Almost every other year the waters roaring down from the mountains after the rainy season would break the dykes and in the bad years this would coincide with mountainous seas, whipped by typhoons, pouring into the areas that lay below sea level.

The worst of these catastrophic floods had occurred on 6 August 1653. Even before the fateful year 1945, 6 August had therefore always been a date that evoked tragedy and misfortune for the citizens of Hiroshima. On that day in the seventeenth century hundreds of houses and all the bridges had been washed away. Records showed that only one locality then escaped, the 'Carp Castle' on its hillock, which was then the seat of the local feudal lord, one Asano. The populace on that occasion was saved from starvation by the action of that prince in opening his supply stores; for weeks on end he fed his people from his private reserves of rice. But even these floods must have been far less terrible than the one that burst upon the unfortunate city only six weeks after its annihilation by the atomic bomb. For days a light rain had been falling, with rarely an intermission; on 17 September 1945 this became a cloudburst; and by the afternoon a storm was blowing which increased in strength hour by hour, until midnight.

The municipal electricity works, which had resumed functioning only a week before, broke down. In the pitch darkness almost all the newly-built houses or shacks that had been quickly put together were either blown over by the hurricane or washed away by the water.

The darkness was still filled with shouts for help and cries of fear when, at one a.m. on 19 September, a weird, torchlit procession began to wind its way from the fishing village of Kuba. On his peregrinations through the ruined city Professor Nagaoka had found, not far from what had once been the Mitsubishi works, splinters of a peculiar sort of synthetic glass, destined for the pilot's cockpits of military aeroplanes. Since he knew that this material burned well, even in a high wind, he now used it as storm lanterns. Dozens of men were soon on their way to Hiroshima, carrying these torches.

The Professor hoped that he would be in time to reach his daughter's house, twenty miles away, where he had stored a valuable library of books dealing with his special subject, geology, as well as his unique collection of minerals. When he approached the house, as dawn was breaking, he saw books floating away on the river's waves. Nevertheless he had arrived just in time to save several microscopes as well as the greater part of his library.

Such luck in misfortune was granted to only a minority among the population of Hiroshima. Thousands lost in the great flood those few possessions that had survived the atom bomb. Houses on the water's edge were, almost without exception, washed away. While the *Pikadon* had destroyed only ten bridges, a further twenty were now rendered impassable, and the various city quarters were effectively severed from one another.

Even Shinzo Hamai, who in the weeks following the first disaster had by his example saved so many from despair, lost courage in face of this new misfortune. When he stepped out on to the flat roof of the Town Hall and gazed across the city, for the first time he felt himself overwhelmed by a profound hopelessness.

'The city looked like a huge lake,' he remembers. 'Beneath its waves it was possible to detect tiled roofs and the outline of much else as well. I felt as though this were the final burial! For what reason had the citizens of Hiroshima been condemned to such frightful sufferings? Suppose the flood waters were never to recede, and it were all to remain drowned forever? In that case, I thought, so much the better. I said this to myself in all seriousness.'

2

Yet the sorely and doubly tried people of Hiroshima dealt with the results of the great flood far more quickly than Hamai, in his access of despair, had guessed. After all, this disaster was, so to speak, a normal, natural catastrophe, a blow of fate of a sort to which the populace had grown accustomed through the centuries. This was something with which they could cope! The inundations left a legacy of dead, wounded, and sick, but did so according to certain rules which were comprehensible and which inflicted no such terrible scars. For as far back as human memory went, the inhabitants of this water-girt city had learned how to deal with the damage left behind by roaring floods and angry seas. On the other hand, when faced with the unexpectedly protracted and variable after-effects of the bomb – and almost everyone was so affected, to a greater or lesser degree – they were bewildered, confused, and lost.

Shinzo Hamai himself was now compelled, several weeks after the *Pikadon*, to seek medical attention. He had suffered only a negligible foot wound on 6 August, but it stubbornly refused to heal. Fortunately, the doctor whom he consulted had attended Professor Tsuzuki's lecture and therefore knew how to treat his patient.

When the doctor had detected a marked fall in the white corpuscle content of Hamai's blood, he ordered the supply chief to take a thorough rest. He was to go up-country, and have a lot of sleep and a highly nourishing diet. Such a cure was usually effective in minor cases of the sickness, and Hamai was soon on his feet again. In more serious cases medical treatment remained, as before, useless. Through the whole of the year following the *Pikadon*, the monthly death-rate in Hiroshima varied between ten and twenty times what it had been before the catastrophe.

During the second half of September a new worry came to plague the survivors. Early in the following month, on 3 October, the first foreign troops of the Army of Occupation were to move into the region. These would be Americans to begin with, followed by Australians.* Indoctrinated for years with the Government's atrocity propaganda and nourished for centuries on the inevitable legends concerning foreigners that resulted from Japan's isolationist policy, the people of Hiroshima really believed that the soldiers who were due to arrive so soon would in fact be devils in human shape. Horrible rumours of what they might expect at the hands of these 'devils' were scarcely modified by the fact that the representatives of the Allied armed forces whom they had actually seen – doctors, war correspondents, and scientists – had been not only decent but positively friendly in their dealings with the natives.

For the first time in Japanese history foreign warriors from across the sea had set foot on the sacred soil of the fatherland. Could, indeed might, the conquerors of a nation which for centuries had believed itself unconquerable be anything other than sub- or supermen, demons disguised as men? Even the very sick who had hitherto stubbornly refused to be evacuated from Hiroshima, wishing at least to die in their homes, now let themselves be moved to the nearby mountain villages. Even as well-educated a man as Dr Hachiya passed many a sleepless night, tormented by the problem of whether or not he should send his wife, sick as she was, to her parents' house, far from Hiroshima. As early as September the Japanese commander of the Chugoku Region, whom the Allied authorities had temporarily confirmed in office, had issued a statement which had been posted up and printed in the newspapers. In the usual pompous official jargon, this warning of perils to come ran as follows:

Subject, *female attire*. Thin, one-piece garments, such as we wear out of doors, will normally be regarded by the foreigners as night attire. This could lead to impulsive treatment with severe detrimental con-

---

* From 31 January 1946, troops of the British Commonwealth took part in the occupation of the five prefectures that constituted the Chugoku Region, in which Hiroshima is located. Apart from Australians these troops included a number of New Zealanders, Indians, and units from the British Isles. The troops were engaged almost exclusively on garrison duty. The actual military administration of the Region remained, as before, the responsibility of the United States Eighth Army.

sequences. You are therefore instructed to wear, whenever possible, the *monpe*.*

Dress properly, and never in any circumstances expose your bosoms!

Watches. These could be regarded as desirable souvenirs. Therefore do not wear them openly. Women left alone at home must take especial precautions, and must ensure at all times that all doors remain effectively locked.

Avoid every sort of nudity. Do not spit in the street. Do not relieve yourselves in public.

In Hiroshima, as indeed throughout the rest of Japan, it was not the custom to lock doors by day or by night. The locksmiths therefore had their hands full fitting bolts and bars. This precaution was one that was soon enough to prove extremely useful, though not against the expected marauding by the foreigners. Rather did it become necessary for the inhabitants to protect their property against hungry fellow-citizens, people who had lost almost everything as the result of the war and the defeat.

3

Dazai, the head of the Security Office at the Prefecture, had prepared an especial diversionary operation for the protection and reassurance of Hiroshima's female population who felt themselves to be threatened. As early as 20 August he had invited a group of honoured businessmen to visit him in his temporary office, which was located in the ruins of the Kangyo Ginko Bank. When they were assembled there, he addressed them as follows: 'Gentlemen, I must ask you once again to put your worthy businesses at the service of the fatherland. Are you prepared to do this?'

These irreplaceable men, who had in surprisingly large numbers survived the *Pikadon*, replied as one that in the prevailing circumstances this was unfortunately quite impossible.

'But the authorities will see to it that you suffer no financial or other loss,' the police official said, in an attempt to win them over. 'Just tell us what you need in order to get your businesses going again.'

---

* Women's long trousers, usually drawn tight about the ankles.

This was language more inclined to win them over. But Motoji Mino, who took part in this conference and whom I have to thank for his report of what happened, now said: 'We have neither bed linen nor kimonos. We've nothing. We haven't even the one commodity essential for our business. That's the real problem: we haven't any girls.'

For Mr Mino, like the other gentlemen here assembled, summoned so urgently by the authorities from the various places to which they had fled after the bomb, was the proprietor of a well-known House of Joy in Yayoi-cho. This had been the red-light district of the port and garrison city of Hiroshima, and had been famous as such throughout all Japan.

Mr Mino, who, when I met him, was a soberly but elegantly clad man in his late sixties, had described the circumstances that then prevailed as follows:

'At that time, that is to say just after the *Pikadon*, I really looked a thorough tramp. I was covered in filth and bleeding from at least fifty or sixty wounds. Under my left eye – look, you can still see the scar – a deep piece of flesh had been torn from my face. I had to carry both my arms in slings, and the only shoes I still owned were a pair of down-at-heel straw sandals. As for what I should do about my business, no, I really hadn't even managed to think about that. I simply hadn't got the heart to try, and that went for my colleagues too. But this Dazai just wouldn't give in. He spoke of "loyalty to the nation" and of the urgent need for "creating institutions that would from the very beginning serve to prevent unfortunate occurrences". Or something of the sort. Anyhow, I know he used a lot of very long words.

'Then he got down to practical matters, and we became rather more attentive. The provincial administration, he said, really was prepared to spend money on this project. Two or three millions were earmarked for us – and this was before the inflation, so that that really was a very large sum. We ourselves would not have to spend a penny, while any profits that might accrue from the scheme would be ours alone.

'Later on, needless to say, that proved to be a swindle. The State never gives anything away. They asked for every single yen back. With interest, of course, and unfortunately there was not a single written proof of all the fine promises with which we had been led up the garden path. But we're a good-natured lot, and we let them talk us into it. We joined together to create a parent concern which we called Consolation Inc. Each of us contributed 20,000 yen. We elected as our chairman Hisao Yamamoto – you may have heard of him, he was later Vice-Mayor – and they appointed me his deputy. Our offices? Well, the police didn't mind, so to begin with we just used theirs. After all, we were all in this together.'

So before the first Occupation troops ever arrived in the Hiroshima Region, Action Iansho (Operation Houses of Consolation) was already under way. During the whole month of September the police launch, *Hoan Maru*, travelled from island to island and from port to port, buying women. They finally collected some five hundred girls. A few of these had already followed this profession in the past. Others – and they constituted the majority – were simply sold by parents or relations who had lost all their money in the war. A further two hundred recruits for the proposed brothels were enrolled in the city of Hiroshima itself.

One month after they had first been summoned by the Security Chief, the brothel keepers were able to report to Police Lieutenant Dazai that they had completed their patriotic duties. In and about Hiroshima they had set up ten *ianshos*. And these were the first post-war houses in the regions to contain something approaching comfort, with in some cases even a trace of elegance and luxury. The biggest Consolation House (Iansho No. 1) was established close to the entrance to the barracks in the suburb of Kaita, where the greater part of the Occupation troops garrisoning Hiroshima were to be quartered. Iansho No. 2 was located in Hiro, near the former headquarters of the Japanese fleet at Kure, which was now envisaged as the headquarters of the Occupation Forces in all western Japan.

On the day that the 34th Infantry Regiment of the Eighth Army marched in, the Houses of Consolation were decorated, beflagged, and open for business. The 'foreign devils' were catered for.

4

But the Americans turned out to be very different men from what Japanese propaganda had described, causing such terror. Ichiro Kawamoto, a young mechanic working in the Saka Electricity Generating Plant, not far from Hiroshima, has described the arrival of the Occupation troops in the following terms:

'On that day the whole sky was filled with foreign planes. All of us, who had learned from our history lessons in school how frightful wars are, had sent our wives and children far away inland. Doors were carefully locked and we were all very nervous when we arrived at work.

'The autumn wind had begun to moan again. All along the road leading to the city Japanese policemen were stationed at fifty-yard intervals. It was said that the American troops would land at Kure and march from there towards Hiroshima. We had heard that they would billet in the Kaitaichi district, where the arsenal used to be.

'During the midday break we all ran to the wire fence around the Electricity Works, to watch the Yankee columns marching past. Jeeps, jeeps, and more jeeps, pulling landing craft on wheels, a powerful, mechanized force. As they drove along, some of the American soldiers were whistling cheerfully. They had to tele-scope their long legs every way in order to fit into the little jeeps. There was no shooting. Quite the contrary. Chewing-gum and chocolate were being thrown to the children by the men of the column. The children had been the first to dare make their way to the edge of the road. The little ones quickly lost all fear and were soon shouting "Hello! hello!" to the soldiers as they went by.

'An agile signal corps soldier shinned up a telephone post and made fast a wire. The march past went on until late in the night. Towards evening two American soldiers walked into our canteen. They were so tall that they almost banged their heads in the little, narrow doorway. The Japanese did not cause any sort of disturb-ances whatever.'

This report is typical of the atmosphere that prevailed when the Americans marched into Hiroshima. The absence of friction with which this region was occupied – a region which only very recently had felt the full impact of war in a peculiarly horrifying manner – came as a surprise to both sides. The G.I.s had expected to encounter in Hiroshima, more than anywhere else, violent outbursts of hatred. Yet what they met almost everywhere was politeness and even hospitality, just as was the case throughout the rest of Japan. The population of this ancient centre of pilgrimage was predominantly Buddhist, and they seemed to be reconciled to their especial fate. Indeed, there were even in the city of Hiroshima at that time people who appeared to find a peculiar source of pride in the fact that they had experienced 'the most powerful bomb in history' and had survived. It was then not realized, needless to say, that the after-effects of this gruesome new weapon would continue to be felt for years to come.

To begin with, the Americans kept very much out of sight in the ruined city. Only a rare uniformed figure was to be seen in the 'atomic desert' that had been the city centre. They usually went there in pairs, in order to take each other's photographs, mostly against the background of the former Exhibition Building, whose smashed dome came bit by bit to symbolize Hiroshima. On one of the gigantic tottering walls of this building, put up in 1913 by the Austrian architect Letzel, it happened that one day there was found, scratched in rusty letters, the slogan NO MORE HIROSHIMAS, written in English. This was to be the clarion cry of the anti-atom-bomb movement throughout the world. Who first coined this phrase – it is assumed that it was an American – has never been discovered.*

For some of the inhabitants of Hiroshima – how many exactly cannot of course be established – it proved impossible to reconcile the harmless and friendly behaviour of the 'foreign devils' with the stereotyped image in which they had hitherto believed. One such was Kazuo M. A few weeks after the arrival of the Americans he wrote in his diary:

* The slogan NO MORE HIROSHIMAS first appeared in print in the London *Daily Express*, as part of a report by W. Burchett. This Australian journalist made his way to Hiroshima, on his own initiative, reaching the city on 3 September 1945. He was thus the first foreign newspaperman to see the atom-bombed ruins.

'White, decent-looking, and cleanly dressed Americans now walk about hand in hand with grubby little Japanese girls. Whenever they come to one of the many puddles that dot the pot-holed streets, he will swing his "girl friend" across and then jump over with one long stride. The sailors walk close beside their little friends, as if to act as living shields, protecting those fragile creatures against damage. The girls are moved to tears by the generosity and kindliness of the American soldiers. It's making them conceited now, and later they'll give birth to half-castes. To me this exaggerated friendliness on the part of the Yankees seems simply ridiculous. . . .'

5

The various administrative offices of the Province and Town of Hiroshima seem to have been somewhat disappointed by the discreet reticence of their foreign conquerors. They had expected their new masters to take the reins of government in their hands at once, and, what is more, to rule firmly and even harshly. For years the officials in the province had grown accustomed to a state of affairs whereby even the smallest details were settled 'at a higher level' and all decisions were made 'in Tokyo'. The Americans had promised the communes a greater degree of self-administration and freedom of choice, and it now began to be made plain that they actually meant what they had said. It is true that certain foreign advisers moved into the offices of the provincial administration and into the Town Hall, but to begin with they remained as much as possible in the background, out of sight, and frequently gave the Japanese officials more freedom and responsibility than those functionaries actually desired or knew what to do with.

When the Occupation troops moved into Hiroshima early in October of 1945, the city was still without a municipal head, for Mayor Kuriya had been reported killed or missing since 6 August. Shortly after the *Pikadon* the city administration had sent a man to the house of its first magistrate, which was located on the river's bank. He returned to say that in the charred ruins he had found the burned remnants of one grown-up and of one small child. This report was regarded as too vague to warrant the announcement that the missing Mayor was dead. It might be that he, like so many others, had fled to a nearby village in the mountains and that he had been too ill since then to manage to communicate with his colleagues of the city administration.

Reliable details concerning the fate of Mayor Kuriya did not come to light until his grievously wounded wife was brought back to Hiroshima for medical treatment.

'My husband is certainly no longer alive,' she was able to say, while on her own deathbed, and her statement was officially recorded. 'On the morning of "the day" he was sitting in the sun on the terrace of our house, explaining to our youngest son the meaning of Buddha's teaching. It was a peaceful moment, which we were all enjoying together. And we were so happy. . . . That little pile of ash that you have found in my house is all that remains of three generations of our family.'

Once this statement had been officially recorded, the city assembly of Hiroshima could at last set about the business of choosing a new Mayor. When they met it transpired that no less than eleven of their members were no longer alive. Most of the other town councillors were also unable to attend, since they were still suffering from the 'atomic sickness'. Therefore it was decided to postpone the choice of a new Mayor until at least a few more councillors were fit enough to take part in the discussion.

The choice of a first magistrate for the city became finally so urgent that it was decided temporarily to fill the gaps caused by the illness of so many councillors by calling in senior Civil Servants in their stead. Thus on 22 October 1945, over two and a half months after the disaster, in one of the few rooms of the Town Hall not totally destroyed by fire, the appointment of a new Mayor took place. Since there were neither chairs nor tables, nor even cushions and straw mats in adequate numbers, the delegates had to squat on a floor covered only with tent-flaps. This assembly of Hiroshima's leading citizens thus resembled rather some robbers' conclave than a reunion of the duly elected representatives of the people. Or so Shinzo Hamai remembers. And Hamai, in recognition of the great services he had rendered his city as supply chief, was now nominated Vice-Mayor.

The first Mayor to be elected by a show of hands was a sickly old man named Kihara, who for many years had represented Hiroshima in the Japanese Diet. In the first instance the Occupation Authorities raised no objection to his appointment, even though Kihara had for years been the spokesman of the extreme right-wing Yokusan Imperial Movement in the Tokyo Parliament. Later, when this first post-war Mayor of Hiroshima was dismissed before the expiry of his time of office owing to his compromised political past, he could maintain with truth that he had never really sought to fill this onerous and difficult position.

'It is my belief,' Shinzo Hamai says, 'that none of the long line of city heads of Hiroshima had ever had to hold office in such trying and thankless conditions as those that prevailed during the mayoralty of Mayor Kihara. The rooms in which we had to work lacked both doors and glass in the windows. Only a few walls were standing, askew and blackened by fire. The floors were uneven. . . . In winter the snow blew into the Mayor's parlour and into his deputy's office, and those rooms were then carpeted white. When the weather was cold, we sat at our desks huddled in overcoats, with our hats on our heads. Lacking coal for heating, we collected any sort of rubbish that would burn, with the result that our offices became filled with clouds of black smoke.'

6

At long last Hiroshima possessed once again something that resembled a municipal administration, but this was an authority without clearly defined powers, almost without means and with scarcely any civil force to ensure that its orders were in fact carried out, for the police force had almost ceased to exist. Most of the policemen, fearful of the 'cleaning up operation' that the Occupying Powers had said would be initiated against adherents of the old régime, had either left the service or were temporarily in hiding as civilians.

On 5 November the local newspaper *Chugoku Shimbun* summed up the amount of reconstruction so far achieved in the following critical article:

In the offices there lie mountains of papers and documents awaiting examination. The rigidity of bureaucratic procedure is primarily responsible for the fact that this general confusion cannot be sorted out more rapidly. The highest office in the city, the office of the mayor, remains entombed in silence.

Housing. The building of houses is to be systematically begun on 15 November. The plan calls for 5,000 houses per annum, with one shop for every twenty-five homes.

Gas. There is no prospect of a gas supply before the end of the year.

Fish. Fish should be available once again in the markets by the end of the year.

Bridges. A typical example of bureaucratic slowness.

Electricity. To date no plan available.

Tramways. At present only ten trams are in commission on the main route, eight on the Miyajima route and five municipal buses. These twenty-three vehicles must cater for an average of 42,000 persons daily. It is hoped that a further five or six vehicles will be made available in the near future.

In the late autumn of 1945 a rumour (later proved false) cast a gleam of hope over the devastated city: it was said that those afflicted with the 'radiation sickness' were beginning to recover. But, in answer to inquiries from the press, the doctors at Hiroshima Infirmary stated: 'The number of patients undergoing treatment as the result of injuries suffered from the atom-bombing declined during November by 300. This decline, however, is due almost exclusively to a decline in the number of those being treated for burns and other maladies not caused by the effects of radioactivity.'

In September the Americans had proclaimed the principle that the press was now free; but their first action was to introduce a press censorship. The censor immediately forbade the further printing of all news concerning the appearance of 'radiation sickness' symptoms among the survivors of Hiroshima and Nagasaki as a secondary consequence of the atom-bombing of those cities. On the other hand reassuring reports (such as one in the *Mainichi Shimbun* to the effect that the number of cases of the so-called atom-bomb sickness had dropped to almost zero) were released without demur by Tokyo for transmission to foreign newspapers.* The result of this was to create a wave of premature optimism, not only in Japan but throughout the world, concerning the consequences to health of the atomic explosions. The coming of spring was to show that the decline in the number of 'radiation sickness' patients in the hospital during the autumn and winter months was due to one cause only: the sick just could not hope to survive the cold weather in unheated wards with neither doors nor windows. During December, Dr Hachiya found himself even obliged temporarily to close his hospital. But this was not because there were less people with the atomic sickness: they were simply being cared for by their families at home, just as soon as those families had a home again.

At about this time a new worry began to appear in Hiroshima, as is shown by a perusal of the files of the *Chugoku Shimbun*. A steep social and moral decline was becoming evident among the populace. Almost every day there were reports of robbery, assault, rape, and murder. No possessions seemed safe any more. Even the first, emergency letter-boxes, which were of wood, were immediately broken up, carried away, and burned for fuel. At last, early in December 1945, this newspaper attempted to summarize and explain the distressing phenomenon of the growing crime wave in the following passage:

The number of crimes reported during the month of November in Hiroshima and the neighbouring district is already as high as the figure for all criminal activities throughout the entire period of the war. The young people billeted in the educational centre of Ujina roam the streets without occupation. Particularly prevalent are crimes of violence. The main centre of infection responsible for the mounting crime wave is the 'black market', where a new and quite unscrupulous type of entrepreneur now flourishes.

* A curious item, worthy of mention, is a report in the *Mainichi Shimbun* for 16 February 1946. This maintained that the effect of the radiation on persons who had been at least three kilometres from the centre of the explosions was positively beneficial, in that it had acted therapeutically in cases of tuberculosis and stomach ulcer.

The newspapers have uncovered the failure of our former military caste, our Government, our plutocrats, and our officer class. A great wave of hatred against our leaders of yesterday has thereby been created. This is now advanced as an excuse for the evil deeds of today.... It is maintained: 'The former ruling class has forfeited its political and military privileges; so today we enjoy the right to steal!'

ORPHANS AND GANGSTERS

1

ONE morning Kazuo M. found that his army boots – which had been issued to him, as to all the other survivors, from former military supply depots – were missing. He immediately suspected the *furoji*, those homeless orphans who were roaming the ruins and suburbs of Hiroshima in their thousands. Only the elder ones among them had actually experienced the catastrophe, for almost all children under the age of eleven had been evacuated along with their school-teachers to villages far away in the country long before the bomb was dropped. When the first horrible news reached these villages the immediate reaction of the grown-ups had been an attempt to conceal the truth from the children. But soon even the most remote hamlets in the highlands and the tiniest fishing villages became so overcrowded with the many refugees from the atomic hell that the schoolchildren began to suspect the worst: something frightful must have happened in the city that they still regarded as their home.

Then the parents or grandparents of an occasional child came to visit him and took him away with them. But most of the children waited in vain. For a long time now they had stopped going to their classrooms. For hours and days on end they stood outside the railway stations or lined the roads that led to Hiroshima, hoping that their loved ones would soon appear.

Finally a few boys, the most enterprising ones needless to say, lost patience. They decided to make their way back home independently in their search for their parents. Others quickly followed this example, and in the end even the girls refused to remain in their foster-homes. On foot, thumbing lifts on lorries, riding stolen bicycles, or as 'black passengers' on the trains, they succeeded in returning to the ruined city.

But only a small proportion found their parents again. Six thousand – some estimates run as high as 10,000 – children of Hiroshima had lost both father and mother in the disaster. So now they set about trying to make their own way in life. A few managed to find a home with relatives who had survived the catastrophe. But grandmothers, grandfathers, uncles, and aunts did not have enough to eat themselves. Furthermore most such relatives were sick, and demanded of the children that they help with the housework or that they 'bring in' something to eat from outside. The children therefore often found that they could do better on their own.

2

Kazuo M. spent the whole day wandering through Hiroshima, in the hope that he might somehow stumble upon the thief who had stolen his boots. Towards evening he found himself in the market near the main railway station, where almost all stolen goods turned up in the end.

The din was audible from afar off, and the bright lights of the rows of stalls that had sprung up all around the *eki* (station) dazzled the eye. Hundreds of people clustered about the little fires that the orphans kept going with splintered wood from the ruins. Many of these fires burned all night. Any person who would come closer, in search of warmth, had first to pay the boy at least a two-yen 'entrance fee'. This was one of the best (and most honest) ways of earning money that the orphans had found for themselves.

Even larger crowds pressed about those 'shops' and 'restaurants' – in reality mere half-open booths, huts made of planks quickly knocked together – which already had electric light. Since the 10th of September the electric current had been on again, at least in some districts of the town, but there was still a great shortage of bulbs. Their cool and steady light seemed a rediscovery, and therefore once again a new 'technical miracle', to the survivors. The narrow streets between the booths were filled with the sharp and acrid smells (they could bring tears to the eye) from the cook-shops where fishes and little crabs were frying in dubious oils of every sort – even machine lubricants were used. Over open fires Chinese cooked thick fish soups, greasy, shiny noodles, and sharply-spiced vegetables; Koreans offered meat roasted on rows of small spits, and it was said that the flesh thus cooked had originated in the pound for stray dogs located on the other side of the railway station.

Duburoku, a home-distilled and particularly strong drink, and methylated spirits, which later drove many addicts blind, were easily obtainable here, near the railway station, as were other commodities for which there was less demand, such as useless wedding gowns or useful but shabby household furnishings of every sort. Particularly sought-after were pots and bottles,which had frequently taken on the strangest shapes after passing through the 'great fire'.

The crowds seeped lazily through the market. What they wanted was to see life again, feel it, smell it, taste it. Here and there a whirlpool would come into existence in the turgid stream. Two drunks would be punching one another. A cry would go up of '*Dorobo! dorobo!* Thief! Thief!' but the pickpocket would have already vanished into the crowd.

Thus Kazuo moved slowly onwards. He carefully examined the contents of every booth where boots were offered for sale.

And at last, there they were – over there! There could be no doubt about it. He recognized them from their size, from their colour, he knew every crease in the familiar leather.

'Hi, those over there! – ' he was pointing with his finger. 'Those boots belong to me. They're mine.'

'Certainly,' replied the dealer. 'For thirty yen. Dead cheap at the price.'

'Those boots were stolen from me last night or early this morning. I'm not going to pay for my own boots. Give them to me!'

The dealer, an undersized fellow with long, untidy hair and a scar that ill became his cheerful features, seemed not at all put out.

'What next!' he said, raising his voice, for he knew by experience that a scene of this sort attracted potential customers. 'Stolen you say? What proof have you of that?'

Kazuo thrust forward his right foot. 'Of course they're my boots. Size nine. I only need try them on.'

His voice sounded slightly uncertain. The boots that had been issued him for nothing had, in fact, always been several sizes too large.

But the dealer appeared to accept Kazuo's argument. 'We don't want any trouble, do we?' he said. 'You can have them. Here!'

Yet when Kazuo leaned forward to take the boots, the dealer pulled them back, with a laugh: '*You* don't want to steal, do you? Thirty yen, please.'

Kazuo flushed with anger.

'But they're my boots. Father and I wear them on alternate days. They're the most valuable thing we still possess.'

'If they're as valuable as all that, thirty yen is dead cheap,' the dealer said cheerfully.

Kazuo was no longer able to control himself. He was close to tears as he shouted angrily: 'I want my shoes. They're *mine*.'

He looked around for help to the crowd that had now collected about the dealer and himself, but there was nobody there prepared to put in a word on his behalf. They were all mere spectators, and their sole interest was in seeing how this little drama would turn out in the end.

Now the dealer made it plain that he was beginning to lose patience with this disturber of the peace. He shouted at the boy: 'I can't waste all day with you. For the last time: thirty yen or buzz off, at once.'

Kazuo was taken aback. Beside himself with rage, he also shouted: 'This is a thieves' market! A nation of thieves! Yes, that's what we've become, a nation of robbers!'

Even insults did not appear to move the crowd. They simply pushed past Kazuo. The 'spectacle' was over. They ambled away in search of the next entertainment.

3

As if to mock Kazuo in his misery about the stolen shoes, an orphan accosted him as he was making his way home through the darkened streets between the ruins: 'Hi, mister, shoe-shine?'

He did not stop, merely waving the child away. The boy was not to be put off so easily, and running beside the reluctant customer he said sarcastically: 'What's the matter with you, *oniichan*?* In a bad mood this evening?'

Kazuo pointed at his wooden sandals.

'Can't you see?' he grumbled. 'Or are you trying to make a fool of me?'

He raised his hand as if to strike the boy. The thief must have been just such a one as this. Perhaps it was this very boy. The child was used to dodging blows, and jumped nimbly aside. When Kazuo saw the fear in his eyes, he dropped his hand and asked: 'No parents, eh?'

The boy nodded, his eyes on the ground.

'*Pikadon?*' Kazuo asked.

'Father, mother, brother, sister . . . .' the boy replied mechanically, as though repeating a liturgy leaned by heart.

'I know how it is,' said Kazuo, laying a hand on his shoulder. 'I myself lost my best friend. He was called Yasuji.'

And he found a crumpled ten-yen note in his pocket, which he gave to the boy, who immediately ran away before Kazuo could change his mind and ask for it back.

'Look after yourself, old chap,' Kazuo called after him in friendly tones. But the boy was no longer there.

Such was Kazuo's first acquaintance with one of the orphan boys, but in the weeks to come he was to get to know many of these little vagabonds. They let him join them on his nocturnal wanderings, and they talked to him as if he were one of themselves. For example, Kazuo noted down the following conversation as typical of many similar ones:

'Saw four or five *furoji*. With them, two very young *panpans*.† They were seated around a small fire, and I joined them.

'"Hi, *niichan*, if you want to get warm, you must pay first. We don't do this for fun." I handed over the usual "entrance fee" and was then allowed to squat close to the flames. My arrival had interrupted their conversation, and they had all fallen silent. Now they began again.

* Old maid.
† A post-war word for casual prostitutes.

"'You can say what you like," said one of the boys who appeared to be the eldest. He spoke emphatically. "You girls are lucky. When you own nothing at all, you've still got something to sell. And even when you've sold it, you've still got it. As for us, we have to steal."

"'Absolute nonsense," said one of the *panpans*. "Maybe we look all right. After all, we have to look good. But I'm telling you, I'm fed to the teeth. If I had the choice I'd rather be a thief, any day of the week."

'And the other girl agreed. "Definitely. One man after another . . . and they do anything they like with a girl. And then you get a dose on top of it all. And over and over and over again, always the same story."

"'That may be. But they hunt us as if we were wild beasts. Anyone would think we stole for the fun of the thing. If they knew . . ."

"'Sanchan, don't let's quarrel," said the younger of the two street-walkers. "Things are bound to go badly in a country that's lost a war, for boys and for girls. I said it before and I say it again: we're just scrap. There's no hope for us.'"

4

But was it true, what Kazuo M. had heard and written in his diary? Was it only physical hunger that had driven the orphans of Hiroshima to thieving and prostitution? Far more was it another sort of hunger, the hunger for excitement, for adventure, for freedom from all restraint, and the vast and unique opportunity that circumstances now offered to satisfy this hunger. It was the appeal of chaos.

Later, when conditions in Hiroshima had become normal once again and most of these children without parents were lodged in orphanages, they would speak with nostalgia of that frightful, lawless epoch, and would all constantly attempt to regain the freedom that had once been theirs. And it must be pointed out that not only were they treated with great understanding in these institutions, but also that they were far better fed than were the average members of the population. But neither words nor gift parcels from overseas could hold them back. In an interview with the *Chugoku Shimbun* an orphanage manager by the name of Kamikuri complained: 'They run away because they miss the excitement of the district around the railway station, and can't forget it. Some of the children have already broken out seven or eight times, and even the most timid ones have done so once or twice.'

There was another factor to be considered: the children of Hiroshima had learned to despise the grown-ups. During the panic they had with their own eyes observed the most disgusting scenes of brutality, of selfishness, of a crass and naked determination to save one's own life regardless of what might happen to others. Grown men had trampled upon the bodies of adolescent boys and girls, had stolen the last drop of water from those feebler than themselves. They had quite ruthlessly shown that they were the stronger. And after the war – as I heard from the manager of the Ninoshima Orphanage – it happened over and over again that relatives would seize the possessions of parents killed in the *Pika-don*, possessions that should by right have gone to the orphaned children. 'The children,' he said to me, 'now think that before the disaster the grown-ups were only pretending, and they have sworn never again to be taken in by their hypocritical lies.'*

With endless patience a few people in Hiroshima attempted, during the post-war years, to regain the confidence of the youth that other grown-ups had destroyed. One of these was manager Kamikuri, already referred to. When on one occasion he discovered that he had punished one of the children unjustly, he assembled the entire orphanage and in their presence, without saying a word, whipped his own left hand until it bled freely.

* The crude generalizations of the children are in part confirmed by a statistical analysis carried out by an American psychologist who examined the emotional reactions during the atomic period and found that, of a typical 'sample' of 589 persons, less than one third (153 persons) had given any assistance to others. And deliberate attempts by those examined to portray their own behaviour at that time in as favourable a light as possible must further be taken into account. See Sparks, Woodbury, *Panic among A-bomb Casualties at Hiroshima*, a mimeographed typescript, Hiroshima, 1957.

Then he spoke: 'I have made an innocent child suffer pain. As expiation for this I have inflicted twice as much pain upon myself. If one of you should still feel anger towards me when he leaves this room, I shall not rest until I have found him and begged him once again for forgiveness.'

Then there was Yoshimaro Mori, a youthful and idealistic gym instructor. He was so moved by the sufferings of the orphans that on his own initiative he founded a refuge for parentless children on the fortified island of Ninoshima, some two miles from the city. But at first the little vagabonds did not willingly follow him either. To begin with he had to catch them, quite literally, and have them transported under supervision to their new home. However, he succeeded eventually in transforming barracks formerly filled with misery (in the First World War they had been a camp for German prisoners of war, while after the *Pikadon* countless sick persons had been moved here to die) into a happy, indeed a model, colony of children. He received no thanks for this. In 1955 he was accused – quite unjustly, as was later proved – for reasons of local political intrigue, of having embezzled money. He committed harakiri in despair at the disgrace thus brought upon his Orphans' Island.

5

Only a fraction of the orphaned children could find help and sustenance in the homes, to begin with. The others gravitated almost without exception into a new segment of society, a sort of anti-society, that became steadily more apparent amidst the ruins of Hiroshima: the gangsters' hierarchy. The 'orphans that roamed the streets' constituted the lowest class of this society. They provided the 'goods' either in the capacity of pickpockets and thieves or as the manual workers who carted the 'black rice', 'black fish', and 'black oil'. They discovered where illegally distilled spirits were to be obtained, they begged and sold cigarettes, they procured under-age girls, in fact they acted as middlemen in every field, serving salesman and customer alike. Not only were they constantly on the prowl for new sources of 'raw materials' but also for new markets in which to dispose of anything whatsoever.

The men who assigned them their jobs, gave them their orders, and in general controlled them were the bosses of the underworld. In this period of anarchy they assumed the role normally filled by the representatives of law and order. For at least six months they were in fact the men who held power in Hiroshima.

It was Dr Hachiya who first told me about the post-war hegemony of the gangsters in Hiroshima. And although the doctor usually spoke bitterly about the general neglect that had been Hiroshima's lot in the period following the *Pikadon*, when talking of the gangsters his tone was almost one of friendliness. According to him they had at least attempted to establish some sort of order, and had intervened energetically to suppress casual theft and robbery with violence.

The doctor said that he had even formed a friendship of a sort with one of the leading gangsters. He had first met Koreyoshi Z. in a tavern that belonged to his friend Katsutani, in the fishing village of Jigozen. Z. had then spoken quite openly over the *sake* of the high position he occupied in the underworld and of the huge sums of money he was making since the *Pikadon*. He was, it seemed, collecting 'protection money' from the booths around the railway station, which provided him with a large and regular income.

Z. maintained that he came of a priestly family, belonging to the Buddhist Nichiren sect, and had himself been born in a temple. In any event he regarded himself as an educated man and did possess a certain gift for expressing himself in words. At least he knew how to tell, in highly dramatic terms, boastful stories of his prowess in various gang fights in which he had invariably played an heroic part. His masterpiece, which the doctor can repeat to this day, was the tale of his great cunning when pursued by a whole pack of rivals whose boss he had shot. He lured them into the big tent of the Yano Circus, where he was 'working' at that time, and got rid of them by letting all the lions out of their cages.

This 'big operator' had lost a leg and wore a wooden one, which squeaked and thereby suggested his nickname, Gitton. When he was not squeaking on foot through his 'preserves' in and about

Hiroshima, he was bumping over the pot-holed streets on his motor-scooter. In either case he was forever on the move. So far as his *coiffure* went, he was in the swim. Like all the other gangsters, he copied the G.I. haircut. All members of the underworld had their hair cut in this foreign style; they also had jackets tailored for them to resemble as closely as could be the tight-fitting 'Eisenhower jackets' sported by the conquerors. Their language was spiced with slang learned at the movies.

Z. had his pride. He was no common thief, but a successor of the *Kyokaku*, those 'knightly robbers' of the folk-tales who stole from the rich and helped the poor. Or so he maintained. Dr Hachiya, therefore, one day took him up on this. 'Look here,' said the doctor, 'for the last few days thieves have been active in this district. They are robbing us, and we have already lost almost everything owing to the bomb. They are taking our last few possessions. They're your *ko-buns* [comrades], aren't they? Can't you do anything to put a stop to such wicked behaviour?'

To which Z. is said to have replied: 'You really feel absolutely at ease with me, don't you, Doctor? Quite right, and don't you worry. If anything of yours is stolen, come and tell me about it straight away. Either the article itself will be returned to you at once, or if I can't immediately lay my hands on it, I'll see to it that you get something else of the same sort only better.'

Dr Hachiya has good reason to believe that the gangsters at that time were not only cooperating more or less officially with the police, but were also meeting and doing deals with representatives of the Occupation Authorities. In order to frustrate action by the so-called 'third nationality' – by which is meant the Korean and Chinese immigrants, who for decades had been treated by the Japanese as second-class citizens – the police were quite ready to collaborate with those underworld organizations of which they had knowledge. Since the Koreans and the Chinese were classified by the Occupation Authorities as members of 'liberated nations' the under-strength Japanese police force was not entitled to act against them. The members of these 'liberated nations' had formed themselves into something resembling military units for the purpose of self-protection, and, more than once, pitched battles had broken out in the railway station district: on the one side would be bands of Koreans in transit, determined to plunder the black market between trains, on the other the local toughs.

Furthermore, the gangs had existed in Hiroshima for centuries. For as far back as human memory went, no building operation (in particular road-making) had been undertaken without the supervision of the *Oka-gumi* (*gumi* means gang). This gang constantly recruited fresh strength from the ever-present crowds of released convicts. Until the bombing, control of the lucrative red light district that used to serve this garrison town had also been in the hands of this gang; they ran the numerous brothels, bars, night-clubs, and gambling joints.

In the post-war period, however, a rival gang quickly obtained both power and prestige. This was the *Murakami-gumi*, among the leaders of which was numbered the celebrated Gitton. It had seized control of the black market. Its bosses became thus the 'protectors' of the booths and organized all the 'smaller operators' such as the pick-pockets, beggars, dope-peddlers, and street-walkers: these latter operated in very large numbers in the railway station district.

Boss Z. had his finger in many another pie, particularly in certain obscure undertakings connected with the reconstruction. It was not for nothing that he appointed the torpedo-manufacturer Ishida, who had made millions during the war, as 'honorary boss' of the *Murakami-gumi*. The gang leader and the war profiteer were not the sort of men to let grass grow under their feet. Whenever they had carried out a really successful deal, they would give a great banquet to the entire population of the little village, not far from Hiroshima, where Mr Ishida had found refuge. On such occasions rice wine, now a rarity, would flow like water, and each of the guests would find in his little wooden food-box delicacies which were not only beyond price, but were actually unobtainable at that time.

When Z. was drunk he would hold forth on his favourite theme. This dealt with 'thieves' honour'. He would maintain angrily that the petty pickpockets and larceny men, who had graduated in the post-war years to more honourable tasks, frequently ignored the 'thieves' code', according to which it was, for example, immoral to steal from people who were starving. He refused to admit that he was himself the adored boss, hero, and model of these very 'beginners' about whom he was complaining, and who saw no way of combining his alleged code of honour with their need for making a living. He said that their admiration filled him with disgust, and the most that they could hope for from him was a contemptuous sneer.

THE TABLET OF THE DEAD

1

So demoralizing had been the effect of the Bomb on the majority of the survivors that very few of them were in any way renewed or strengthened by their experience of frightfulness. One exception, however, was Ichiro Kawamoto.

I first got to know him twelve years after 'that day'. He was then, quite literally, a frog. Some time before, he had begun to work as a sandwichman for a Hiroshima hotel. He was costumed as a *kappa*, one of those fabulous creatures that are said to carry on a weird existence in the pools of Japan's temples and that do live a life of sorts in the creative imagination of its advertising experts.

'To begin with I thought I'd never be able to put up with this job,' he told me. 'Humping this placard on my back through the crowded streets in the centre of the city became almost unbearable after an hour, and I felt that all the people were staring at me, not at what I was carrying. At first I had to wear a *happi-coat* [a short coat], with a black bandage over one eye. Like a pirate. I looked really absurd, and I felt ashamed that all the people should see me. Then one day a little girl of about eleven ran up to me. She walked along beside me for a bit and sang a little song that Ryo Ikebe had first made popular in some film or other. It goes: "Sandwichman, sandwichman, you're the friend of everyone." I stroked her hair and said: "Thank you, thank you!" Since then I haven't minded being stared at and I quite enjoy this *arubeit*.* It's only four hours a day, four days a week – Tuesdays, Thursdays, Saturdays, and Sundays, from six to ten each evening. That gives me plenty of time for other things.'

It was in order to learn more about these 'other things' that I had arranged to meet Kawamoto. Almost everyone in Hiroshima

---

* A German word, *Arbeit*, adopted into the Japanese language. It means hard casual labour, done in a man's spare time to supplement his income from his normal job.

who talked to me about the after-effects of the disaster and about the reconstruction period had at some time or other mentioned this simple day-labourer. Yes, it was true that everybody knew him in Hiroshima. This, however, was not because he lugged placards through the streets four days a week, either on foot or perched upon an ancient, rickety bicycle. It was because he gave something which nobody else in the world seemed willing or able to spare: he gave his time.

Whenever a sick or unemployed survivor of the *Pikadon* needs help, advice, an extra pair of hands, someone to patch up a quarrel, or simply just a baby-sitter to look after the kids for a couple of hours, the little man with the long nose and the sad eyes is always available.

He could have lived a safe, calm, and obscure existence as an electrical mechanic, and by now he might even have risen to the rank of engineer, but the Bomb blew all his plans asunder.

'In an age when such atrocities can happen, what is called "making a career for oneself" really becomes totally unimportant.' Such is Ichiro Kawamoto's opinion. 'This is a time in which people should devote all their energies to their fellow-men, helping them, serving them, explaining things to them, and fighting to make sure that nothing of that sort ever happens again.'

He expresses such sentiments quite simply and without grandiloquence, but rather with a timid smile as though asking forgiveness for the big words. I assume he would not have uttered them at all, had I not questioned him.

2

My conversations with that day-labourer and friend of humanity, Ichiro Kawamoto, have now been going on for over two years. They began in his dilapidated house beneath the shadow of the 'atomic cupola' beside the entrance to which is a sign that reads *Atelier pour la paix et l'amitié*; and they went on, with our mutual friend Kaoru Ogaur acting as middleman, week after week, in the form of an interchange of letters. I thus learned Kawamoto's entire life story bit by bit. There was only one period concerning which he would not, for a long time, tell me anything at all: this was the period that began on 6 August 1945.

When I asked Ogura what the reason for this was, he wrote to me:

'In reply to your question as to why he only ever speaks of events subsequent to 1948, he [Kawamoto] explains that he could only write about the earlier period if he had a great deal of time and was also fully in control of himself. For those had been years of extreme poverty for him, and therefore he cannot talk about them casually, after a full day's work.'

But at last it happened. I had reckoned that he would tell me nothing, and had decided that the manuscript of this book was now completed. Indeed my publishers had already announced its publication date, when suddenly, day after day, Kawamoto's reminiscences of this most terrible period began to arrive at my home. He now had the time: a motor-cycle had run him down in the main street of Hiroshima, and he was having a lengthy convalescence in the clinic. Here in the hospital ward he dared, for the first time, conjure up his memories of the beginning of the post-war period. Indeed, he even found the courage to describe to me one of those shattering incidents which, as he had frequently implied, had altered the whole course of his life.

It had happened shortly after the *Pikadon*. Kawamoto, who was then just sixteen years old, had volunteered for a salvage operation. Employees from the Saka Electricity works, who had watched the destruction of Hiroshima from a safe distance, began on 7 August to make regular and systematic visits to the city, daily coming nearer and nearer to its centre, in search of relatives and the possessions of former work-mates. Despite the gruesomeness of it all, these rescue operations always began in an atmosphere of excited expectation, even of something approaching merriment. Many people who had survived the catastrophe found themselves, at that time and despite the horror that met their eyes everywhere and the sense of tragedy, in the grip of an almost euphoric sensation of happiness, of high spirits, of well-nigh hysterical gaiety.

For example, on one occasion the rescue team was driving in from Saka, in a commercial lorry that bore the pennant of the

firm to which it belonged. They passed a company of soldiers
making their way along in disorder. The exhausted soldiers, seeing the pennant, thought that this lorry must belong to some
senior officer, leaped to attention, and saluted. This misapprehen-
sion struck the young people on board the lorry as so hilariously
funny that they were doubled up with laughter for minutes on
end.

But what sobered them up at once was 'the atrocious stink that
almost makes a man faint'. They saw corpses 'rolled up like the
monkeys and snakes in a Chinese apothecary's'. They passed by
convicts, recognizable as such owing to their blue armbands, who
were 'fishing corpses out of the river with instruments that resembled a harpoon. They simply spitted them, then hoisted them
on to a sort of iron roasting-grill, as if they were fish to be cooked'.

On 10 August, the day that was to have such a significance in
Kawamoto's life story, the rescue team from Saka had headed for
home earlier than usual. Silently, with heads lowered, cloths
covering their noses – and in some cases their eyes as well – they
were on the way back to their own, almost undamaged homes.

It was then that it happened. In order to avoid a puncture or a
blowout, the lorry had to go especially slowly. Over and over
again it would stop, because rubble, glass, nails, or other obstacles
blocked the way. During this hesitant progress Kawamoto had
ample opportunity to observe, in detail, the faces of the dead that
lined the roadside. But that one over there. Its eyes were opening!
They were staring at him! The body of the 'dead man' remained
as rigid as before, there could be no doubt about that, but its
white eyeballs were slowly rolling from right to left, up and
down.

'He's alive, that one's alive over there!' Kawamoto shouted
down from the lorry at the soldiers who were engaged in clearing
the streets of corpses, using their long harpoons for this purpose.

One or two of the soldiers glanced up. Apparently they had not
understood. Meanwhile, the lorry driver, delighted to see a
stretch of clear road ahead, had stepped on the gas, and they were
gathering speed. 'Don't take that one, don't burn him. He's alive.
That one's alive!' shouted Kawamoto once again. But they had
already gone too far, and the men with the bamboo hooks were

out of earshot. They waved after the lorry, a tired gesture, as though Kawamoto had shouted a greeting, and then they returned to their gruesome tasks.

That night Kawamoto was unable to sleep. Without respite the question tormented him: 'Why did I not jump down from the lorry at once? Maybe I wouldn't have been too late to save a human life. Did they toss his body, still alive, into . . . ?' He dared not complete his thought.

In the middle of the night he awoke a colleague, sleeping beside him in the dormitory of the Electricity Works. He shook him, and whispered: 'Tell me, why didn't you tell the driver to stop? You must have heard me shouting. You must all have heard. And you saw them lying there, too.'

'Leave me alone,' was the answer he got. 'Why not complain to the *B-san** which dropped the Bomb. That man lying beside the road – he'd had it, in any event. *Shikata ganai* – there's nothing to be done. Go back to sleep, boy.'

3

'*Shikata ganai,*' that's what they all said in Saka. But was there really nothing to be done, to stop the frightfulness? At least a beginning should be made. But how? Memories of what he had seen in Hiroshima and in the emergency hospital at Saka tormented Ichiro like the demons in the temple pictures which his mother had once shown him.

She had been a pious Buddhist. Which was why, after her husband's death, she had returned, accompanied by Ichiro, then aged ten, from Peru, the land where they had emigrated, to their old home. 'Those who have done evil in their past life will be reborn as horses or as oxen,' the mother used to teach her son. 'Their masters will beat them, and when they are no longer capable of work they will be slaughtered. Many an evil spirit also comes back in human shape, but it is then arranged that his new life on earth will be as cruel and as filled with work as is that of the beasts of burden.'

* Japanese expression for the B-29 bomber.

Now, as he tossed on his lumpy *futon* (mattress), unable to sleep because of the day's events, Kawamoto began to wonder. 'What crimes can those many, many people have committed that they should have such unspeakable sufferings inflicted upon them, over there on the charred patch of ground where Hiroshima once stood? It can't be that they all were guilty of evil deeds in some earlier life. And even so, are we not taught that birds and butterflies are to be regarded as the reincarnation of good people? If so, why should thousands of them too have died such a horrible death in the *Pikadon*?'

Years later, when telling me of these first doubts concerning the beliefs that he had learned at his mother's knee, Kawamoto was to add: 'An outsider like yourself will surely laugh at such religious fantasies. But for me this new perception came as a great shock. I could not help it. And then a truly shattering thought occurred to me: if all that I had hitherto believed was not true, then it followed that there could be no Supreme Being.'

It was in this state of spiritual turmoil that shortly after the armistice the young man happened to visit the neighbouring village of Okugaita. It was there that during the last few weeks of the war he had undergone a rapid form of military training. Maybe the head of the school would be able to help him. 'He greeted me in friendly fashion and we talked about all sorts of things,' Kawamoto says. 'Finally he advised me to copy out, twice daily, the *Imperial Edict concerning Education*. This task should give me back my certitudes as well as the courage to go on living. And I actually did this. But after a month I gave it up, because I had come to realize that it was of little help to me.'

But without realizing it himself Kawamoto had in fact at this time found the beginning of the path that he was henceforth to follow. It had been shown to him by the example of two people whom he did not know. On one of the trips to Hiroshima to evacuate the people still there, he had observed a girl who in most touching fashion was trying to do something to help those for whom there was no hope. Later he saw a policeman who with the utmost patience was feeding moistened bread to a small child whose mother had collapsed on the roadside. In the midst of the fearsome chaos all around it seemed to him that these two people were the only ones doing something which really made sense.

Kawamoto writes:

'The more I think back over my experiences, the more clearly something within myself tells me: "The most important thing in life is to help all those who are in need and who suffer." Indeed, it is almost as if a voice spoke those words aloud to me.'

In the days that followed, Kawamoto tried to dismiss the memory of those dying people whom he had passed by, and he did this by devoting himself to those so seriously wounded that they were beyond hope. These hopeless cases lay in the school and in the kindergarten at Saka.

He reports about this: 'Once I carried a man whose whole body was one great wound to an emergency hospital a couple of miles away. There were only a few of us who had volunteered for this sort of work, and we were often at it all through the night, by candlelight. To begin with we washed our hands in ordinary water. Later, when the rumour became general that the Bomb must have contained poison, we used to go down to the beach every time. There we would scrub the dirt from us with salt water and sand, until there was no longer any trace of the smell of sickness on our bodies. Because we wanted to live. We had no wish to die miserably, as we had seen those others do.'

4

After days without sleep and almost without food the delicately built youth had become wellnigh incapable of doing his work properly. His arms were weak, and his hands could hardly grip anything. On one occasion he dropped a heavy submarine battery on to his foot, while carrying it from the Naval Base to the electricity works; and he had to spend several days in bed as a result. His workmates offered him no thanks or recognition for the help he was giving voluntarily to the sick and the dying evacuated from Hiroshima to Saka. On the contrary, they mocked and teased him: 'Weakling! Good-for-nothing! You knock-kneed bag of bones! Milksop! Leave it alone. I'd rather do it on my own. It frightens me just to watch you try.'

For a while Ichiro put up with their jeers. He did his best to avoid his workmates. That they might not see his thin body, covered with a rash ever since the *Pikadon*, he slipped into the washroom after the lights had been put out, when the water was almost cold. He felt himself to be sick, ugly, wretched, despised by all, and there was no one with whom he could talk.

But the greater his efforts to remain inconspicuous, the more they mocked him and tormented him in the factory:

'Why don't you eat a bit more, Kawamoto? Don't you want to get strong? Why are you so thin?' It went on day after day, at work and at rest. Out of pride the boy would not tell his persecutors that he was giving his rations to the sick and that for weeks now he had been living almost entirely on grasses, seaweed, and crabs' shells that he collected upon the seashore or on the cliffs. So his only reply was: 'I guess that's the way I'm made. . . .'

'Then it's a pity you were ever made at all,' said Engineer Shitahara, whom Kawamoto had hitherto regarded as one of his friends.

'Did I ask it to be this way?' Kawamoto shouted at him. 'I certainly did not.' He felt a senseless fury against his dead parents for having brought him into this sad, vulgar, loveless, senseless world. The fury overpowered him.

Kawamoto jumped to his feet. He ran into the dormitory and pulled something out from under his mattress. It was a tablet of the dead, bearing the names of his forebears. He himself had carved and painted it. Now he hurled it, with all the strength that he still could muster, against the wall. But the tablet did not break. It was of solid wood and only tore a hole in the paper that covered the sliding door.

His workmates realized that this time the joke had gone too far. They came running after Kawamoto, and called to him: 'Stop, Ichiro, stop. It's madness! There's a divine punishment for what you're doing!'

'Devil take it!' he shouted back at them. 'I wish I'd never had any parents. Then you wouldn't be able to push me about the way you do, and I shouldn't be a burden to anyone.'

Before they could stop him he had run into the kitchen. He had lost all trace of self-control. When he came back into the dormitory, he was carrying an axe. He was wild-eyed and breathless.

The workers glanced at one another. They were afraid that he was going to attack them with his axe.

But Kawamoto paid them not the slightest attention. He stood by the window and began to hack the tablet of the dead into a thousand pieces.

Then he threw himself down on his mattress, pulled the blankets up over his head, and fell into a deep and dreamless sleep.

2

A New Beginning

(1946–8)

THE DREAMERS

1

EVEN before the first, cruel winter 'after the bomb' was over the city administration of Hiroshima had at last won a considerable victory over the forces of indifference and illegality.

Since the *Pikadon* the water mains had been dry; for, in a desperate and fruitless effort on that 6 August to check the holocaust, the taps had been turned full on in the houses and allowed to run for hours on end. As a result, water pressure had fallen so low that finally only the hydrants in the streets were still working. Their stop-cocks had had to be forced open during the fire, and the heat was then so great that the water had shot out close to boiling point or even in the form of steam. The final reserves had been squandered, so that in the days that followed the catastrophe yet another torment was sent to plague the survivors – thirst.

It is true that the reservoirs belonging to the water works were soon refilled, but to re-establish the degree of pressure needed to send that essential element coursing through the pipes again it was necessary first to replace the many pipes broken by the explosion. Engineer units from the Navy and squads from the Technical Emergency Service, therefore, rapidly set about this task, digging under the ruins in the search for breaks which they could then mend. But for every hole that they plugged by day, two or three more came into existence each night. For the thirsty population had meanwhile discovered that by boring holes directly in the underground network of pipes they could get a few cupfuls of water at least. So on their own initiative they proceeded to sink a multitude of such 'springs' in this atomic desert.

There thus came about a highly unequal struggle between the city authorities and the citizens. The official demand that the population should, in their own interest, preserve at least a rudimentary discipline, and should draw their water exclusively from the few taps that were functioning at widely scattered points throughout the city, was simply ignored. A few dozen municipal bureaucrats – who could not now rely on any police assistance – found themselves face to face with tens of thousands of tired and thirsty people. The head of the Water Supply Department, Shinohara, went to see Hamai and complained: 'It's more than we can cope with.'

In January 1946 the first of the released prisoners of war began to come home from the South-West Pacific theatre. Among these, fortunately enough, was an energetic civil engineer by the name of Masao Teranishi. He said that he was prepared to undertake this particular struggle and told the poor city fathers, now at their wits' end: 'It's a simple matter of endurance. We'll just have to see who can hold out longest.'

Vice-Mayor Shinzo Hamai immediately appointed this enterprising man Head of the Water Supply and gave him complete freedom in the choice of his subordinates. There were plenty of tough young men in search of work among the returning soldiers, and Teranishi chose the ones who seemed to him to be the most adventurous. When recruiting these men, the new Water Chief made no bones about the dangers that their work would involve. They would have to work primarily by night in those parts of the city dominated by the least trustworthy sections of the people, and they would have to reckon on being resisted with force, for certain gangster elements had meanwhile organized the sale of water as a highly lucrative racket and, as a result, would presumably do their best to hinder the re-establishment of the normal methods of supply.

So night after night, while the citizens of Hiroshima slept, the monotonous sound of hammering re-echoed through the city. It was Teranishi's men, mending the broken pipes. Since they were armed with knives, and operated in squads well equipped for self-defence, no one dared to interfere. First results were visible after only one month; a few drops of water began to trickle from the taps.

'It's not over yet. You must be patient for a little longer,' Teranishi advised his fellow-citizens. 'But you now see with your own eyes the progress we're making. But wait a little, and every one of us will once again be able to use as much water as we want.'

And the citizens really began to trust him. Fewer and fewer became the customers buying 'black' water from the water merchants or drawing it from the hydrants or from their private water holes. And in fact one day it suddenly began to drip, to trickle, to run, to gush, through every pipe and from every tap.

This return of the normal water supply meant much more to the surviving citizens of Hiroshima than a mere relief from thirst and dirt. For it showed them that it might again be possible to live properly and decently on the scorched and ashen patch of ground where their city had once stood.

2

Early in January 1946 a new department was created within the municipal administration of Hiroshima: its principal task was to make preparations for the reconstruction. The departmental chief was Toshio Nakashima, a civil engineer with experience of town planning. He was assigned a group of thirty leading citizens of Hiroshima – principally businessmen and politicians – who constituted a 'Discussion Group for Problems of Reconstruction'. They had advisory powers only.

This Committee set to work with great enthusiasm and a plethora of ideas. Apart from the city of Sapporo in Northern Japan, there had been no single urban community which had been created according to a plan. Japan's cities had grown wildly and without any sort of control. As a result not one of them had proved in any way capable of dealing with such problems as overcrowding and communications. Narrow, twisting, attractively old-fashioned alleyways, and small private gardens had been characteristic of the Hiroshima that had existed before the catastrophe; now it was to be a city of wide streets, skyscrapers, open parks, and was to aim at winning the title of 'Nippon's most modern city'. 'We must transform our misfortune into a stroke of luck'; such, according to Shinzo Hamai, was the slogan with which the Reconstruction Committee set to work.

At their very first meeting profound differences of opinion became apparent. Before the basic plans for the new city could be decided upon it was essential that they should have made up their minds what the primary purpose of this 'new Hiroshima' was to be. For the city was compelled, as it were, to change its profession. During the Sino-Japanese War of 1894–5 the Emperor Meiji had set up his headquarters, his *Dai-hon-ei*, in this place, and ever since that date war had been Hiroshima's principal source of income. The Russo-Japanese War, the 'China incident', and finally the 'Greater East-Asian' War of 1941 had all brought the city an increase both of population and of wealth. A succession of arsenals, supply depots, barracks, parade grounds, and munitions factories had come into existence. Now, after total defeat and disarmament, the question arose as to what Hiroshima would live on in future.

Describing these fundamental debates, Hamai says: 'One member of the Committee believed that the city's future lay in tourism, and he found a considerable amount of support for this view. Others were of the opinion that Hiroshima should become primarily an administrative centre, a town of Government offices and training establishments. This proposal met with no applause. What is interesting is that in the end all the members of the Committee agreed on one thing: a city of peace and culture must arise here.'

Some Committee members produced ideas that can only be described as fantastic. They dreamed, for example, of a 'Venice of the East'; canals were to be dug between the rivers, 'Bridges of Sighs' built, even gondoliers imported from Italy, with riverside or floating restaurants and much else as well. Others envisaged a Japanese Monte Carlo, with casinos, yacht basins, and waterside promenades. The railway station was moved – on paper, naturally – from the outskirts to the centre of the city. There was talk of spacious boulevards, of enlarging the university by building a library to specialize in problems of peace. Someone suggested that Picasso be asked to preside over an international artists' colony for which art galleries of a suitable size and number would be provided.

This planning fever, originally limited to the official department concerned with such matters, soon spread throughout the entire city. It assumed epidemic proportions. 'Everything must start anew!' exclaimed the young people back from the wars. Hiroshima, the symbol of atomic war, was to become a beacon whose rays would spread across the entire world.

3

When the Discussion Committee for Reconstruction met, one question of primary importance arose immediately. Should the accursed, poisoned, burned soil on which Hiroshima had once stood, and which was constantly threatened by the danger of floods, be abandoned forever? In fact should the new Hiroshima be built elsewhere? But new buildings – even if most of these were mere huts – were already springing up on all sides, and the opponents of this radical resettlement plan advanced this fact as a sort of people's protest against it. Also an actuarial summary of the situation rapidly made plain that the only partly damaged 'infrastructure' of the city (the labyrinth of pipes, wires, and so forth beneath the streets) was still so valuable, and its replacement at post-war prices would be so costly, that the city could not afford simply to abandon it.

These debates were still in progress when something happened that gave new courage to those people who doubted whether Hiroshima could ever rise again.

To the south of the Town Hall there stood a pair of smoke-blackened cherry trees. The municipal administration had saved them from the fate that had befallen all the other trees of Hiroshima. They had in fact not been burned as fuel during that first, bitter winter.

They stood there, hideous mementoes of what had happened, their painfully twisted and tortured branches an unforgettable reminder of the great fire. Shinzo Hamai would glance repeatedly out of his office window at these two survivors. In their agonized convulsions they seemed to him, particularly at night, to stand there like a couple of ghosts.

Then, one morning in April 1946, the Vice-Mayor looked up from the papers that lay so thick upon his desk. He gazed for a long time. For what met his eyes was a sight he had scarcely hoped ever to see again. He ran down the stairs as fast as his legs would carry him, and only now, when he was standing immediately beneath the branches of the trees, could he be sure that his eyes had not deceived him. The blackness of the branches was dappled with the brilliant white of cherry buds opening into blossom.

In the days that followed hundreds of people made a pilgrimage to the two sad cherry trees that had, overnight, come to life once again. Only now did they begin really to believe that their city was not condemned to remain an atomic desert for close on one hundred years.

4

Sachio Kano is an immigrant from Hiroshima whom I met in one of those endless grey suburbs that surround Chicago. When he recalls that first spring after the defeat in his home town the air of depression leaves him, his face lights up, and he is vivacious and gay:

'In those days we really thought that the world had been born anew, and that we people of twenty or so might henceforth live in this just, free, better, more beautiful world. We had plenty of optimism, and plenty of words in which to express it. That was the way we used to talk when we met in the Musica Tea-room, on Enko Bashi Street, amidst a décor of Swiss chalets, over weak coffee or even weaker cups of tea, and to the accompaniment of endless classical music played on the phonograph. (Somehow or other the Chinese proprietor had managed to save his really first-class collection of records.) Those marvellous, endless conversations, how well I remember it all.

'Like most of my contemporaries, I had only recently been discharged from the forces. I had been trained as a "one-man torpedo" and that was pretty well all I knew. So now I had to set about looking for a career. I found one quite by chance. In one of the newspapers, I came upon an article signed by Hata, the poet. He was complaining that in Hiroshima, since the death of the Sakuratai Company in the atomic explosion, there had been no theatre at all. I had always dreamed of becoming an actor. So now I went to see him, and with his help I started a company that we called the Porte-Manteau Group, because our ambitions did not go beyond serving as "coat-hangers" for the ideas of modern, and particularly of foreign, dramatists.'

It did not take long to collect sufficient actors and actresses to form this group. Money for clothes, make-up, scripts, and advertising was also finally available, though this was come by in a somewhat unusual fashion. A member of the group happened to discover that the municipal administration was subsidizing new firms. In an attempt to get business going again, each such firm was given a special allotment of rice wine, normally rationed in the strictest fashion. It should be explained that a few bottles of *sake* form part of the essential inventory of any Japanese business concern.

Owing to their extreme rarity these bottles of *sake* could be sold on the black market for sums many times in excess of their nominal value. So before they even staged a play the young actors 'created' a few dummy firms with fine-sounding names. These only 'ran' until the *sake* ration had been received and passed on to the black market. The fine, new world wanted a drink too. . . .

They had got it into their heads only to produce Western plays, thus underlining their break with the traditions of 'Old Japan'. They rehearsed Ibsen's *Ghosts* at Hata's house, not far from Hiroshima. In the waiting-room of Hiroshima station, only partly repaired since the bombing, and in front of several hundred enthusiastic and enraptured people, they enacted this play that deals with the problem of inherited disease, a very real problem for the people of Hiroshima, even though here shown in the comparatively idyllic circumstances of the pre-atomic nineteenth century.

As with all such groups, the actual productions that were staged were of less importance than the feelings of comradeship derived from rehearsing and acting together. The young people who formed this circle were among the first in Hiroshima to associate in a hitherto unknown, free, and 'Western' manner. It became possible, for example, for unmarried young men and girls to meet without complicated subterfuges and stratagems. Although the 'emancipation of women' had been ordered from on high, women played a very subordinate role in the provincial city of Hiroshima. With these young people this was no longer the case. At first only one girl had dared join the company, and plays with an all-male, or almost all-male, cast had therefore to be found, for the young actors would have regarded it as contrary to their programme of 'modernization' if young men had played female parts, as was customary in the traditional Japanese theatre.

Bit by bit, however, other girls gained sufficient confidence to join the little company.

'There was one occasion when the part required that a young girl, who had only recently joined the company, should appear in a sleeveless dress,' Sachio Kano remembers. 'She started by producing every possible argument against wearing such a dress. But finally she gave in to the producer, burst into tears, and went away to change. When we saw her on the rehearsal stage, we understood and felt deeply ashamed. Her arm was hideously scarred by a huge atomic cheloid. "Apart from my doctor, I've never dared show it to anyone," she said, still sobbing. "But you . . . you're all my friends."

'She became our best actress. But only when she was with us did she feel healthy, normal, and free again.'

What subsequently happened was perhaps inevitable. Evil-minded people maintained that Sachio Kano was only interested in chasing the girls, and that rehearsals were the equivalent of orgies. It was also rumoured that he introduced Communists into the company, and was busy making propaganda.

'Both statements were slanders,' Kano insisted. 'We acted Lord Dunsany, Elmer Rice, Synge, Dickens. Are they supposed to be bolsheviks? No, the truth is that we offended the "old people". As you know, I myself emigrated from Japan when I realized – 1950 or thereabouts – that my hopes of a brave new world were coming to nothing, and that the men in charge were almost identical with the people who had been running Japan before the war.'

I left him at the dirty-white gateway of a meat-packing factory in one of Chicago's dismal 'coloured quarters'. He earns now just enough money for himself and his family to be able to visit the theatrical section of the Arts Institute in the evening. So at least a fragment of his dream has not faded away.

5

Among those who frequented the Musica Tea-room during that first, hope-filled spring after the war there was a thin, unhealthy-looking poet by the name of Sankichi Toge, who was soon to be the centre of a whole new literary movement. From a political and artistic point of view he often seemed, to the adherents of this movement, too moderate, but they detected in him a moral strength and an artistic incorruptibility which elevated him far above the rank of ordinary propaganda writers. Therefore, in July 1946, he was elected chairman of the Seinen Bunka Renmei (Assembly for Young Culture), a strongly left-wing organization to which most of the surviving artists and authors of Hiroshima belonged.

Toge had been born in February 1917. He came of a family which for many years had been prominent in the fight against Japanese militarism. His elder brothers and sisters had worked in the illegal trade unions and anti-war organizations. The younger of his two brothers had fallen into the hands of the police and had been tortured to death. Since reaching manhood Sankichi had suffered from a malady of the lungs, which meant that he was frequently bedridden. In hospital he had developed an interest in Christianity, and in 1943, that is to say in the middle of the war, at a period when it was dangerous to show such an interest in ideas that 'smelt of butter' (i.e. Western ideas), he had had himself secretly baptized.

The frightful experiences of the *Pikadon* gave a new meaning to the poet's work. He tried to express the unspeakable experiences through which he had passed. Furthermore he was a patient, clever adviser of other young writers of talent. He urged them not merely to describe perfected, ceremonious moments in their verses, as was done in traditional Japanese poetry, but to find a 'new beauty' in the bustle and fullness of contemporary life.

Toge was of the opinion that every human being contained

T–D

within himself a poet or a painter. He therefore urged his fellow-citizens to write 'poems of everyday life', for to every man is given the longing for artistic form. And Kaoru Ogura has told me that in post-war Hiroshima it really happened: hospital orderlies, patients, factory workers, in brief human beings from every class of society, began to write. In verses without any strict form and without rhyme these simple people tried to describe, and so to discover anew, their daily life.

To obtain the basic necessities of life and also as a sort of demonstration to prove 'the survival of God's beauty amidst the ugliness of destruction wrought by human pride', in the autumn of 1945 Toge opened Hiroshima's first flower shop. It was called Midori (Green). In August of 1946 he also opened the first post-war bookshop.

In this bookshop, which he called Hakuyo Shobe (The White Water Willow), discussions about certain writers' latest work would often go on until the early hours of the morning. One book that caused particular excitement at that time was the diary of young Shinoe Shoda, whose father had been one of Hiroshima's leading armament manufacturers. This small volume, entitled *Sange* (Remorse), was a confession of family guilt in the war that had ended with that family's destruction in the atomic disaster. Another book which attracted a great deal of attention was *Natsu no hana* (*The Flower of One Summer*), certainly the very first novel about the *Pikadon*. Tamiki Hara, a writer who had moved to Hiroshima from Tokyo during the war, had dedicated this novel to his wife, killed in the explosion. Later, in March of 1951, fearing that the Korean War would develop into another atomic war, the author committed suicide.

For the survivors the most impressive of the documentary reports about the catastrophe which they had lived through seemed even in these early days to be *The City of the Dead* by Yoko Ohta. When Tokyo was devastated by a napalm-bombing in June 1945, the authoress of this book had fled to Hiroshima, in the hope of finding safety there. Caught by the atom bomb, she had spent three days and nights in the open, surrounded by corpses, and had entered hospital with symptoms of the 'radiation sickness'. For one month Mrs Ohta lingered between life and death. In October and November 1945, while still sick in bed, she wrote down her experiences. The book, however, could not be printed at once, for the Occupation Authorities – referring to Paragraph 3 of MacArthur's press law – declared its publication to be 'contrary to their interests'. For Mrs Ohta had said that the 'self-destruction of humanity' which she had been compelled to witness in Hiroshima had not in fact begun with the explosion of the atomic bomb, but much earlier, with its 'invention and creation.'*

Of the many poems then written about Hiroshima, one touched particularly deep and powerful chords. It appeared in March 1946, in a collection of poems entitled *Chugoku Bunka* (*The Culture of Chugoku*). The poetess, Sadako Kurihara, describes in particularly impressive fashion the 'voice of hope in the midst of despair':

REBIRTH

Through the deep cellar, where only shadows live,
Shadows of the living and the dead, a cry breaks,
A cry of pain through darkness,
No cry of joy, yet a consolation,
Drowning the thousand other cries that still
Re-echo shrilly through their heads,
An answer comes. From among those shadows
'Cry as you will, woman,' comes the answer.
'I know the way. In such hours of heaviness
It was my daily task to be with you
Up there.'
                    And this too helped:

* By various stratagems the censor of the Occupying Powers even prevented the publication of a Japanese edition of John Hersey's famous *Hiroshima*, which originally appeared in the *New Yorker* in September 1946, but which was not allowed to be printed in Japanese until March of 1949. Almost all works by Japanese authors dealing with Hiroshima were originally censored: only after lengthy appeals and much protest were they finally allowed to be published. But MacArthur's headquarters refused to give way in the matter of the documentary film made in August and September of 1945 by the Nichiei Film Production Co. in Hiroshima and Nagasaki. The fifteen reels of negative were seized in February 1946. Even lengths of film that had been taken out of these in the cutting-room had to be handed over. But the producers had secretly made a copy, which they had buried, risking thereby the most severe punishment.

Thus, unseen, a new life came,
Born of darkness. Out of darkness
Into light, for surely he
Was destined for the light.
Yet those who helped him then,
The consolers and the helpers, might themselves
Never again see light. Before the first
Gleam could reach into their cellar, they
Had been forever snuffed, like candles.

6

Yoko Ohta told me that in the spring of 1946, when one of her friends had outlined to her one of those many fanciful projects which were then in the air, she had asked the sensible question: 'And where is the money coming from?'

Mrs Ohta is a Marxist. But Shigajiro Matsuda, director of the motor-cycle factory Toyo Kogyo and one of Hiroshima's leading industrialists, was in the habit of asking precisely the same question of the 'dreamers' who abounded in those days. At the long and animated meetings of the Reconstruction Committee he tried to inject a note of economic reality into the debates by repeating almost *ad nauseam*: 'These are castles in the air. Magnificent though your plans may be on paper, the question we must answer first of all is this: what financial sources can we draw upon? Only when that question has been answered will we know what we can actually undertake.'

One of this industrialist's proposals was that the city should buy up as many plots of land, and the ruins that covered them, as possible – while property values were still low. Once reconstruction had begun the value of land was bound to go up, and the resultant profits might then well be used to finance costly communal projects.

But even to do this an initial capital was needed, and the coffers of the city administration were quite empty. For the time being there could be no question of borrowing from the banks or from industry. They would understandably prefer to invest their capital, which was scanty enough, in safer reconstruction projects than an atom-devastated city. In the cautious financial circles of

Tokyo the rumour that the soil of Hiroshima was 'poisoned', and would probably remain so for several generations, was still current. This was enough to make those circles even more cautious than usual, and extremely reluctant to grant credits.

What about the Government? The Mayor, Kihara, the chairman of the city council, Yamamoto, and a delegation of councillors went to Tokyo for the purpose of obtaining special credits for the reconstruction of their city. The answer they received was not encouraging. 'At this moment of history the entire nation is passing through a serious financial crisis. One hundred and twenty of our towns are in ashes as the result of enemy air attacks. Hiroshima cannot ask for, nor expect, specially favourable treatment merely because the disaster there was caused by an atomic bomb rather than by incendiary bombs.'

So the only remaining hope was the Americans. They seemed to be touched on a particularly sensitive spot whenever Hiroshima was mentioned.

Already, on the occasion of a visit by foreign journalists in February 1946, Mayor Kihara appeared to be aiming at this spot when he said: 'This entire tragedy was brought upon us by the Americans. Therefore the United States should devote very special attention to the reconstruction of Hiroshima.'

To which one American journalist had replied angrily: 'Do you happen to know what the Japanese Army did in Manila and Nanking?'

'I don't,' answered Kihara.

'What were you doing during the war?' the cross-examination went on.

'I was a member of the Upper House.'

'It is quite impossible that any man occupying such a position should have no inkling of these matters,' a reporter began. And, from then on, the conversation was about the atrocities that the Japanese troops had committed and not, as the Mayor had hoped, about the reconstruction of Hiroshima. In arguing about the relative vileness of yesterday's crimes, today's needs were forgotten.

Despite this initial failure, Mayor Kihara decided, after the Japanese authorites had refused a special subsidy in the summer of 1946, to try his luck with the Americans once again. But on this occasion he adopted subtler tactics. He did not immediately ask for money, but only for advice, confident that if the advice were given the money would surely follow. The Americans sent him as adviser a young lieutenant by the name of Montgomery, whose proposals, as Shinzo Hamai recalls, were 'at least always quite innocuous. He examined our projects in detail, and then pronounced them first-rate.'

But Lieutenant Montgomery had had only limited practical experience, while the influence that he could exert on Allied Headquarters, that prime source of dollars, was disappointingly small. Nor did he remain for long in Hiroshima. But for years he sent a telegram each year, on 6 August. Even today everyone remembers him with affection, because he spoke fluent Japanese and was an unobtrusive, unpretentious man; however, it must be admitted that he was of little practical help.

He was replaced by another foreign adviser on reconstruction, the Australian Major S. A. Jarvis. This man set about his job with real earnestness, for he was aware that he was confronted with a very large task. His plans for the 'new Hiroshima' were even more grandiose – if that were possible – than the ideas advanced at the meetings of the Reconstruction Committee, and he fought fiercely against those plans for compromise which had meanwhile been put forward by the municipal administration, and which would retain from the large-scale town-planning of the early months little more than a projected park and a single boulevard one hundred yards wide.

There was no effort that Major Jarvis did not make in his fight to ensure that this unique oportunity for a model rebuilding of Hiroshima should not be wasted. Not only did he confer with the responsible authorities at MacArthur's headquarters, but he even obtained an audience with the Japanese Emperor's brother, Prince Takamatsu, with whom he pleaded for special financial assistance for Hiroshima. It was all in vain. The Japanese were compelled to count their pennies, while certain Allied politicians felt that any special help for Hiroshima would imply an indebtedness, perhaps even an admission of guilt, towards the city. The Japanese could not, the Allies would not, do anything.

Disappointed, his health broken, the Australian at last sent in his resignation. In a farewell letter addressed to the city administration he expressed his regret:

'I have caused the Mayor a great deal of trouble, because I desired the impossible. But while travelling through Japan I had noticed that there is not one single city which is built according to the basic principles of town-planning, and so I told myself that here, on a somewhat smaller but nevertheless ideal scale, this should now be attempted. In time to come it would not only be your town's citizens who would have profited from this, but other towns as well, for which yours would have served as a model. But the more I came to know about conditions in Japan, the plainer it became to me how difficult it would be to carry out such an undertaking. I only hope that I will not be misunderstood, for my intentions were honourable.'

7

Meanwhile, the provisional 'uncontrolled' rebuilding was going on apace. The first schools had been reopened – and this was the city fathers' chief concern, even if, to begin with, the children had to have half their lessons in the open air, in the so-called 'Blue Sky Schools'. Streets were cleared of rubble and resurfaced. A few fresh, green trees were even imported into the shadeless city from the surrounding countryside. Without inquiring too closely into property rights or paying too much attention to the city administration's blueprints, which laid down a minimum street width of one hundred and twenty feet, the homeless built themselves house after house. First a post would be driven into the chosen plot, and to this would be nailed a board bearing the future householder's name, electrical cables would be connected, only the most conscientious citizens bothering first to obtain the permission of the Electricity Workers; and in three or four weeks yet another family had a roof over its head. A reporter writing for the American Army paper, *Stars and Stripes*, may well have found the right comparison when he described the Hiroshima of 1946, that city of the Far East, as resembling some mining town in the Far West during the Gold Rush period.

The Japanese Government had explicitly forbidden population

movements into those cities which had been particularly damaged by the war. This however did not prevent strangers who happened to be in Hiroshima from settling there. Nor did it stop others from coming into the city with the returning evacuees or those who had fled elsewhere. Even if the authorities had had the heart to enforce these regulations, they lacked the necessary means. These new settlers were in most cases men, women, and children who had now been uprooted for the second time; having gone overseas to colonize the Japanese-controlled territories, the defeat had now compelled them to come home again. As the pioneers of the Japanese 'new Asia' they had been the representatives of a self-conscious and often arrogant ruling class in Korea, China, Manchuria, Indochina, Indonesia, Burma, Formosa, and Malaya, where they had lived like princes. Now utterly depressed and discouraged, after weeks of running the gauntlet amidst the foreign populations whom they had so recently oppressed, they disembarked at Hiroshima's port, Ujina, that same port with its 'Hall of Triumph' from which a few years ago the soldiers of Nippon had set sail to conquer an empire overseas.

They were in most cases penniless, driven from their homes with nothing, exhausted by hunger marches or by their time in a 'reception camp', frequently broken in health. Having got as far as Hiroshima they went no farther. Here they felt more at home than they would elsewhere, for the survivors of the *Pikadon* had emerged from the war as poor, as sick, and as wretched as themselves. 'In Hiroshima nobody looks down on us,' remarked one of these new citizens, when asked to explain why they should have chosen to settle in this most war-damaged of all the Japanese cities – a choice that at first glance seemed a strange one. Others said, with a frankness verging on brutality: 'Before the war four hundred thousand people found living space here. Only a hundred and fifty thousand of them still exist, so there's bound to be room for us.'

Similar calculations attracted ambitious men, hoping for success, from the Osaka district to Hiroshima. The citizens of that great sea port are known throughout Japan for their business acumen. It is said that when an Osaka businessman trips and falls, he will certainly have pulled off a deal before he gets to his feet again. Now they reckoned, quite correctly, that in a place so totally destroyed as was Hiroshima a shrewd operator could surely amass a fortune in a very short space of time.

Soon many of these hard-working, ambitious, and high-spirited settlers achieved positions superior to those of the original citizens of Hiroshima. Even before the war the inhabitants of the Chugoku region had been regarded as somewhat slower, more stolid, and less enterprising than were the men from the metropolitan centre of Japan. To this was now added the fact that even one whole year after the *Pikadon* the majority of the survivors were still suffering, to a greater or lesser degree, from the after-effects of shock, deliberately attributable to the extraordinary experience through which they had passed, and simply lacked the strength to compete with the tough and resourceful newcomers on equal terms. As a leading article in the *Chugoku Shimbun* put it at the time, months after the catastrophe they were still 'somewhat deafened'.

There were thus two classes of persons living in Hiroshima. There were the 'survivors', who, to begin with, constituted the majority of the population, but who were soon only half, then a third, and finally only amounted to one in five of Hiroshima's inhabitants. And on the other hand there were the 'new people' steadily on the increase both in importance and in numbers. The result of this was conflict, which, while seldom openly in evidence, came to constitute an integral part of the 'new Hiroshima'.

There was one incident, however, which caused a public outcry. One 'new man' from Osaka went so far as to attempt to acquire the whole business of selling atom-bomb souvenirs, and thereby threatened to deprive a real victim of 6 August of his livelihood, a man named Kikkawa whose very body bore the burn-scars of that day.

A hateful public slanging match ensued. The 'intruder' from Osaka asked sarcastically by what right his competitor should describe himself, as he did in his advertisements, as Atom-bomb Victim No. 1. Finally this business struggle, fought in the very shadow of the 'Atom Dome', reached such proportions that a bitter jest went the rounds of Hiroshima: 'What those two would really like, if they could, would be to atom-bomb one another.'

BAMBOO-SHOOT EXISTENCE

1

PILOTS and air-crews who flew over Hiroshima during the first six months that followed the dropping of the atom bomb tell of having experienced a deep and choking sensation of guilt at the sight of the huge, dirty, grey-and-rusty-brown stain that disfigured the green landscape of fields and forest. By the spring and summer of 1946, however, Hiroshima was itself green once again. As seen from the air it now resembled a single, gigantic market garden. Wherever a patch of ground remained open, this was rapidly ploughed. Opposite the Town Hall corn sprang up, and beneath the shadow of the 'Atomic Dome', in whose rusty ruins swallows were nesting, there was a crop of potatoes, tomatoes, and cabbages. That first harvest was a meagre one, and this was ascribed to the belief that the radiation which followed the bombing had exterminated the bacteria in the soil. On the other hand the rice crop was more abundant than usual, and certain vegetables assumed so gigantic a size that people stared at them in wonderment. Such wonderment, it must be admitted, contained a greater element of worry than of joy.

These auxiliary crops proved, however, quite inadequate to provide even half the food needed to feed the population of Hiroshima, which was once again approaching the two hundred thousand mark. The reserve stocks that had survived the war had meanwhile been exhausted, and almost the only food to be obtained with ration cards was a sort of meal made of potato leaves and 'railway grass'. 'The housewives,' reported the *Chugoku Shimbun*, 'maintain that all they can do with this stuff is to feed it to their rabbits. But they only say that in public. In truth, in the privacy of their houses, they make all sorts of "grass cakes" out of this bitter-tasting powder.'

Any person in those days who still had any possessions moved them out, bit by bit, into the country, where they were traded for food. A poetic phrase had been invented to describe this prosaic necessity, a phrase which became current during this period of living hand-to-mouth: *takenoko-seikatsu*, 'bamboo-shoot existence'. For the heart of the young bamboo consists of many delicate leaves laid one close above the other, and they are eaten as a European eats an artichoke, leaf by leaf, until at last there is nothing left at all.

At this period in Japan, as in war-torn Europe in the immediate post-war months, the houses of the peasants were soon crammed to the roof with valuables and money. The mistrustful country folk insisted on cash payments and locked the banknotes away in their strong-boxes. In these days there were celebrations and festivities in the villages, known as *issaku-iwai*, or 'one foot feasts'. On such occasions the peasants would make towers of their banknotes, which often reached a height of a foot or more; they would then gloat over their new wealth.

Saka, the suburb of Hiroshima where Ichiro Kawamoto lived, was half town and half country. Many of the men who worked for the Electrical Company had a secondary job as well, working on the land. Thus Kawamoto was in a position to observe precisely how the farm produce would be quickly hidden away when the controllers responsible for proper delivery and distribution were in the vicinity, and how it would be brought forth again with equal speed when the *katsugiya* – the representatives of the black-market operators in the city – came to call.

It is true that the Americans did try to help, and issued yellow corn meal from their own supply stores, a form of food, incidentally, hitherto unknown to the Japanese; but these auxiliary supplies were totally inadequate to the need. Not only in Tokyo and Osaka, but also in Hiroshima did the May Day festivities of 1946 – celebrations which had been forbidden for years by the Japanese military régime and which were now resumed for the first time – take the form of hunger demonstrations. On a banner made from an old black air-raid curtain there was to be seen, for all to read, in black and white: WE STARVE! The week-end holiday, another innovation of the newly-established democracy, had to be spent by most workers at this time searching for weeds and edible barks, or else doing heavy manual *arubeit* for some peasant in exchange for a few handfuls of rice.

The Occupation Authorities made a demand of Shinzo Hamai: in his capacity as a senior official he should set a good example to the other civil servants and should openly announce that from now on he would never again buy 'black rice'. He accepted this order and for a few weeks he and his wife endured the greatest privation in consequence. At last, however, he was compelled to abandon this display of civic virtue and turn to the black market once again. There was also a story in the papers at that time about a judge who found himself faced with the dilemma of either breaking the law in order to eat or of slowly starving to death: the only solution that he could find to this problem was to commit suicide, which he did.

It was said that smoking stilled the pangs of hunger, so countless 'cigarettes' were rolled in pieces of newspaper. In order to forget their miseries and misfortunes most people got drunk whenever they could. In their choice of alcoholic drink many of them were completely careless. They even drank industrial alcohol. Numerous drinkers died in consequence, while others went blind. And Kawamoto tells me that persons so blinded would maintain they had lost their eyesight in the atomic bombardment, with the result that those people who had really been blinded by the *Pikadon* were frequently not believed – and dismissed and insulted as lying drunkards. *Hiropon* became very popular. This was a drug that simultaneously killed appetite and induced a sensation of great well-being and energy. It had been issued to *kamikaze* pilots before their death-flights, as well as to troops about to take part in an assault landing. The dope-peddlers had got hold of it by plundering the old supply depots.

At the Saka Electricity Works during this period drinking bouts were also the daily custom. Rice wine and whisky being only rarely available here, they made do with a milky-looking, sour-smelling brew made of water and fermented potato peelings.

Kawamoto had hitherto never participated in one of these drunken evenings. But at last he could no longer resist the pressing invitation of his workmates nor stand up to their teasing. A bowlful of the stuff was held under his nose, and they encouraged him with these words:

'Come on, boy, you must build up your strength. Just try a swallow!'

They stood around him, five or six of them, and watched him as, with eyes tight shut, he forced down the foul-tasting brew.

'He's drinking it! At last! He's made it!' they were all shouting together. 'Like the taste, boy? Warms you up, what?'

Kawamoto shook his head:

'It's sour. Did you make it properly? There's something wrong with it.'

The others roared with laughter. 'That's how potato spirit tastes. That's all. Come on, have some more!'

It was with a splitting headache that Ichiro lay down to sleep that night, swearing that he would never drink again. And next morning he was as hungry as before.

In order to get over the empty feeling in his stomach, Kawamoto's first action in getting up was to drink a glass of water. Then he ran down to the drugstore, where they were already waiting for him. In order to earn a little extra money, and then be able to buy a little extra food, he had taken on the job of delivering newspapers before starting his normal day's work.

It was a hard job, for most of the farms to which he had to deliver the papers lay on hilltops or amidst fields. When it was raining Ichiro would be soaked to the skin, for he did not own an umbrella. Often the newspapers that were not printed locally would fail to arrive on time, owing to a railway accident or a breakdown of the electric current. Then he would have to do the whole exhausting round a second time, after his day's work.

By that time it would usually be too late for him to travel into Hiroshima and spend the money he had earned on rice cakes in the black market near the railway station. So Ichiro would go back to bed even hungrier than when he had got up, his stomach rumbling emptily after the hard day's work.

2

There was one advantage to his *arubeit* as a newsboy: it allowed Kawamoto to quench his parching intellectual thirst, for he could read the papers to his heart's content.

'I would sit down under a tree in which the summer cicadas were singing, and read. . . .' So runs a sentence in his diary, where he faithfully described the political and social developments of the immediate post-war years.

Noteworthy are the entries dated 1946 in which he describes how the initial admiration for the Americans was slowly turning to scepticism. He observes incidents in which American soldiers had 'interfered' with civilians; he comments critically on the Occupying Power's increasing tendency to intervene against the right to strike; he records the emergence of 'anti-Americanism' in his own circle. But Kawamoto continued himself to be friendly disposed towards the Americans. He even tried to learn English by correspondence course. A certain Professor Matsumoto visited Saka, to lecture on American institutions, and Kawamoto went to see him with the request that the Professor help him emigrate to the United States. The lecturer, however, could offer him no help at all, for the American immigration authorities offered only a minute quota of immigration permits to 'Asiatics'. By way of consolation, however, he sent the boy a few copies of the *Reader's Digest*.

When the next winter came, Kawamoto tried to obtain work with the Army of Occupation. The direct reason for his taking this decision was the loss of his fitter's wrench, which he carried day and night, attached to his belt. The tool, however, had never been his property, but only a loan. It belonged to the firm, and the young man did not dare face his employers again until he had found it, for in the conditions then prevailing a wrench was an almost irreplaceable treasure.

So Kawamoto reported sick and began an intensive search for the valuable object he had lost. But though he retraced all his steps of the previous day, the wrench was nowhere to be found. It had probably been stolen, and had made its way to the black market long ago.

'There's only one thing to do now,' Ichiro said to himself. 'I must find another job, one where I can earn enough money to replace the wrench. Until I have done that, I can't possibly face my workmates.' So next morning he reported sick again and took the train to Kure. He knew from his reading of the newspapers that

the Americans were constantly advertising for men to work in
their 'Air Force Camp' at Hiro.

The young Japanese had no sooner passed through the gates of
the military installation than he found himself in a world that was
to him both new and strange: jeeps and cars bearing a white star,
barbed wire, pin-up girls, and notices in a foreign language. Although his train journey had taken him only a few miles, it was
as though he had arrived far, far from his home.

The new arrival was directed to the Employment Office, where
he was first of all given a questionnaire, which he was told to fill
in exactly. 'Then I asked about my quarters,' Kawamoto remembers, 'and I was told that I would be given a bed in the camp, but
that I must bring my own bedding. When I heard that, my reso-
lution began to weaken. All I possessed was my thin *futon*, which
was almost in rags and which I'd left behind in Saka. I couldn't
bring that here. But without bedding I'd surely be unable to sleep
for cold in these draughty barracks, even if I kept all my clothes
on. . . .

'Well, there you are, the dream's over. That's what I said to
myself, and I felt deeply disappointed. All the same I hung about
a bit longer, not knowing quite what to do, watching the others
filling in their questionnaires, and the men in uniform who took
them away . . . . After I'd been waiting for half an hour, or maybe
an hour, it began to snow outside. A middle-aged Japanese soldier,
who maintained that he had served in Manchuria, was the first
to pass the "examination". They also took on another big,
strong lad of about twenty. . . .'

Another young man was standing by, shifting uneasily from
one foot to the other. He must, Ichiro reckoned, be about two
years older than himself. He found this stranger sympathetic at
first glance. He wore no hat to hide his black unruly hair, and
there were holes around the elbows of his jacket. He too seemed
undecided as to whether he should continue to await the American's decision or should leave at once. Suddenly he lost patience.
He turned sharply on his heel and stamped out, into the whirling
snow, heading for the railway station. Without knowing precisely
why he did so, Ichiro followed him, at a distance of some thirty
yards.

The long winter rains and now the damp snow had quite destroyed the surface of the road along which they were walking. Only where the tyres of the jeeps and army trucks constantly passed had the earth been pressed down to form two smooth ribbons. Along one of these narrow paths *Moji-moji-san*, or Gollywog, as Kawamoto called the other man in his mind, was carefully picking his way. And he was doing this so skilfully that his feet remained both dry and clean despite his dilapidated footwear. 'He knows his way about,' Ichiro said to himself, and followed in his footsteps.

3

There was a wait of almost two hours before the next train would be leaving Hiro for Kure and Hiroshima. There were five of them seated in the icy, empty waiting-room, three women who were too tired or too hungry even to gossip together, and the two young men. Kawamoto would willingly have entered into conversation with his contemporary, but he was too shy to address him without a pretext. The tall young man was attempting to warm his hands by thrusting them into the sleeves of his shiny, threadbare jacket. 'Should I lend him my fitter's gloves?' Ichiro wondered. He was already tugging at one of them, with the intention of offering it to the stranger, a wordless gesture of incipient friendship. But the other's head was sunken, his eyes on the ground, and when he looked up again Kawamoto had lost the courage to repeat his shy offer.

So they sat there in silence, staring out at the whirling grey snow, at the millions of white flakes. Each flake, alone and separate from its fellows, fell upon the hard, cold ground.

At last the train arrived. It was pretty full. Ichiro sat down on one of the two unoccupied seats in the coach. He could not help looking at 'Gollywog' and he watched him burrowing deep in his pockets, from which he drew forth first one banknote, then another, and proceeded to compare the two of them with a sceptical grimace. Kawamoto gave him a sympathetic smile of understanding. He knew that the other young man was amusing himself by examining the design of the new ten-yen notes issued by the Americans. On each of these there was reproduced the Imperial chrysanthemum emblem, encircled with an ornamental design which, according to many Japanese, resembled a prisoner's chains; they also bore a picture of the Diet Building within a frame that was said to look like a prison window. There were even persons who were reluctant to accept these notes, on the ground that they regarded them as a symbol of 'Japan's enslavement'. Kawamoto was on the point of opening a conversation on this subject when all of a sudden they were plunged into total darkness. They were entering Kure station. Those who wanted to get out here were crowding towards the door, but the tall 'Gollywog' waited until all the others had alighted before he got up, ran to the exit, and in one leap was down on the platform.

'Should I follow him? But what does he mean to me actually? Why is it so feverishly important to me that I get to know him?' Kawamoto got to his feet, with the intention of following him, when 'Gollywog', who must have been thinking it over, suddenly changed his mind and leaped back on board the train which was already in motion.

He sat down in his old place and began to dig in his pockets once again. His face was expressive of anxiety, even of despair. 'He's exactly as unhappy as I am myself. Something has gone very wrong for him,' Ichiro decided. 'And he's got nobody he can talk to about it. Again, just like me.'

At this point a very crumpled piece of paper fell out of Kawamoto's travelling companion's side pocket. Quickly Kawamoto leaned down, picked it up, and handed it to him.

'Thanks,' he said, and tucked the scrap of paper away in the outside breast pocket of his jacket. Then in the tones of one making a confession he added: 'That is precisely what I've been looking for all this time. This piece of paper is worth . . .' He hesitated, looking for the right word, 'worth a fortune to me. A very, very large fortune.'

The train was screeching over newly laid rails, an emergency repair to the line.

'Would you care to know what's written on that piece of paper?' Gollywog now asked, hooking it out of his breast pocket once again. He held it out. 'Take it, please.' It was a *yosegaki*, one of those greetings containing words of affection and encouragement, such as are given to friends before they set out on a journey according to the old Japanese custom. On the creased piece of paper, near to disintegration after so many foldings and unfoldings, was written:

> *In China it was cold. In Japan it is icy. Don't forget me. Look after yourself. 'Noppo'* [Thin-leg].
> *Keep strong and healthy. Do nothing foolish. 'Mindanao'* [Philippines].
> *I'm already rejoicing about your pay-day in Hiroshima. Keep your chin up, brother. 'Kutsuken'* [Little boot].

And finally:

> *As a present I'd like a little bit of chocolate and some chewing gum. 'Chibiko'* [Tiny].

Kawamoto told me:

'I quite forgot that I was in a moving train. Opposite sat Mojimoji-san, watching me tensely as I read and reread the note. I had forgotten all about my wrench, the bedding I hadn't got, yes, even the hunger and the cold. Now Gollywog explained to me, with a sort of pride, what those greetings really meant, while I interrupted from time to time with "Is that really so?" or "Ah ha!" or simply with a sigh.

'I did not learn Gollywog's real name either then or at a later date. But he did tell me what his real nickname was. They called him "Kutsuhei", which means Big Boot. He also told me a certain amount about the authors of the *yosegaki*. "Mindanao", who had come back from the Philippines, was twelve years old. His friend "Noppo" was two years older, also an orphan, and had made his way back to Hiroshima from China. "Chibiko", who was eight years old, had lost her mother in the *Pikadon*, and her father had been a soldier, posted as missing, believed killed. Finally "Kutsuken" was the younger, fifteen-year-old brother of my new friend "Kutsuhei".'

As he listened to Gollywog's story, Kawamoto began to understand why he had behaved in so extraordinary a fashion when the train had stopped at Kure station: he had wished to jump out there because he could not bear the idea of returning to his four protégés in Hiroshima with empty hands.

'I'm what you might call the head of the family,' he explained. 'And now I haven't got a tiny bit of chocolate for Chibiko. They had all hoped so that the Americans would take me on. But it was no good: you see, I don't own any bedding of my own!'

They were passing by the hill of Saka, and Kawamoto never so much as noticed it, so intently was he hanging on Kutsuhei's words.

'I met my brother,' he was saying, 'quite accidentally, in Hiroshima station in October 1945. For weeks he had been looking for our mother and sister, and he kept on returning to the station because he hoped that they might have fled during the first panic and would eventually come back. Well, they had obviously gone on a longer journey. But I – who had been given up for dead by the whole family when I was sent to the front – I did come back. They'd discharged me from the army and I possessed nothing whatever in the world except a single blanket. This I shared from then on with Kutsuken.'

'And the others . . .?'

'During my time in the army I'd really only learned one thing: how to dig foxholes. So I simply dug a larger one now, somewhere between the rubble, and made a nice little dug-out, according to army regulations, as a home for my brother and myself. We earned our daily ration of rice by polishing shoes. Then one evening a tiny, sweet little girl – sweet, I tell you, really charming! – came and begged from us. That was Chibiko. We kept her to live with us right away. After all, somebody had to look after her. As, for example, when two hooligans snatched the rice-balls from her that she'd just begged off a traveller. We set off after the louts at once, caught them by the collar, gave them a good beating so that they began to howl for mercy, and from then on they too belonged to our little band. You know their names already, Noppo and Mindanao, and I wouldn't care to say which of the two is the cheekier. You'll get to know them, because you'll come and visit us soon, won't you?'

'And that's how we two orphans, too poor even to possess any bedding of our own, were brought together by a scrap of paper,'

Ichiro says; 'for hours we had sat opposite one another in silence, and now we were suddenly old friends. We parted, in mid-sentence as it were, at the Kaitachi station and I promised to visit him and his friends for sure in the near future. Next day, my courage restored, I went back to work, and the first thing I did was to report the loss of my monkey wrench. I had expected that I would be severely reprimanded, but the foreman and my workmates forgave me and told me not to worry. They said I shouldn't get so upset about losing my wrench. It wasn't a tragedy, they said. But would Kutsuhei, who was unemployed, forgive me for having a regular job again?'

So ends Ichiro Kawamoto's description of his futile flight to Hiro. He had found something quite other, and far more valuable, than what he had sought: a comrade who had shared his fate. This man, he felt, was the first real friend he had ever had in his life.

4

Kazuo M. too had at last got a job. Ever since the *Pikadon* he had been roaming the streets, with no real occupation, though almost every evening, as soon as it grew dark, he would attempt to do business with those American soldiers whom he saw accompanied by Japanese girls.

A respectable organization, the Hiroshima Savings Bank, had now taken him on as an assistant clerk. Then he was able to turn to good account the training that he had had as a 'conscript worker' during the last few months of the war. At the age of sixteen he found himself the sole 'breadwinner' of his family. Father Setsuo had insisted that the boy should not resume his schooling, which the war had interrupted – he spoke of school as 'a waste of time' – and therefore now treated him in a slightly more friendly fashion than heretofore.

Kazuo left his parents' home punctually each morning carrying a schoolboy's satchel made of coarse canvas which contained his midday meal, and would hurry into the makeshift city of booths and lean-tos. It was usually night by the time he got home again. He was proud and contented with his new life.

But a few weeks later he arrived back home one day at noon.

'What's the matter, *Oniichan* [little brother]?' his sister asked in surprised tones. 'You're quite pale. Have you been fighting again?'

Kazuo had no wish to explain. When his anxious mother came hurrying out of the kitchen, he only growled roughly: 'Nothing to worry about, Mother.'

He was happy that ever since 'the day' his mother had given up asking questions; but today he would have been pleased if she had, for once, insisted and had cross-questioned him. But she for her part had grown accustomed since the *Pikadon* to others being moody and depressed, including her own son. In such moods she preferred to leave him alone.

For an hour or two Kazuo lay on his mattress with his eyes shut. He had rolled up his empty luncheon bag, and was using it as a pillow.

'I won't need it now,' he said to himself. But, as he told me later, what he would really have liked to do would have been to shout at the top of his voice:

'Cowards! Robbers! All of you!' Later, according to a habit he had recently acquired, he noted down what had happened to him that day:

'A girl named Kyoko shouted at me "*Kazuchan*". I'd only been working in the office a short time, and here she was calling me "*Kazuchan*" as if we were old friends. I reckon she's about two years older than me. Not particularly pretty, but always acting stuck-up, so everyone can see right away how well brought up she was.

'Never could stand the way she talks to me. And, that business today, well that's put paid to her so far as I'm concerned, And, as it happens, she's my immediate boss.

'It happened during the midday break. Four or five of the girls were talking and giggling together and then they began laughing so much that it was actually more like squealing. This girl had been shouting "*Kazuchan*" for some time, and I'd been acting as though I'd heard nothing. After all what could I answer? "Little Kazu, what's the matter with you?" she asked me, and came right close up to me now. Her face was only a few inches from mine.

'"Kazuchan," she asked softly, "wouldn't you like to earn a bit extra?" These girls ask the dumbest questions.

'"Of course I would. Money's always useful."

'"In that case we've something to discuss with you." And now suddenly the other four girls had crowded close around me.

'"Are you really prepared to join in?"

'It was only at this moment that it occurred to me, for the first time, how terribly poor we were. We couldn't even give my sister a full *bento* [breakfast tin] to take to school with her.

'"But what is it you want me to do?" I asked.

'"You know everybody's got to be pretty smart to get along today," Kyoko said suddenly.

'When I didn't say anything to this she went on more softly: "It's a question of finding out which families were completely wiped out by the atom bomb, with nobody left alive at all. Near the Aioi Bridge and in the Dobashi Quarter there must have been lots that happened to. . . . We'll check in the files and see which ones had an account. When they did, we'll produce a duplicate of their savings books. But for ourselves! The supervisors won't notice anything. It's all so obvious! These people will have lost everything except their savings, and now they – that is to say, in reality, we – want to draw them out of the bank. Don't look so stupid. We've tried it all out, and nobody noticed anything. Well, what do you say, Kazuchan? Won't you have a go, little Kazu?"

'Now I remembered what I had heard a few days ago. I hadn't paid any attention to their remarks: "You, how did you do today?" "A good haul." "Mine was pretty thin." "But you hit the jackpot yesterday. . . ." "True enough, hee, hee!" That was the way they'd talked, and I'd wondered at the time what it was all about. Now I knew. These corpse-robbers had been boasting to one another about their successes.

'I pulled myself together. "No," I said, "that's not the sort of thing for me." I looked them straight in the face, one by one, as I said it. My answer seemed to take the girls aback. For a moment they just stood there, and I could see surprise in their eyes, and fear too.

'Then Kyoko shouted:

'"Obviously Kazuchan is still wet behind the ears. That's why he's so scared of everything, no matter how small."

'The girls now began to screech with laughter, to cover up their embarrassment.

'"What's that got to do with it?"

'"Ho, ho, look at him, he's going all pink, the little boy! Look how angry he's getting! Isn't he sweet?"

'Next moment one of the girls had rubbed her cheek against my cheek, and her sparkling eyes were gazing invitingly into mine. All I wanted to do was to get away from those eyes. I don't know why, but had I looked away it'd have been all up with me. So I pulled myself together and stared straight back into her eyes, and then I slapped her right across the face.

'"I'm not coming back. . . ." I announced and walked out of the office. The girls just watched me. They were so astonished they didn't know what to do.

'And now what? Father and Mother have been sickly ever since the atom bomb. They rely on what I earn. Sister has set her heart on an aluminium breakfast tin. No hope of it now. But something like that, I really couldn't take part. . . .'

5

On the first Sunday of February 1947, Kawamoto, as he had agreed with Kutsuhei, caught the seven a.m. train from Saka to Hiroshima. It was not a passenger train, but a train consisting of goods wagons which, as was not unusual at that time, were used to carry passengers. 'Since there were no windows,' he recalls, 'we had to keep the side doors open, or it would have been as dark as pitch inside. A bitter wind blew in and all the passengers tried to avoid the middle of the truck, where it was coldest, and crowded together near the front. The ones standing by the walls stretched out their arms to cling on. The ones in the middle had nothing to hold on to. Each time the train took a curve we would be tossed about, falling over each other and trampling on one another's feet, apologizing all the while.'

Despite the earliness of the hour the square in front of the railway station was already full of people. Ichiro looked around for a shoe-shine boy, for Kutsuhei had promised to meet him, and for a moment, amidst this crowd of strangers, he felt as lost as he had done a few days ago when he had been staring into the snow falling outside the barracks at Hiro.

Then he saw, far away, a hand waving a blacking brush. Golly-wog came towards him with a smile. With one hand he was pulling little Chibiko along behind him. She gave him a dignified bow, as if she were not wearing a torn *monpe* but the most beautiful kimono.

'Are you the brother from the Andes?' she asked.

'Needless to say I've been boasting about your having been to Peru,' Kutsuhei explained. 'We're all particularly proud that our new friend should be so widely travelled.'

'May I carry your parcel for you?' Chibiko asked. She was already carrying a parcel of her own, a bundle wrapped in old newspaper.

'No, thanks. I am sorry that you had to come here in such cold weather to meet me.'

'Not at all. Besides, Chibiko has already been working.'

He nodded towards her bundle, and winked.

In the sharp sunshine of that icy February morning Hiroshima seemed to the visitor to be entirely changed. Now the town had something of a hastily constructed fairground about it, for in the past twelve months the number of places of entertainment had increased remarkably. Whole amusement districts had sprung up in the neighbourhood of the station and near the city centre, streets of bars, night-clubs, brothels, cinemas, and gambling dens, complete with brilliant advertisements and balloons waving in the wind. The largest of these new quarters was called, arrogantly, *Shintenchi*, the New World. A grotesque and crazy new world!

Apart from a single housing project in the Motomachi quarter, the city authorities had so far been able to do almost nothing by way of finding accommodation for the many homeless. Therefore everyone was busy attempting to make a roof for himself by his own endeavours.

'We've found a real posh district for ourselves,' Gollywog remarked as they set off. 'In Noboricho, which is where our little home is, only the most respectable people lived in the old days.' They were walking through a bewildering chaos of corrugated iron and wooden huts, an untidy settlement without any recognized arrangement of streets. All of a sudden they found themselves in front of a waist-high fence which looked, if anything, even less respectable and civilized than did the other shanties.

A little beyond were the remains of a ruined wall, skilfully utilized; the rest of the building consisted of rusty metal, blackened planks, and straw mats in more or less advanced stages of decomposition, which gave to the edifice something of the appearance of a huge basket.

'This is our *Himawari-jo* [Sunflower Castle],' said Kutsuhei with an exaggerated wave of the hand. 'When we're in a less boastful mood we call it the Worm Basket.'

From within voices were audible:

'Come in, brother from the Andes! But quickly, or we'll all freeze. Mind your head! Be careful, you've got to make yourself small in here.'

It was dark as a cave inside the windowless interior of the shack. Gradually the candlelight lit up the heads and faces of the inhabitants.

Formal introductions took up a considerable time, for the 'Band' insisted on the most punctilious manners. When for example Kutsuken, the brother of Moji-moji-san, tried to introduce himself in a manner that was contrary to etiquette, Chibiko reprimanded him at once:

'*I am* is what you say. *I am* Kutsuhei's younger brother. You must never leave out the "I am". It would be impolite to the guest.'

'What's to eat?'

Chibiko emptied her parcel: rice, fish, seaweed, even a piece of pickled white radish. 'A good morning's begging, little one.' It did not strike the orphans as at all shameful that they should beg from strangers. But when they were all together a decree laid down by Kutsuhei, the 'Paterfamilias', was absolutely binding upon them all: they did not beg from one another.

Kawamoto too had brought a contribution.

'I almost forgot,' he said, feigning absent-mindedness. He untied his old red *furoshiki* (bandana). Out of it he took a small, flat piece of 'American Bread' made of corn meal which he had baked himself in the furnaces of the Saka Electricity Works.

Soon the odour of the meal being warmed up over the fire permeated the entire dark room. They broke the bread with their fingers, and sipped hot water, as if it were the most delectable tea, from tiny cups that they had themselves made out of old cans.

Kawamoto now began to notice the room. The beds consisted of piles of dried leaves, which were brought down from the mountains. 'They're much softer than an ordinary *futon*,' Noppo boasted. On the walls hung their straw hats, army capes, and a few other garments, properly arranged in order, for Kutsuhei insisted on tidiness.

In the middle, nailed to the wall, was a photograph. One of the children must have torn it out of a newspaper. It showed a tiny child, clinging to a grown-up's hand. It was clearly a woman's hand, perhaps that of the child's mother. Whether or not this was so it was impossible to say, for there was nothing written under the picture, which indeed was not even the whole photograph. What the rest may have been was left to the imagination.

'A lovely picture,' Ichiro remarked.

'Hm . . .' said the children. They had no wish to say more.

6

Thenceforth Ichiro Kawamoto spent every Sunday, and as many week-day evenings as he had free, with his new friends from 'Sunflower Castle'. He recalls many a conversation and many a tale told by the children concerning their adventures and their triumphs, but it is one afternoon that he remembers with especial pleasure; this was the occasion when he invited his friends to go to the pictures with him.

A new cinema had recently been opened, immediately behind the railway station. Its auditorium still reeked of fresh plaster, paint, and new wood. This was quite in order, and indeed suitable for the film, for what was being shown was Charlie Chaplin in *The Gold Rush*. The crudely knocked-together shacks of the Californian miners' settlement, the saloons, the rough housing – it all reminded the children very much of their own city of Hiroshima. But what pleased them best were those scenes in which the little moustachioed and bow-legged man indulged in his grotesque hunger fantasies.

For a long, long time after they had left that dark cinema the children and Kawamoto continued to live *The Gold Rush*.

'Oh. . . . Oh . . . I'm doubled up with hunger,' the spindly-legged Noppo would squeak, pulling the most fearful faces all the while. 'What is this I see before me? A delicious spring chicken, is it not?' And he would make a grab for Chibiko, who would run away, screeching with laughter and fear. 'Don't flutter your wings so, my pullet,' he would go on, and his victim would run away from his clowning, squealing nervously, to hide behind a hut.

Kutsuken, the shoe-shine boy, had particularly enjoyed the scene in which Charlie with enormous relish devours a boiled boot. He would try to snatch the sandal from Kawamoto's left foot.

'You've no idea what a delicious, juicy beefsteak that'll make,' he would say. 'Please. I'll pay you a whole gold bar for it, I want it so much.' Then he would press one of the many blackened roof tiles that had been scattered everywhere since 'that day' into his hands, run off with the sandal, and leave Ichiro to hop about on one foot, weak with laughter.

But when at last they had reached their 'Worm Basket', Kutsuhei, who already possessed the common sense of a grown man, put an end to the clowning. 'Enough nonsense,' he said. 'To-morrow you may be really hungry again.'

7

From Ichiro Kawamoto's diary:

'6 August 1947. I bought some chocolate for Chibiko. Since genuine chocolate is expensive, I could only afford the *ersatz* sort. But Chibiko was delighted with it all the same. I didn't tell her that today was the anniversary of that day when the atom bomb was dropped. All I said was: "I want to give you a present." But Kutsuhei and Kutsuken were in a bad temper all day. They couldn't even bring themselves to say anything about the fried potatoes that I'd brought for supper. They didn't talk about it, but I noticed that they knew exactly what sort of a date this was ... Noppo and Mindanao only ate half their potatoes too, and then slipped out as if they had something on their conscience. I went out as well.

'"The red roof on the green hilltop . . ."

'Noppo began to sing the song called "The Hilltop where the Bell Rings out". He sang it softly.

'Chibiko joined us. Her voice was louder than Noppo's timid treble:

> The bell rings out, chin kon kan,
> It rings, it rings, it rings,
> The mother and the father say:
> Little ones, watch out!

'Noppo's thin voice and Chibiko's loud one merged and were audible inside Sunflower Castle.

'"Kutsuken, Kutsuhei, come on out, friends, and join in the singing!" That was what they called, but they got no answer. I crept back into the dark hut.

'"What's up? You're not sitting in here crying like a couple of little babies, are you?"

'"Brother from the Andes, do not you too feel terribly alone?" Kutsuken asked, the tears rolling down his cheeks. Outside, the singing went on.

'"Alone? Why alone?"

'"Why are our mother and our father no longer with us? Why?"

'"Yes, it's true, your parents are no longer alive. But you two are here, despite everything, and you're grown men." I was attempting to give them encouragement. "Why give in like this? You and Kutsuhei ought to pull yourselves together, yes, particularly you two. Noppo and Mindanao would give in completely if they were to see you like this. Normally you give the three out there strength to go on living. And if you'd like to know the truth, you've given me strength too."

"'Thank you, brother from the Andes," said Kutsuhei. "But sometimes it's really too much to bear. Whatever we do, we get blamed for everything. If anything is missing around here, or even if a couple of windows are broken, the cops, and the nasty old women too, immediately say that it must be us who did it. And then they all go for us. They scream at us and throw stones. They deliberately dump all their garbage right beside our hut. Even their chamber-pots are emptied here. Have you ever been as badly treated as that?"

"'Yes, when I spent three months in my *honke* [family home], at every meal they said spiteful things about my dead parents. I was so upset by this that I wouldn't even sleep in that house, and I used to creep out every night and curl up in the entrance of a nearby temple. Also they often used to blame me when in fact the others had broken things. But in the long run I've always found people to help me over the bad patches . . ."

'For a while they said nothing. Then Kutsuhei got up and spoke in a voice that was far more grown-up than usual: "It's warm in here, Kutsuken. Why don't we go swimming?"

"'Okay . . ." They had picked up this expression, like so many others, from the Americans.

'We climbed the stone steps to the Ohta. These were the same steps up which so many hundreds of people had run, driven almost mad by fear: it was the same river in which they had sought safety on that day, flaming, living torches.

'We lowered ourselves cautiously into the river. The water was chilly and refreshing. The two brothers swam in a somewhat comical fashion, a wildly thrashing free-style. Even in the water we could still hear the others singing . . .

"'We want to swim too!" Mindanao and Chibiko had followed us, and were taking off their ragged trousers. With shrill screams of delight they jumped into the water and began to splash each other frantically. This flowing river was the same one in which Chibiko's mother had drowned on the night of the *Pika-don*. And now Chibiko and Mindanao were enjoying themselves in its water, while Kutsuhei and Kutsuken wanted to show what good swimmers they were. But from the banks came the smell of incense, where the survivors had lit sticks in memory of those who were already half-forgotten. It was the only reminder, on this day of anniversary. Later I went with them to the market in front of the station, and we bought mostly noodles (shockingly expensive). We were so hungry, we wolfed them down.'

8

'How many potatoes have you, Chibiko?'

'Three. Is that right?'

'Quite right. Now we're going to eat them. You'll get exactly the same amount as Kutsuhei, Kutsuken, Noppo, Mindanao, and myself. So how much potato do you get?'

Chibiko counted on her little fingers, her lips moving silently as she did so.

'Think carefully, Chibiko. One . . .'

'One half!'

'Very good. From now on we'll call you Chibiko-san [Miss Chibiko]. Like a grown-up young lady.'

Whenever he could spare the time these days, Kawamoto gave Chibiko lessons. She had herself asked for this. She had seen, as summer ended, that the Hiroshima schools were beginning to re-open – some in the open air, others in new buildings, others again in the cellars or the ruins of the old schools – and had watched the other children learning how to read and write and do arithmetic. So she had asked Kutsuhei why she was not allowed to go to school too. 'I'd still have enough spare time for my work,' she had added.

The elder children had tried to explain to her that it wasn't quite so simple. Any child applying for entrance to a school would be immediately put into an orphanage, so that she wouldn't be allowed to stay with her friends in the Worm Basket. And the newspapers carried disagreeable descriptions of life in those institutions. It appeared that in some of the orphanages there were real 'bosses', themselves children, who modelled themselves on the gangster bosses, and who compelled the other children to surrender a portion of their food rations and to work for those bosses like slaves.

'But we'll teach you everything we know ourselves, Chibiko,' Mr Gollywog had announced, and so they took turns giving the little girl her lessons. They showed her how to form her letters, how to tell the time, and they even taught her to paint a few Japanese ideographs.

Kawamoto was particularly preoccupied with the little girl's education. He showed her how to wash properly, how to comb her hair, the different ways of speaking to different sorts of people according to their age and class. But what the child loved best was when Ichiro gave her her 'geography lesson'. Then he would tell long stories about his own childhood in South America, about the people he had met there, about the tropical foods and fruits that he had eaten as a boy.

So Kawamoto came almost every day to Sunflower Castle, and the children would come running out joyfully to greet him. Thus Ichiro was all the more surprised when one evening they could hardly bring themselves even to wish him a good day. They stood about their hut, evidently in the worst of moods, each one with a longer face than the next.

Mindanao took the 'brother from the Andes' aside, and whispered: 'Kutsuhei has brought a girl here. The sister of a friend. And we're not allowed into the house until she goes.'

Kutsuken was so angry with his elder brother that he would scarcely address a word to Ichiro. Instead, he kept muttering to himself: 'Ever since she showed up, we've had no more fun, no fun at all.'

Only Chibiko seemed to derive a certain pleasure from this novel situation. 'Soon Kutsuhei will be a bridegroom,' she chirruped. This made Kutsuken so angry that he would certainly have boxed her ears, had she not skipped nimbly out of the way just in time.

A couple of days later Mr Gollywog and his new friend vanished from Hiroshima. He had not so much as left a message for his brother and the other children.

Kawamoto immediately took a whole day off from work to

console Kutsuken. The other three that had been 'left behind' also did not go to their work in front of the railway station.

'Kutsuken, it's up to you now to take Kutsuhei's place,' Ichiro told him. 'You're the "head of the family" from now on. Keep your chin up! When your brother first took on the job of looking after you all, conditions were really very much worse than they are today.'

But Kutsuken went on sulking. His comrades all did their best to improve his mood. They sang songs, pulled faces, imitated Charlie Chaplin's unsteady walk. Today, though, there was nothing they could do to make 'Little Boot' laugh.

At last with a sigh Chibiko made her great decision. She crept into the corner where her sleeping-bag filled with leaves lay, and from behind it drew forth her 'treasure', which up till now none of the others had been allowed to touch, or even to look at. It was a bundle of carefully smoothed and folded silver paper. For months Chibiko had been collecting the silver paper from old cigarette packets and chocolate wrappings thrown away in the streets. She had often followed American or Australian soldiers for hours on end, in the hope that they would throw away a sheet of glittering tin-foil. Whenever a G.I. or an Aussie gave her a sweet, she always saw to it that it was one wrapped in silver paper.

Without a word the little girl offered the moody boy her most prized possession. Now at last he did seem to be somewhat impressed, and he stroked her hair gratefully. But all he said, in a voice that was still sulky, was: 'What shall we do with this now?'

'I suddenly remembered my own childhood,' Kawamoto recalls. 'My mother was unable to buy me a mouth-organ. So I got a thin sheet of paper and walked about blowing through it. The paper would tremble gently, and by blowing now hard, now soft, now here, now there, I learned how to get a tune out of it. I did this now. I took the silver paper from a packet of Peace* and on it I blew the tune "The Hilltop where the Bell Rings out". They all gazed at me in amazement.

'"Not bad, eh?" I asked them.

* A type of imitation American cigarette, popular in post-war Japan.

'"Oh, oh, WANDAFUUL! Very, very guud," cried Chibiko, imitating the American soldiers and their accent. She took another of the pieces of silver paper and tried to blow a tune on it. But all that happened was a humming sound without any real tune. Noppo and Mindanao tried next. They too could not manage a tune. They were holding the paper too close to their lips.

'"Just keep on trying, you'll get it eventually. But now you boys whistle, Chibiko shall sing, and I myself will play the silver-paper mouth-organ."

'So our song about the Bell on the Hill rang forth. Three days later they'd all learned the trick except Chibiko. Kutsuken turned out to be a remarkably good performer, and it seemed as though this had really consoled him for the departure of his brother.'

9

Only a few days later something happened which Kawamoto had been dreading ever since Kutsuhei's disappearance. He arrived at Sunflower Castle, to find it deserted.

At first he thought that the children were playing a joke on him. He pulled up the straw mat that covered the entrance and peered into the dark interior, calling out as he did so: 'Don't hide. I'll find you quick enough!'

There was no answer, not even a laugh. He lit a match, and saw at first glance that the hut had been entirely cleared out. Hanging from the low ceiling, and stuck to a candle-holder, there was a message. Kawamoto took the note out of doors, where he read: 'We can't go on like this. The brother from the Andes can't bother about us every day. Kutsuhei is in Okayama. I'm following him there tomorrow. Good luck! Kutsuken.'

The note did not say what had happened to Chibiko, Noppo, and Mindanao. Had they gone with him? Or were they somewhere in the city? Perhaps. No, they must be! Kawamoto became obsessed with the idea that he must find the children. For how would they manage, all on their own? Day after day, when he had finished work, he would wander through the new city that was arising from the ruins of the old, poking into corners, talking to black marketeers, gangsters, prostitutes, and countless other *furoji*. It was all in vain. There was no trace of the children. On those Sundays when he was free, Ichiro widened the circle of his search, going as far as Kure. He even visited the orphanages, because it occurred to him that the three homeless children might have fallen into the clutches of the authorities for the protection of children.

Each time that Kawamoto crossed that part of the town where Sunflower Castle had stood, he hoped that in the hubbub of voices he might suddenly distinguish Chibiko's laugh or Noppo's thin and childish treble, or that Mr Gollywog's unruly crop of hair would emerge from the 'Worm Basket', or Kutsuken try jokingly to steal one of his sandals.

And each time Ichiro had to observe how the 'Castle' was deteriorating more and more, from week to week. First a board fell in, then one mat after the other vanished, and finally the corrugated iron roof made its way to the black market. Those charming neighbours were looting it, systematically.

So it disappeared piece by piece, as happens when a bamboo heart is eaten, leaf by leaf. Finally all that remained was the square hole which had been their fireplace and the foxhole that Kutsuhei had originally dug in October 1945, when he had come here as a freshly-discharged soldier home from the wars and was creating a shelter for his brother and himself.

Then came the snow which covered everything, flakes whirling down on to Hiroshima from a dull, grey sky. Thousands and thousands of them, each one a tiny, separate star.

'ATOM BOY'

1

THE first anniversary of 6 August, that day on which their city had been obliterated in a fraction of a second, had been celebrated by the citizens of Hiroshima with quiet dignity. Thousands upon thousands of white lanterns, each bearing the name of one person who was dead or missing, had been floated down the Ohta and out to sea. A man by the name of Seichiro Kakihara, who before the war had neither borne a famous name nor held high office, had pronounced the oration commemorating the dead. Amidst all the flurry of reconstruction it was he who first reminded the living of their own people who had passed on. It was on his initiative that in the summer of 1946 an artistically tasteless Tower of Spiritual Peace had been built, inside which were preserved the names of all the victims of the bomb.

How different it all was one year later, on 6 August 1947! For three days there was singing, dancing, and drinking. There were masked balls, processions, fireworks. From early morning till late at night the streets were filled with noise.

It is understandable that the foreign observers who attended this so-called 'Festival of Peace' should have been shocked by the lack of piety and of taste. They were silenced by being told that it would be wrong to judge the Japanese according to Western standards. In the Far East such ear-splitting memorial services in honour of the dead were absolutely normal, or so they were informed.

But it was not the Westerners alone who voiced such criticisms. The loud indecency with which the memory of so unspeakably agonizing an event was celebrated caused deep displeasure to many of the survivors as well, and they protested in the strongest terms against this transformation of a solemn memorial day into a coarse, popular festival.

Their cruellest, and unfortunately not unjustified, complaint was that 'people' – by which they meant the traders and merchants of Hiroshima – 'were cashing in on the dead'. In fact the project of having a great 'Festival of Peace' had originated in the newly reorganized Chamber of Commerce. The chairman, Totaro Nakamura, on the occasion of the opening in March 1947 of the new Association for the Advancement of Tourism, had proposed that the attention of Japan and of the entire world should be focused on Hiroshima by means of an International Festival of Peace. The first person to express doubts about this idea was Shinzo Hamai. But one month later he was promoted from Deputy Mayor to first Mayor of Hiroshima, and in his new capacity he had no choice but to do his best to forward this project, despite all the reservations that he had expressed.

On 6 August at 8.15 a.m., that is to say at precisely the hour at which the bomb had been dropped, the new and active First Citizen of Hiroshima declared the Festival open, standing on a plinth at the foot of the bridge. Peace bells rang out. At the same moment hundreds of 'peace doves' fluttered skywards. There followed a short prayer for the victims and the reading of a message from General MacArthur. Then came many, many speeches (all previously cleared with the censor) in which no single reference to the horrors of the atomic bombing was allowed. And finally Mayor Hamai read an impressive 'Declaration of Peace'.

Throughout the whole day two Buddhist priests chanted prayers from the Tower of the Dead, close to the tribunal. But their voices were soon drowned by the din of dance music.

The reporters of the *Chugoku Shimbun* have described this macabre carnival in the following words:

Darkness and light played a duet in the joy-filled city of Hiroshima. Those many persons who had lost their nearest and dearest wept tears of memory, prayed at the Buddhist Ceremonies for the Dead, or sat at home and read the scriptures. But no sooner did they pass through their front doors than they were met by strident dance music played upon gramophones, and by processions of masked dancers moving through the streets. Seventy or more young girls in the most beautiful kimonos came pouring out of the Shintenchi quarter. They wore flowers in their hair and danced the new *Heiwa-Ondo* [the Peace Dance], the words of which are:

Pika to Hikkatta	(The atomic ball
Genshi e no tama ni	loosed sharpest lightning,
Yoi-yaga	Yoi-yaga!
Tonde agatte Heiva	They fly upwards,
No Hato yo....	the doves of peace....)

By midday at least five times as many people as usual were in the streets. And in the business district the shopkeepers were saying to themselves that now was the time to cash in. They hung up lanterns, with the announcement: '*Great peace sale!*' Sweat poured from the brows of the young shop assistants and they calculated that their take would be three times that of a normal day. Dancing went on until late into this summer night.

Among those who resented such commercialism, and who therefore kept away, was Kazuo M. The entry in his diary for this day runs:

'Everywhere in the town there is now jazz ... Cinemas are springing up like bamboo shoots after the rain. Dance halls are raking in the money. I sometimes ask myself whether this is the "Peace" for which we have longed. True reconstruction, however, should consist of more than the building of houses and the laying of streets (I hear we are to have one a hundred metres wide!). What is happening about spiritual reconstruction....? I suddenly found myself on the road that leads to the Cemetery for the Unknown Dead on Hijiyama Hill. I felt that I must visit Yasuji and Sumiko.... The sun was just sinking, and in the cemetery I came upon an elderly woman. She was kneeling, and crying out: "Hajime, Hajime...." That must have been the name of her son, or grandson. I could share her feelings. Since I had no wish to disturb her, I slipped away. Above the streets of Hiroshima the city lights cast a brilliant red glow....'

Kazuo's notes for the years 1947 and 1948 are even more deeply permeated with emotional outbursts than are the earlier entries in his journal. He was coming to feel even more clearly that his attempt to remain 'pure' in an environment pulsating with lust for life – an environment of a heartlessness and a corruption that disgusted him – could scarcely succeed. His protests against the post-war epoch grew to screams of hatred. His inability to live in and with this changed, new age was bound to lead him into ever sharper conflicts and increasingly perilous situations. In his diary he describes this period of his life as 'The Story of my Wandering from Job to Job'. There I read:

'X Month, X Day, 1947. Today I started work in the Asahi Theatre, a medium-sized cinema, in the advertising department. Got the job through a newspaper "Positions Vacant" ad. Since I enjoy drawing and painting, I thought it would just suit me. So I'll try hard to keep it.

'First day: Washed out sixty paint brushes. They were encrusted with old paint, hard as wood. Thought to myself: how can anyone have allowed such fine brushes to get in so disgusting a state? Cleaned them as thoroughly as possible. Then came the sticking up of the posters. Not at all easy. But taken by and large a pleasant day. The head of the Advertising department seems a nice man.

'X Month, X Day, 1947. Today I quarrelled with the cinema projectionist. Subject: *hiropon*. Told him that night-work makes me tired. So he advised me to take *hiropon*. Presumably he meant it well. I told him stimulants are bad for the health. This annoyed him. Finally he called me a coward, and I shouted back "*Baka-yaro!*" [fool]. The head of the advertising department separated us, and we stopped quarrelling. He said to me: "I see what you mean, but night-workers can't get by without *hiropon*. You can act sensible and scorn it today, but just you wait: one of these days you'll be asking for a couple of shots yourself. The thing is, you're so young. . . ."'

2

'X Month, X Day, 1947. I'm still worrying about what the department head said to me the other day. Maybe I really am too "green", but at least I can tell the difference between right and wrong. I keep thinking: If only Yasuji were still alive. Since I lost him I've really been entirely alone. Actually, I often used to quarrel with him too. We would then say horrible things to one another, but deep down each of us thought about the other: He's really a grand chap! If I was ever unhappy, he would always cheer me up. For me it's still as though I'd only lost Yasuji yesterday.

Yet sometimes it seems as if it were many, many years ago. I don't even know how he spent his last months on earth. If only I could cry out "Hi, Yasuji!" and he were to be standing there saying "Here I am!" If . . . yes, if . . . If he were alive. . . . If he were to come back. . . . Nonsense! Yasuji will never come back again. Good night, Yasuji. . . .

'X Month, X Day, 1947. I swore to myself I'd never get into a quarrel again, but hardly six months have passed since I made that promise to myself and already I've broken it. It was a funny business. The head of my department – he says he's a Communist – was praising Soviet Russia. Marx says so and so, and Lenin says this and that . . . I had no wish just to sit there in silence, listening to him the way a man listens to his boss, nodding from time to time. "Soviet Russia played a dirty trick on us," I said. "They waited till Japan was knocked out, unable to defend itself – till we were as helpless as carp before they're tossed into the cookpot – and then they took advantage of our misfortune . . . declaring war on Japan and pretending they'd defeated us . . ."

'But he's not the type to accept he's beaten and be silent . . . Since he's my boss he ordered me to meet him in the auditorium after the performance. Nothing looks so forlorn and sad as an empty cinema. I sat down beside him. For a while he stared at me in silence. Then his lips began to twitch. So I saw how angry he was. He said to me: "If we're going to quarrel, I shall win!" But we didn't quarrel. Instead he yelled at me: "Fool! Worm! You're fired as from tomorrow!"

'He was already disappearing through the public door. It all happened in a moment. I just sat there as if I'd been pole-axed. The words "fired . . . as from tomorrow" had knocked me out more effectively than a straight left to the chin. Sat there, not knowing what to do, in the deserted cinema . . . So here I am, for the second time, a failure who can't keep a job. . . .'

3

'X Month, X Day, 1947. "If there is a God who lets a man fall, then there is another who picks him up again." So runs the saying. Only three days after my dismissal I was enabled, thanks to the intervention of a neighbour, to start work with the firm of Kirita & Co. This firm deals with the installation of waterpipes. I've been taken on as assistant to the man responsible for the planning of tank installations. This is a real solid firm, and not only externally so. The more one gets to know it, the solider it proves to be.

'We are fifteen or sixteen assistants, busy with plumb-lines and spirit-levels. The work requires such a high degree of concentration that none of us even glances about him. A job like this not only seems fine to me, but it fills me with self-respect. It's often so quiet that you can hear yourself breathe. Engineer Terada, who is instructing me, shows me what it's all about. Since I'd already begun to study draughtsmanship in the Middle School, my progress is rapid.

'X Month, X Day, 1948. At last I got a couple of days off, and walked around as I used to do, aimlessly, through the streets. There are still spots that remind me of "that frightful day". But the *Hime-mukashi-yomagi**\ that used to grow wild everywhere is no more to be seen. Everywhere there's the sound of hammering, everywhere new houses are springing up. . . . At the foot of the bridge was standing an ex-soldier in a white robe. He wore a bowl hung about his neck, and called to the people walking by: "Please, please . . ."

'X Month, X Day, 1948. For the past month a rumour has been going around the factory that we're moving. Today it was announced officially. I'm being sent to the Occupying Power in Kaitaichi. The department head explained to me: "We've been given the job of installing a heating system in Camp Kaitaichi. We'll be needing five or six stokers, two or three engineers, and one assistant. You're the assistant . . ."

'In the afternoon a truck brought desks and draughtsman's materials to the new office in the camp. Boiler room, washrooms, offices, everything smells of new paint . . . I was busy arranging the desks when an Australian soldier walked in. "*Kon-nichi-wa*," he said, and I was amazed, because he had no accent at all. He smiled at me, and repeated his entire Japanese vocabulary to us:

* A weed that covered the ruins after the *Pikadon*.

ojo-san [girl], *arigato* [thank you], *ikura-desu* [what price?], *Hanako-chan* [a girl's name], *mo-takusan desu* [enough, enough]. Meanwhile he gestured with his hands and feet, explaining what the words meant. We all laughed. For half the day he was there, helping us move the desks and chairs. That there could be such men among the Australians too! My opinion of foreigners is beginning to change a bit. His name is Johnny and he calls me "Kassu-san". We can half understand one another pretty well. He even gave me a bit of chocolate.

'X Month, X Day, 1948. It seems that Johnny isn't his real name. He brought another N.C.O. with him. This one said he was called Johnny too. Maybe they've got the same name. A confusing state of affairs. I'm just going to call them both Johnny. This other Johnny is eighteen years old and six foot tall. I told them both about the catastrophe. I told them about Yasuji and Sumiko as well. It's a pity my English is so bad. All the same they understood what I was saying quite well. "Oh, atom bomb, Hiroshima," they said softly, and at the end, when I said "No more Hiroshimas", they repeated it after me.

'As assistant to the engineer I've had to test whether the steam in the pipes reaches all over the big camp. So I have also had to go into that part of the camp which is marked PROHIBITED AREA FOR JAPANESE NO TRESPASSING! To do this I was issued with a special pass from headquarters. I felt insulted that as a Japanese on Japanese soil I could not go where I pleased without special permission. My anger increased when I read on the back of the pass that once I had completed my job I was to hand it in again at once. After all, this is our country!'

4

'X Month, X Day, 1948. A bearded Australian soldier, waving a little stick in one hand, shouts angrily: "No loitering!" And the half-starved Japanese labourers work as if they expect him to hit them with his stick . . . "Hubba, hubba, hubba. No loitering!" Each time he brandishes his stick it makes an unearthly whistling sound.

'Here there is no pretence even of that minimum of respect which surely every conqueror must give to the conquered. The relationship is exactly the same as that between men and beasts. And in addition to that, in this case the "animal" is of a particularly inferior sort, debased below the level of swine and snakes. And we poor devils must accept all this humiliation as if we enjoyed it.

'When I'd done my usual round and was back in the office, I heard that there had been trouble there too. One of the stokers was maintaining that his wrist-watch had been stolen. Needless to say by one of the soldiers. They do whatever they please. Recently a stenographer was raped by three soldiers, one after the other. I heard tell that one of the laundry girls had simply been kidnapped, taken off to one of the barrack huts, and was kept locked up in there. "They're the conquerors and that's all there is to it. There's nothing to be done." That's what our people say. In most cases the victims have no choice but "to weep and go to bed", as the Japanese saying has it. I advised the stoker he ought to go to headquarters and demand the return of his watch.

'All day long, disagreeable occurrences of this sort.

'X Month, X Day, 1948. Checked the steam ventilators in the soldiers' sleeping quarters. From one room I heard a woman's voice. She was shouting. I ran across quickly, opened the door a few inches, and put my head in. A woman, stark naked, in a man's arms. I must say I didn't at all get the impression that she had been forced to do this. Without realizing what I was doing I said "Ah!" because I was so surprised. The two figures jumped apart, as if they'd had an electric shock. They both stared at me. When the female saw that I was young she gave me a cheap smile.

'What I wanted to do was to shout "Traitress!" at the top of my lungs. But my emotion was so great that when I did say the word it was in a hoarse, low voice. Then the woman's expression changed. She reached for a glass standing beside her.

'She's going to throw it at me, I thought, and at the very same moment it crashed against the door and broke into a hundred pieces.

'"Get out, you filthy guttersnipe!" she screeched at me. She had jumped up and was screaming the vilest things. Her naked body was very light-skinned. I spat and ran away. The tart went on screaming at me till I was out of earshot.

'When I was back at my drawing-board I could not get the picture of this whitish body and her snake-like arms out of my head.'

5

'"Hi, atom boy!"

'A soldier walked into the boiler room. It was Nixon. He would often walk in here, hit the stokers, and when they didn't hit back he'd amuse himself by throwing lumps of coal at them. As a joke, naturally. He was supple as a worm and a pretty good boxer.

'Now he walked up to me, pointed to a can of beer he was holding, and began to mumble something very quickly. The only words I caught were: "Beer . . . hot . . . boiler . . . shovel . . ." I reckoned that what he was trying to say was: "Put the beer on the shovel and heat it in the boiler." Had I known English better, I'd have answered him at once: "I'm not your servant. And I'm certainly not going to do you any sort of kindness, because of the horrible way you always treat the stokers." But unfortunately I couldn't express all this. So I replied simply, but violently: "No!"

'His face assumed an expression of fury mingled with astonishment.

'"Shut up!" he screamed. At the same time he was winking, as if to show me what fun he was having at my expense. His right hand lay clenched against his chest, while with the left he aimed a couple of blows in my direction.

'Normally I do not pay much attention to humiliations of this sort. But I was still in a high state of nervous tension, as a result of the earlier scene with the naked girl and the soldier, so I said to myself: "If he so much as touches me, he's had it!"

'I grabbed a shovel that was close at hand. Almost at the same moment Nixon kicked out at me. His foot caught my elbow. This caused me such pain that I dropped the shovel. "Eeeeei!" I was half unconscious. "Devil take it!" I seized the shovel again and swung it through the air. Once, twice, the third time I felt that I had hit something.

'"Kazuo-san, you've . . ."

'When I was myself again I found that two or three of our workers were standing around me. They were gripping my arms. My hands felt sticky. It was blood. Blood everywhere . . . even on my overalls. Frightful. And at my feet lay Nixon.

'I must have killed him . . .

'I know there is no direct connexion between my fight with Nixon and the fearful misery of the atomic bomb. But deep in my heart there remains a tragic scar, a scar caused by fire. Scar-tissue on the face, the hands, the feet, can sometimes be removed by surgery, and a certain degree of healing achieved. But the cheloid in my heart can never vanish altogether. . . . And whenever I see a foreigner the wound opens again.

'So it was with Nixon. He had not even taken part in the destruction of Hiroshima. He had killed neither Yasuji nor Sumiko. No, indeed not. But he exploited the fact that he belonged to the conquerors in order to humiliate and despise every Japanese. For that reason alone I cannot forgive him. And if my body must be cut into a thousand pieces for it, I shall still avenge the destruction of Hiroshima! Only a victim of the atom bomb could understand this feeling. And only my heart can conceive this blind fury of mine.'

6

'"Kazuo-san, run away, quickly. . . . Run, hurry!" That is what my workmates were shouting at me, and I could hear the fear in their voices.

'"Why should I run away?" I shouted back at them. "I don't regret having killed Nixon. Nixon isn't an American, it's true. But all the same he's a foreigner and a conqueror. . . ."

'"Okay, okay . . . But now disappear, and fast."

'I turned around. There stood the two Johnnies and, to my delight, they didn't look at all angry.

'"All right, Kassu-san, leave the rest to us. We'll sort this one out. If you hang around, it'll be that much harder."

'How cowardly, to run away now! But they were all so excited and upset. So I made up my mind to go home.

'I told the whole story to my parents right away. "If I've really killed Nixon," I said, "the Military Police must be after me by now, for questioning." When I'd finished Mother began to cry loudly, and her tears fell in a pool on the floor. Father's face was pale; he kept staring into a corner of the room.

'"Stop crying!" Father told Mother sharply. He acted as though he were completely unconcerned, though of course in reality this was not so at all. "Kazuo," he said, "this is your business, and you alone must bear the responsibility for what has happened. . . . You must go at once to the firm, talk to the directors, and decide what you want to do."

'I got up. I heard a car drawing up outside the door. "They're here already," I thought.

'I went outside at once. There stood the two Johnnies, an interpreter, and a director of the firm. There was no sign of any Military Policeman.

'"*Kon-nichi-wa*," said Johnny No. 1, and winked at me. . . . And the dark, heavy feeling that filled my heart was blown away by this wink as if by a gust of wind.

'The interpreter explained that Nixon wasn't dead. His left cheek had been ripped open by the sharp edge of the shovel and had had to be stitched up. He was mad with rage, and kept roaring "Jap! Jap!" So it would be dangerous for me to go to work next day. To save the firm embarrassment it would be highly advisable for me to ask to be dismissed at once. . . . Because of his rough manners Nixon was extremely unpopular with his fellow-soldiers too. The two Johnnies had had a private conversation with him and had persuaded him not to make a fuss about what had happened.

'The director concluded: "The incident has surprised us, but we don't reproach you. You have shown that we Japanese do not lack guts, even today. Fortunately, thanks to the action of these two Australian soldiers, the incident will not become a public scandal. You've been lucky. But you'd better be more careful in future."

'They immediately drew up a letter, to be signed by myself,

requesting that I be dismissed. Father and Mother were very happy when they heard that that would be the end of it, and all I had to do was give up my job with the firm. They thanked the two Johnnies over and over again.

'And so that's how I lost my third job.'

MISS WOODSTICK

1

ICHIRO relates: 'Quite a while before the girl entered the school-room, we could hear her coming.

'*Toc, toc, toc*, re-echoed from the cement floor of the Quonset hut where the Hiroshima Foreign Language School held its classes in elementary English, three times a week. Fujita, once a "suicide sailor", would dig me in the ribs and murmur: "Attention – here comes your Miss Woodstick."'

Ichiro had naturally already heard the tapping of her walking-stick upon the stone floor. Feigning indifference he would gaze straight ahead, while hoping that she would choose a seat immediately in front of his own, because then her two thick plaits would be dangling immediately before his eyes for one whole hour!

He no longer regretted the fact that Fujita, like himself a fitter with the Saka Electricity Works, had persuaded him to attend the language course. Ichiro had only given in to his workmate's insistence because he knew that he must find something to do in his free time, so that he might forget the loss of his friends from Sunflower Castle. The first time he entered the school building, and saw the Cross hanging above the door, he nearly turned on his heel and walked away again. He certainly had no intention of letting the Christians catch him! After all it was 'Christian soldiers' who had dropped the atom bombs on Hiroshima and Nagasaki.

At that time many people in Hiroshima felt this way. Nevertheless the Christian missions in Japan, whether Protestant or Catholic, were enjoying a success in this immediate post-war period such as they had never had before. Their schools and their charitable institutions also attracted many who were interested only in what they had to offer or in the chance for free schooling. Others came for even less respectable reasons. They knew that the religious foundations had money and goods to give away and they hoped that as pupils of Christian schools they might get treatment almost as preferential as that given to baptized 'Christians'. A favourite hiding place for extreme nationalists and even for war criminals on the run was the homes of Christian clergymen. Thus, for example, Flight Captain Kusuda, one of the pilots who had taken part in the bombing of Pearl Harbor, was for a time assistant (using a false name) to the best-known Protestant clergyman in Hiroshima.

Ichiro certainly had no wish to be one of those who nowadays posed as more American than the Americans and who did their best to ape the conquerors in speech, dress, and behaviour. On the other hand he did not like the coarse way in which their enemies mocked the Christians, shouting 'Amen! Amen!' after them in the streets and despising them solely because of their beliefs. It was out of a spirit of opposition to this opposition that he finally decided to attend the Christian language school. He said to himself that it could do no harm to find out what went on there.

Since the appearance of 'Miss Woodstick', Kawamoto had attended the evening classes regularly. He had lacked the courage actually to speak to his fellow-pupil. The nearest he had dared come to approaching her was secretly to slip an English-language newspaper on to the girl's desk, hoping that she might take it home with her and then find the unsigned message that he had laid between the pages.

After the lesson Ichiro remained seated at his desk, pretending that he had something to write, and waiting to see if 'she' would take the newspaper away with her. And it happened: 'Miss Woodstick' leafed through the paper and found the note: 'No longer needed. Don't hesitate to take it.' 'Good, good, it's come off,' thought Kawamoto, and he ran off to catch Fujita, with whom he travelled back to Saka each evening.

'Don't you even know her name?' asked the former member of the Tokkotai (Suicide Patrol). For his taste, Operation Woodstick was going rather too slowly.

'No idea. The teacher never calls us by our names.'

'But she comes to every lesson. Why don't you just go up and speak to her?'

'She doesn't come when it's raining,' Kawamoto corrected him.

'Probably because of her bad leg. I can hardly bear the boredom of it when she's not there. And incidentally I think we ought to refer to her as *Geta-san* [Miss Wooden Sandal]. They go clop-clip-clop too.'

'Why on earth?'

'"Miss Woodstick" doesn't sound nice. Poor girl, I wonder what's wrong with her?'

'That I don't know. But there's one thing I do know. You're in love with her.' And Fujita rolled his round, black eyes most comically.

'Nonsense,' said Kawamoto, 'I've got no interest in girls whatsoever.'

2

Before Tokie Uematsu's accident at the age of twelve, she had wished to be a dancer. Her teachers, who had instructed her in classic Japanese dancing, had all been enchanted by her beauty, grace, and powers of endurance. In 1943 Prince Takematsu, a member of the Imperial Family, had visited Hiroshima to take the salute at a march past of the fighting forces and of the 'patriotic youth'. In honour of the occasion the little girl had been given a new pair of sports shoes with rubber soles. Just before the parade was due to begin it occurred to her that she had left something behind in her classroom. She ran up to the second floor, slipped, and fell down the stairs. She was carried home with a complicated fracture of the shin-bone.

Her father was a smith whose little workshop had expanded during the war until it was a proper factory. He now spent a fortune securing the best possible medical attention for his daughter. For one of the many painful operations that Tokie had to undergo he was charged a thousand yen. The neighbours came crowding into his house to see, and if possible to touch, the thousand-yen note with which he proposed to pay the surgeon. For in that part of the city no banknote of so high a denomination had ever before been seen.

All the prayers, all the voluntary fasting on the part of the Uematsu family (one sister swore to abstain from tea until Tokie could walk again), proved unavailing. At last a professor summoned from afar found a form of treatment which promised to cure the young girl. It involved the wearing of a plaster cast, reaching from her chest to her toes, for months on end.

Tokie was just beginning to take a few cautious steps in her plaster 'corset', and was outside her parents' home, when the 'great lightning' struck.

Before she had really grasped what was happening she heard, in her own words, 'a noise like a roar from ten thousand throats. It was as if an entire mountain were collapsing, and I was thrown to the ground in the garden. My last thought before I lost consciousness was that my bones would be broken again.'

Unfortunately her fears were correct. Another compound fracture dispelled once and for all her hopes of eventual recovery. During those August days of 1945 such doctors as were still alive had far more urgent cases to deal with than broken bones. So Tokie found herself compelled to be her own doctor and nurse, helped only by one of her sisters. She was successful in that she managed to close the wound, the festering stopped and the bones grew together again, though crookedly. But henceforth and for the rest of her life she would be a cripple. At that time she wrote in her diary: 'I am fourteen years old. I naturally do not know how long my life will last, but I should prefer to skip the happy years, sixteen and seventeen, and become an old lady of sixty to eighty at once.'

The Uematsu factory, which was on the vine slopes of Ozumachi, was completely destroyed by the *Pikadon*. For some time her father could not find a job as smith, for he was suffering from the results of radiation and quite simply lacked the physical strength needed to follow his old trade. Mr and Mrs Uematsu began by running a stall in the neighbourhood of the main railway station where they hawked socks and underclothes. When Uematsu-san's health started to improve, and he was able to touch his savings, he began to speculate with raw materials in a small way. Finally he invested his money in soap. Against cash payments he bought soap in bulk, huge blocks that he himself cut up into normal-sized cakes, which he then sold retail. On the occasion of one such deal the soap was delivered to Mr Uematsu in huge casks. When he opened them he found that they did not contain the normal hard soap, as he had expected, but a thin dirty grease that he could not dispose of. Since he had paid cash for this, almost all that remained of Tokie's father's fortune was wiped out by this swindle.

'I too must earn some money, so that our family shall have enough to live on.'

Such was the conclusion that Tokie drew from the conversations she was forced to listen to when her parents came home late at night after a day spent hunting for a little money.

That was why the girl had determined to attend the Christian language school at Matobacho and learn English. She hoped that this would lead to her obtaining a secretarial job.

But, as with Kawamoto, so Tokie had hesitated before taking this step. Should she, ought she to, learn the language of those people who had brought such misfortune on herself and her family?

She asked her father for advice. He reminded his daughter of a conversation they had had in the old and happy days, when Tokie was a gay schoolgirl with a golden future before her. She had been in the fourth form at that time, and one day she had come home with a terrible great bruise on her head and her clothes all torn. She had been fighting twenty other children in defence of a little Korean boy, whom the Japanese children were reducing to tears by shouting after him that he smelt of garlic. Tokie had often seen them tormenting the child, but on this occasion it had been too much for her.

On that evening, long ago, Uematsu-san had said to his favourite daughter:

'You know that a girl shouldn't fight. Please never do so again. But so far as the cause went, you were quite right; no human being is worse than another simply because he comes from a foreign country.'

'And what I said to you then still applies today. . . .' Father Uematsu said, thus ending their conversation about the advisability of her taking English lessons. This was how Tokie began to learn the language of the people whom she had hated ever since the *Pikadon*.

3

In order to test himself and also Fujita's assertion that he was in love with 'Miss Woodstick', Ichiro let the Electricity Works send him by ship to Shimonoseki. He had already made one such trip on the inland sea, to buy food for his workmates in the islands. But this journey was a longer one, to more distant places. It would keep him away from the language school for at least a week. Would Miss Woodstick, he wondered, notice his absence?

They were four men who set sail one stormy day on board the motor-ship *Kyoei Maru*. They were to collect heat-resistant tiles needed for the boiler room of the Electricity Works.

Towards midday the sea grew calmer. In the dull light of a late winter's day the ship was ploughing through the straits of Miyajima. They saw the beautifully proportioned lacquer-red *Torii* of the famous island shrine, outlined against an almost violet sky. The wind was beginning to rise again, whipping the sea until the waves were topped with a thousand crowns of foam, a glassy meadow where the flowers bloomed their finest in the moment that they broke asunder.

At last light the *Kyoei Maru* cast anchor in a harbour the name of which Kawamoto did not know. The little houses with their grass roofs were completely undamaged, nestling peacefully between the bright beach and the tall, dark pines. And this was a deeply moving sight to the boy whose eyes had grown so accustomed to the ruins and shanty-towns of Hiroshima that these now seemed to him normal landscapes. He took out a little sketchbook which still contained some drawings by Chibiko (skeletons of houses, shacks leaning drunkenly this way and that, the windowless ruins of the Nagarekawa Church) and drew the idyllic scene. Then by the light of the cabin lamp he wrote a letter to his language teacher, the Rev. Tsukushimo, to Fujita-san, and finally, after much hesitation and with a beating heart, to 'Miss Woodstick'.

On the following day the little ship struck foul weather. It had begun to rain as soon as they had left the island of Ube. Then a

stormy wind rose and within a few minutes it was blowing a gale.
The *Kyoei Maru* began to pitch badly. More dangerous than the
great waves were the black masses of seaweed which the turbulent
waters had torn loose from their fastenings on the sea-bed and had
tossed up to the storm-racked surface. They clutched at the screw,
and though the engine was given full power the clutches of the
blue-grey strands of weed seemed stronger than the steel blades
now fighting with all their strength to cut through them.

Then the engine stopped altogether, and the little boat was
whisked about, helplessly, in circles. There was only one hope
left. Somebody on board must try to cut loose the clutching seaweed. Held only by a narrow leather thong, Kawamoto leaned
overboard, so far that almost his entire body was out of the boat,
and tried to cut loose the green hydra, using for this purpose a
long *tobi* – that same instrument which, since the corpse-burning
after the *Pikadon*, had been so indelibly impressed upon his
memory. A tremendous wave knocked him out. Now the captain
himself took a hand, and at last he succeeded in freeing the screw.

They fought their way on, through mountains of water and the
jungle tossed up from the sea-bed. Four times the screw was
caught, and four times Kawamoto thought that the end had come.

In his thoughts he wrote many a farewell letter to Miss Woodstick, and with silent lips he said much to her that he had hitherto
not even dared to say to himself. When at long last they reached the
harbour of Onada, and before he had even got out of his wet
clothes, Ichiro scribbled a few lines to his beloved far away. Yet
these contained no word of all that had passed through his mind
when his life was in mortal peril.

He addressed this note to: 'The Young Lady with the Beautiful
Pinewood Stick, care of the Foreign Language School, Hiroshima.'

4

When Ichiro Kawamoto was home again and entered the school
for the first time since his journey, Miss Woodstick gave no sign
to show whether or not she had received his note. Though the
'bold adventurer' was certainly disappointed by this, his feeling

of relief was almost stronger. With any luck the letter had gone astray! For he feared that the girl of his choice might have been offended by his unsolicited confidences, and to punish him might stop coming to the class. Gradually this hope that the postal service had let him down became a certainty. For 'she' appeared at the school with precisely the same regularity as before, and remained just as remote towards him as she had always done.

Now one evening Tokie had indeed found a postcard on her desk, which was entirely covered with English letters. Beneath these was a pretty drawing of a harbour at sunset. And the card was signed: Ichiro Kawamoto.

'At the time I had no idea who this could be,' Tokie has told me, 'and unfortunately I must now admit that I failed to understand one single word of his English. I hunted in my English-Japanese dictionary but could not find one of the collection of foreign letters. And I wanted so much to know what was actually written on the card! So I went to our teacher and asked him: "Sensei, would you please translate this for me?"

'The teacher looked at the card for a moment and then broke into a loud laugh.

'"Uematsu-san, do you really mean to say that you can't read this on your own?"

'"No, I can't. But I'll try to do better, and make more progress."

'"Ha ha! This letter is in Japanese, only written in English characters."'

Now, by deciphering the foreign symbols, Tokie could at last discover what the meaning of the note was. But who was this Ichiro Kawamoto? He must be the same person who left newspapers on her desk with such regularity. Once or twice she had found sweets there too. But since the teacher never addressed his pupils by name during the classes, and since she was too shy to ask him for help again, Miss Woodstick had to rely on guesswork.

'At the end of each lesson,' Tokie says, 'two of the students always remained behind to tidy up. One of the two was in the habit of singing at the top of his voice – much too loud – and also ran about a lot, to attract attention. The other worked in silence and seemed to enjoy it. It became gradually clear to me that

Kawamoto-san must be the noisy one, and that he was trying to attract my attention by his loud singing.

'At that time besides going to school I began to attend the Christian religious services. I there learned that the word God is to be found in the Bible. This was, for me, like rain falling on to parched soil. The word God soaked into my being . . . I made up my mind to devote my life to the faith, and I asked the teacher if I might be baptized. In addition to myself there were five others for baptism.

'Then one day the cheerful singer came up to me and pressed a note into my hand. It read: "Try to learn these words for your baptism. Kawamoto."

'The one who had handed me the note said: "Ichiro asked me to give it to you."

'It was like a light being turned on. I'd been wrong. He wasn't Kawamoto. Kawamoto was the other one, the still waters that run deep.'

5

On one of the last days of November the clergyman had said to all the students of the language class: 'If any of you wishes to be baptized at Christmas you can apply now.'

'What does "baptized" actually mean?' Kawamoto asked his friend Fujita.

'Well, it means becoming a Christian,' replied Fujita, who was never a man to waste words.

Apart from vague childhood memories of Peruvian altars decked with gold, and occasional church attendances on Sunday in Hiroshima – undertaken principally in order that he might admire Miss Woodstick – Ichiro at that time knew for all intents and purposes nothing about Christianity.

Nevertheless, he made up his mind to offer himself as a candidate for baptism. He himself, writing about this at a later date, has said:

'My motive in doing so was at that time less that of faith than of an unspecified feeling. For I was looking for responsibility. And I thought that if ever I should find myself in a tricky, slippery situation, the fact that I had been baptized would act as a sort of barrier, an invisible promise you might say, a contract that I would be bound by. I hasten to add that it was not some deep idea within the Christian teaching that particularly moved and attacked me. If the evening class had happened to belong to some altogether different religious community, with other ideas, I should probably have adhered to this sect instead.'

On the Sunday before Christmas six candidates for baptism met in the corrugated iron church of Matobacho immediately behind the Hiroshima railway station. It was bitterly cold. Once again persons unknown had, during the night, cut the expensive and almost irreplaceable glass out of the windows. The wind blew through the building with such force that the candles were being constantly extinguished.

Apart from Ichiro Kawamoto the other candidates were: a man of sixty by the name of Nishikawa, who, as he said, had finally given in to his wife's insistence 'in order that he might have a little peace and quiet in the house'; Miyake, a student at Tokyo University; Okamoto, who was studying at the Sanyo Agricultural College; Fujita, the former 'suicide sailor'; and Miss Woodstick.

The six candidates were led in through the left-hand side door. They went right up to the altar, beside which stood a large, decorated Christmas tree.

Now they were told to kneel. But little Tokie could not bend her crippled leg.

Ichiro, who was standing on her left, whispered: 'Shall I fetch you the little chair from the children's corner?'

This was the first time that he had ever addressed her directly.

'Please don't bother,' the girl whispered back. She was so confused that she could scarcely utter the words of the baptism service, which she had learned by heart.

When it was all over and the new converts were to have a meal together, it was discovered that Tokie had disappeared. They looked for her everywhere. Finally it came out that she had told someone she must go home at once.

Ichiro was unable to enjoy the baptismal dinner, even though it was the best food that had been set before him in years. He kept repeating to himself: 'Perhaps I offended her when I thrust my offer of help on her.'

Only much later did Ichiro learn why Miss Woodstick had run away. That a stranger should speak to her in such friendly terms, that a man should bother about her, the cripple, fate's outcast, at all, had moved her deeply. She had long ago resigned herself to what she believed to be her destiny and was prepared to live a life without friendship or love. And now? Did not her whole future look quite altered? Tokie wished to think this over in peace and undisturbed. But first she must collect herself.

Immediately behind the church there was a cinema. This was the same cinema to which Ichiro had taken his friends from Sunflower Castle to see the Chaplin film. Tokie bought a ticket and found a seat in the darkened hall.

'I can still remember what the film was called. It was as if it wanted to mock me, because its title was *First Love*. But what the story was about, I couldn't say. During the two hours I sat there, there was far too much going through my mind.'

3

The City of Peace

THE INDIVIDUALISTS

1

'HALLELUJAH!' The voice was outside, but it was clearly audible within Tokie's room.

'Your telegram boy is there again,' her older sister mocked her. 'Why don't you tell him to come into the house for once?'

Miss Woodstick limped to the door. Ichiro Kawamoto was standing in the entrance. As happened each day, he had brought a little present for Tokie. And besides that, of course, a letter. For they had been writing to each other every day for some time now. But since the post usually took more than one day to deliver a letter, they exchanged the letters they had written before they said good-bye.

Since the baptism Tokie had given up coming to school. One day Ichiro had mastered his shyness and had called on her. As a pretext he had brought with him the English Language Bible which, after endless delay, had at last been issued to all the pupils of the Foreign Language School. He said that, as he happened to be passing his former schoolmate's house, he had thought he would just drop it in, had excused himself, and had pretended that he intended to leave at once. But although the unexpected visit had thrown Tokie into a real state of confusion, she still had enough presence of mind not to let her visitor depart immediately and she engaged him in conversation.

Since that day much had resulted from this brief conversation outside her front door. Ichiro now came to see her almost every evening after he had finished work. But it had taken one whole month before he set foot across her threshold for the first time. 'I should not care to cause your family any embarrassment,' Ichiro had said, by way of excuse. His sensitivity was such that he felt immediately how embarrassing it must be for the once wealthy Uematsu family to be seen by a stranger in their present poverty.

The family's financial position had once again deteriorated

since the beginning of 1948. 'It's true that my sister was earning a little money with her sewing-machine,' Tokie recalls, 'but everything that Father and Mother tried, in order to get on their feet professionally once again, turned out badly. We had potatoes, and only potatoes, to eat, day after day. For a change we made ourselves a sort of caramel, using ordinary domestic sugar. Sometimes I managed to save my share of the caramel, which I could then exchange for books.'

When for the first time there was a little money in the home Tokie's sister invited the shy Ichiro to dinner. A table was laid in the hall, with two plates, two spoons, and between them a vase containing a single bough of blossom. But Miss Woodstick was so overwhelmed to be dining alone with a 'strange man' that she could scarcely swallow a mouthful of the wheat curry.

'That evening I wrote in my diary: "Thank you, *Nesan* [elder sister]!"' Tokie relates. 'The rest of the family left the house to go for a walk, leaving us two alone together. Ichiro asked me: "Do you write in your diary every day?" "Yes, every day," I replied. "Could you show it to your *Niichan* [brother]?" "Well, yes . . . I could give it you to read. But if I do, then you must let me see yours in exchange. . . ." Ichiro said: "I should think that over. But of course you can read my diary."'

Before Tokie was prepared to hand over her diary, she had to correct it. 'Because the name Ichiro-san occurred in it far too often,' she says. 'So I couldn't show it to him the way it was. At this time my thoughts were almost entirely preoccupied with Ichiro. But unfortunately I would never be able to tell him this. A person like me, with this crippled leg – what business had I with emotions of love? I was convinced that Ichiro-san must surely despise me if he even so much as suspected such a thing!'

It was a more than normal shyness that held Kawamoto back from simply telling Miss Woodstick that he was in love with her; and it was more than this feeling of bodily inferiority and of being no longer worthy of consideration as a woman that led Tokie to hide her true feelings from Ichiro. Both were suffering from the deep-seated after-effects of a fear of life and a weariness with living which had affected the inhabitants of Hiroshima after the *Pikadon*. This had been plainly visible on the survivors' faces, and the

doctors had given it the name of *muyoku-ganbo*, or 'no more will'.
If in addition to the hundreds of scientific papers that now exist
dealing with the physical consequences of the atomic bombing
there were an equivalent number concerning its psychological
effects, it would be apparent that this 'fear of love' which was to
be seen in the remarkable reticence and generally peculiar behaviour of our two young people was typical of countless people
in Hiroshima at this time.

The sociologist Nakano, Professor at Hiroshima University,
has in recent years devoted particular attention to the orphans of
the bombing who have subsequently reached marriageable age.
He has established that a fear of forming attachments and of
producing children of their own is overwhelmingly great among
the majority of these young people. He explicitly connects this
with the fear of possible radiation damage to the genes and of
misbirths. Yet in reality the cause of this anxiety seems to be even
deeper.

Ichiro Kawamoto and Tokie Uematsu – and countless other
survivors like them – had been through more than a bombing:
they had experienced 'the end of the world'. This shock must have
affected one of humanity's most fundamental urges, namely the
will to conceive and give birth to children and, through them, to
ensure one's own continuity.

2

After his baptism Kawamoto had begun to attend regularly the
meetings and Bible classes of the Young Men's Christian Association. Soon after this he took on the telling of fairy tales and
other stories to young children, illustrating these with funny
drawings which he inserted into a wooden frame. Tokie helped
him with these weekly *kami-shibai* (paper shows). And in his
story-telling Ichiro was so good at imitating the noises made by
all the animals who figured in them that he soon enjoyed a sort of
fame among the children who lived in and about Hiroshima.

Performances were soon being held in Saka, too, as well as in
the orphanage Shinsei-gakuen. The children ran up to him as they

did to no other grown-up, and many parents asked the uneducated day-labourer, Kawamoto, to look after their offspring. Though they were all Buddhists they did not object when he followed his fairy tales with a Bible class.

On the other hand when Ichiro and his brother-in-baptism Fujita wished to practise the Christian hymns, they had to do this in a distant corner of the works where their singing could not be heard. For their workmates in the factory maintained that class-conscious members of the proletariat could never be Christians and mocked them accordingly.

'Jesus intervened on behalf of the poor and against the rich,' Kawamoto would say, defending his faith. 'And another thing. He also preached: "Love your enemies." You hate too much, and always pretend that you know best.'

However, in order to show that man could be simultaneously both a Christian and a trade unionist, from now on Ichiro took an active part in the struggle for higher wages and against the constant cutting down of those democratic rights which were theoretically guaranteed by the new constitution. In the third year of peace the internal political situation in Japan had taken a turn for the worse. The continuing food shortage, rising prices, and inflation had led to repeated struggles for increased wages; demonstrations and strikes were the order of the day, and the industries of Hiroshima, only now beginning to get on their feet again, were not spared these. At this time delegation after delegation of workers marched to the City Hall, to protest against the galloping devaluation of the currency. Mayor Hamai reports: 'From early morning till evening – and often until late into the night – these delegations would come, and would force their way into my very office. On many days this happened more than one hundred times, and we really could not get on with our work at all. They produced demands which a local authority such as ours was quite incapable of meeting. In exceptional cases men would leap on to my desk, without even removing their shoes, and would attempt to make speeches. . . .'

In order to control political agitation throughout the entire country, Tokyo decreed a 'Law for Securing Public Order', which gave the police increased powers and made demonstrations illegal unless prior notice had been given. The detailed implementation of these exceptional measures was left to the discretion of the local authorities; significantly enough this decree was not submitted to the Japanese Parliament for its approval.

The Mayor of Hiroshima was not himself a party man, but in this matter he shared the point of view of the left-wing parties, which not only maintained that such political oppression must fail as a cure for social maladies, but also declared that the decree was directly contrary to the principles of freedom of thought, freedom of speech, and freedom of assembly as guaranteed in the new constitution. Hamai was firmly convinced that the outbreak of demonstrations such as those from which he himself suffered was only a temporary, post-war nuisance, whereas the 'Security Law', were it to be enforced, must deal a severe blow to the very foundations of the democratic fabric that was just beginning to assume a certain solidity. Furthermore, he believed that this law could easily be misused as a pretext for further acts of political oppression.

To worried workers who protested to him about this controversial law Hamai declared: 'I don't intend to enforce decrees of this sort here in Hiroshima. But I am hoping that you will display self-discipline.' Shortly after this the city's Chief Magistrate was summoned to the headquarters of the Occupying Powers in Kure. The authorities there were extremely annoyed by his reluctance to act in the spirit of the new law. In almost all other Japanese cities the Mayor and council had not hesitated to obey the instructions they had received from 'higher up'.

Hamai dug his toes in. 'If I should obey you, this would mean that I was damaging our new constitution,' he declared.

'Mr Mayor,' replied the American officer, 'leading Japanese legal experts have pronounced this law to be perfectly constitutional. Do you imagine that a simple Mayor is entitled to have his own opinon about such a matter?'

'That is a matter of interpretation. In any event a local authority cannot simply authorize such far-reaching measures. If such a law is really needed, then it should be debated by all the people's representatives in a proper atmosphere of calm and with due respect for the constitution.'

With an ominously threatening remark – 'Please think the matter over carefully once again!' – the Mayor of Hiroshima's interview ended. The pressure from 'on high' did not let up from then on. Hamai was summoned more than once to Kure and finally felt himself compelled to work out a compromise; this took the form of a proposal that, whereas the citizens would be bound to inform the authorities of any planned demonstrations, the authorities for their part would not have the right to forbid it.

A few days later Hamai, together with the Chairman of the Municipal Council, Nitoguri, was summoned to the office of Military Government, located in the Provincial Prefecture Building in Hiroshima. There he met a Captain Caswell, who was introduced to him as a legal expert.

'I should like to repeat to you, word for word, what my superiors wish me to say to you,' the officer began. 'My commanding officer is extraordinarily disappointed by the Mayor's interpretation of the Security Law. The most important portions of that law are not being enforced at all. We therefore are in doubt as to the Mayor's goodwill.'

When the two representatives of Hiroshima remained silent, Captain Caswell went on: 'I have simply repeated what my commanding officer told me to say.'

With the utmost dignity Mayor Hamai now said: 'We have no other wish than to preserve the democratic institutions that have been bestowed upon us. We deeply regret that our sincerity should be called in question.'

The foreign captain hesitated a moment before answering, then he spoke slowly and in a very low voice: 'I am only the mouthpiece for my superior officer, and I have no choice but to obey his instructions. My personal view, Mr Mayor, is that you are right. But in view of the way matters stand at present I have no alternative: I must obey my commanding officer's orders.'

For a few days Hamai was engaged in a silent, internal struggle with his conscience. Should he continue to resist, or not? On the one hand he had accepted certain responsibilities towards the workers which he had no wish to ignore, for he shared their apprehensions. On the other, it was clear to Hamai that if he were to be adamant in his attitude there would be little chance of his obtaining help for Hiroshima from the Tokyo authorities in days to come.

So he decided to give in and was even compelled himself to present the proposal for such a 'Security Law' to the Municipal Assembly. To save his face he had at last added a somewhat weak clause to the bill, whereby public demonstrations would 'be permitted whenever possible'.

But it soon became apparent how easy it was in practice to use the 'rubber stamp law' to ban all forms of public assembly. For a long time part of the Hiroshima working class would not forgive Hamai for having given way in this matter.

Hamai learned later that the Mayor of Hakodate, confronted with the same dilemma as himself, had resisted to the end and had never given in. And he admits today: 'So I felt bitterly that I had acted like a coward.'

3

In other matters too, more important and with greater signifi-cance for the future, Hamai felt himself forced to act against his better judgement at almost this same time. As early as mid 1947 a young American scientist by the name of Lieutenant Neel had come to see him, accompanied by a Japanese doctor named Takeshima. Neel had informed him that the American Govern-ment, in cooperation with the Japanese authorities, proposed to set up a research institute in Hiroshima to study the after-effects on health of the dropping of the atomic bomb. Although in almost all the official reports and newspaper articles of that time the assertion was repeatedly made that the dropping of the two atomic bombs on Hiroshima and on Nagasaki had produced no enduring ill-effects on the survivors' health, it was well known in Hiroshima – where even the strictest censorship imposed by the Occupying Powers could not, after all, render invisible what all eyes might see – that a very large number of men, women, and children were suffering from various complaints which were lumped together in the popular mind and were collectively referred to as 'the atomic sickness'.

Mayor Hamai was therefore highly pleased to learn that the

Americans were now going to look after these sick persons, and he immediately told the Construction Office to find the most suitable possible spot for the new clinic.

It was proposed that the Research Institute should be built in Koshamochi, near the city centre and on the spot where the garrison's powder magazine had stood before the *Pikadon*. At first this proposal was greeted with genuine approval. The clinic would then be within easy reach of all. Furthermore, it was seen as an impressive symbolic gesture that at the very spot where an arsenal of war material once had stood there should now be an Institute devoted to healing the wounds caused by war.

The approval of the higher American authorities had still to be obtained, but this was more or less taken for granted. Then one day an American officer came to see Mayor Hamai, and told him that the government could not accept this site: a building erected here, he said, might well be damaged by water if there were another flood such as had devastated Hiroshima in September 1945. The irreplaceable documents and laboratory material that the clinic would contain would be too valuable for any such risk to be tolerable. As a 'proof' of this argument the officer in question had brought with him a map of Hiroshima. This, according to Hamai, must have been very old, for the river's delta, which had been intensively built over for decades, was shown on it as forming part of the open sea.

In order to be on the safe side, therefore, the American insisted that a new site be selected on higher ground. He proposed as a suitable location the Hijiyama Hill, which rises steeply on the western outskirts of the city.

From the very first Hamai was strongly opposed to this suggestion. He said: 'On this hill there is a park for which my fellow-citizens cherish particularly strong emotions. For in its northern sector there once stood the Emperor Meiji's headquarters, when he resided in Hiroshima. Since that date this had been regarded by us as hallowed ground. In the southern part of the park there is an old military cemetery. We Japanese have feelings of especial respect for the graves of our warriors. If you were to put your building on either of these sites you would, from the very beginning, antagonize the inhabitants.'

In an attempt to make the Americans alter their plans, the Mayor took them to the Futaba Hill, which is no great distance from Hiroshima, and also showed them Yoshida, another district quite free from the danger of flooding. But these gentlemen showed less and less inclination to change the site that they had chosen. Finally Hamai said to them in terms that brooked no misunderstanding: 'I am here as the representative of my fellow-citizens, and I know that they will never approve a plan such as yours. Therefore I cannot agree to your proposals. Please don't imagine I am simply being stubborn and uncooperative. I am convinced that the work of your Institute will be of very great importance, but you will only succeed in achieving what you have in mind if the people of Hiroshima are ready to work with you of their own free will.'

This seemed to put an end to the argument, at least for the time being, and early in 1948 the A.B.C.C. (Atomic Bomb Casualty Commission) occupied provisional offices in what had previously been the Hall of Triumph in Ujina harbour.

At the end of December 1948, when Hamai had almost forgotten his successful struggle to save Hijiyama Park, he suddenly received a visit from the head of the Department of Health and Public Welfare in General MacArthur's 'cabinet'. This officer demanded once again that the Mayor of Hiroshima hand over the park to the A.B.C.C. When Hamai refused to do this, repeating all his original remarks about the inadvisability of such an action, his visitor informed him that he already had in his pocket the approval of the Japanese Government, and that since the land in question was national property, the city could no longer refuse its consent.

Early in 1949 another visitor came to see Hamai, this time from the Japanese Ministry of Welfare, who lectured the stubborn Mayor of Hiroshima in the following terms: 'If you continue to make difficulties, the Government will find itself in a most disagreeable position. This would not only be prejudicial to the nation as a whole, but would also cause harm to your city itself.'

This argument proved decisive. The old military cemetery had to be moved, so that a site could be found for the new clinic. How justified Mayor Hamai's objections to this had been were to be shown in the years that followed.

4

In the arguments about the 'Public Security Law' and the site for the A.B.C.C. Clinic, Shinzo Hamai would presumably have followed a less conciliatory line, if he had not hoped that by giving way in these matters he might save a project which he had very much at heart. This concerned a special law which should finally help Hiroshima out of its financially hopeless situation. In order to ensure the passage of such a bill in Tokyo, the Mayor needed a great measure of goodwill in the Dai-Ichi, MacArthur's headquarters, as well as in the councils of the Liberal-Democratic Party, which formed the majority and which was committed one hundred per cent to the Americans' policy.

In April of 1948 a 'League' had been created in Hiroshima, containing representatives of every section of society, with the sole purpose of obtaining from the authorities in Tokyo a special increase in the Reconstruction Grant for the atom-bombed city. But though members of their 'People's Lobby' had travelled in their hundreds to Tokyo and had submitted appeal after appeal in the hope of thus bringing pressure to bear on the ministries responsible, when the budget for the current year was published there was no special increase to Hiroshima's grant, which remained fixed at the usual figure.

When Mayor Hamai thereupon threatened to resign, his political friends advised him to make the 'Help Hiroshima' cause the basis for a bill to be submitted to the Japanese Parliament. Only if the representatives decided by a majority vote that Hiroshima should be given preferential treatment, in the form of credits for purposes of reconstruction, was there any chance of securing special financial assistance for the city.

With this object in view Hamai had drafted a lengthy petition, in which he spoke of the 'historical significance of Hiroshima's catastrophe' and suggested that great advantages would accrue to the country as a whole if one of Japan's cities were to be officially designated a 'Mecca of Peace'. This must lead not only to an increased awareness all over the world of Japan's desire for peace, but should also prove advantageous to the Japanese economy as a whole in that it would attract a stream of tourists from every land. Finally – and here we can detect a remnant of the dreams of the Reconstruction Committee and of Major Jarvis's high-flying plans – such an 'ideal modern city' could serve as a model for all the other towns of Japan.

Sickness prevented Hamai from personally circulating the petition (which was explicitly entitled *Petition for an Integral Reconstruction Policy with regard to the Atom Bomb Victims of Hiroshima*) in the corridors of the Parliament Building in November 1948, as planned. But the delay proved to be wholly advantageous. The elections of January 1949 showed a marked swing to the left. The Government party, with a decreased majority, now felt that if it were to regain the ground it had lost, it must henceforth devote more attention to measures designed to win popular support. Therefore when Hamai arrived in Tokyo in February 1949, he was immediately received with unexpected friendliness by the deputies of the majority party. Both in the Upper and the Lower House he had no trouble in finding deputies prepared to sponsor such a bill. At the same time the responsible Ministers announced that they were prepared to set up a special committee at once, to work out a five-year plan for the reconstruction of Hiroshima.

The Mayor took it upon himself to obtain approval of the Occupying Authorities, which was essential if his hopes were to be realized. Accompanied by Deputy Takizo Matsumoto, who had lived for many years in the United States, and by Nitoguri, the Chairman of the Hiroshima Council, Hamai called on Mr Williams, MacArthur's liaison man with the representatives of the Japanese people. After Matsumoto had given a brief description of the essentials, the American reached for the English translation of the *Hiroshima Peace Memorial City Construction Bill* and read the draft with extreme care and very slowly.

Time seemed to stand still while Williams 'attentively and without the flicker of an eyeball' studied the document. He spoke no word, nor was it possible to judge from his expression whether or not he approved of what he read. The fact that the Occupying Powers' censorship had hitherto done everything in its power to blot out the memory of Hiroshima from the public's conscience indicated that the approval was unlikely to be forthcoming. On the other hand MacArthur's published statement of 6 August 1947, on the occasion of the first 'Peace Festival', and the world-wide applause that this had received, at least seemed to indicate the possibility that the Americans would not refuse permission.

Hamai recalls the almost intolerable suspense as the minutes ticked by while he waited in the American official's office: 'I felt unwell. I stared at him, in the hope of discovering what his reactions were. If he were to say "No" then our project was doomed in Parliament. But when at last he raised his eyes from the paper before him he said: "This is wonderful! It will be important politically both internally and externally. You must do your best to make sure that this bill is debated and passed at once. As soon as the representatives of Parliament are ready to discuss the bill with me, I'll take it to General MacArthur and get his approval."'

The three Japanese were overjoyed, and shook one another by the hand. As they emerged from the headquarters, the Chairman of the City Council repeated over and over again: 'It's in the bag! It's in the bag! Now the draft bill is bound to be passed!'

And indeed the idea that Hiroshima deserved especial treatment among war-damaged cities now and at last seemed to be accepted in Parliament. Even Prime Minister Yoshida, whose attitude up to now had been one of reserve – neither he nor any of his predecessors had hitherto found the time to visit the atom-bombed city – said to the Mayor: 'Naturally we'll do something for you. I'm always repeating, when dealing with representatives of the Allies: "Talk as you will about your love of humanity, the Hiroshima incident makes you appear in an altogether different light." Then they usually change the conversation, saying: "We'd rather not talk about *that*!"'

So at long last, on 10 and 11 May 1949, the Japanese Parliament finally passed the law which declared officially that Hiroshima was a 'City of Peace'. Simultaneously not only were large special grants assured for the city, but also one of two great plots of land which had hitherto belonged to the military was now legally returned to the city.

At the last moment an unforeseen difficulty had indeed arisen which nearly halted the passage of the new bill. The Nagasaki deputies had suddenly intervened to say that their city, as the second victim of the atomic bomb, should be given treatment at least as favourable as that now being bestowed upon Hiroshima, and should also be designated a 'Mecca of Peace'. Therefore a Reconstruction Act for Hiroshima and Nagasaki should replace the present bill at once. Were this not done, all the Liberal-Democratic deputies representing the Nagasaki district were determined to resign from the Government party. Bamboku Ohno, one of the sponsors of the Hiroshima Act, was so disgusted that he shouted at the Nagasaki deputies: 'Where else in the world are politics played like this? It's not possible to prepare a substantial meal for someone else and then, when it's all ready, to say: "We want to eat it too."'

A compromise solution was worked out in great haste. Nagasaki was honoured with the title of 'City of International Culture'. For the rest, the second atom-bombed city received only a third of the meal that had been cooked up in the party-political kitchen.

5

The population of Hiroshima's initial joy at the assurance of future grants was soon to be dampened by another occurrence.

An economic adviser to the United States Government by the name of Joseph Dodge had been sent to Japan. He was instructed to give his views as to what should be done to combat inflation, and early in June he published his report. In this he proposed that in order to get the Japanese economy on a sound basis there must be a drastic and immediate reduction in State subsidies, a general credit squeeze, and a rationalization of industry. This meant that the five-year plan for the industrial reconstruction of Japan, only begun the previous year, would be set aside for the time being, and in Hiroshima it was generally believed that the new reconstruction plan for the city, so recently and joyously inaugurated, would suffer the same fate. This fear was reinforced by the fact that the over-cautious politicans who had drafted the bill had avoided specifying the size of the grant that the State would be giving to the 'City of Peace'.

As a result of the 'Dodge Plan' over two thousand workers at Hiroshima's second largest factory, the Nippon Seiko Co. (the Nippon Steel Works), were dismissed in mid June 1949; for the railway administration had cancelled for the time being its entire order for railway lines, previously placed with this company.

All the trade unions in the Hiroshima district protested at once against these dismissals. Since their demands failed to obtain the men's re-employment, a general strike was organized for all Hiroshima and the surrounding area.

The employees of the Saka Electricity Works were among those who voted in favour of this protest strike, and they sent all their union members to join in one of the big demonstrations which took place on 15 June in front of the buildings of the Nippon Steel Works. This was the biggest and most excited demonstration that had so far taken place. Ichiro Kawamoto, who carried the banner of his work group, was there.

When the Saka delegation marched in, a great bell was rung and they were greeted by the applause of thousands of clapping hands.

But soon the police too began to arrive, in trucks. A communication from the Governor of Hiroshima Province, Kusunose, was read aloud. He ordered the immediate dispersal of the protest meeting. Amidst all the shouting of slogans, the singing, and the chanting, few of the demonstrators heard the Governor's message. As dusk fell, clouds of mosquitoes settled on the crowd and began to sting them. The men would not budge, however, and so arranged themselves that those who were physically the strongest, who happened to be the members of the Korean Trade Union, occupied and held the entrance gate to the mills.

Alarm bells roused the demonstrators from their half-sleep. 'The police are attacking! The police are attacking!' And indeed in the flickering light cast by the torches it was now possible to make out bodies of men in uniform marching towards the mill.

But they too were carrying banners and placards. Then it turned out that they were not the police but the railwaymen, who could only now join the demonstration, their day's work completed.

The police waited until dawn. Only when they believed the demonstrators to be sufficiently tired and hungry did they attack, with the purpose of 'cleaning up' the area around the steel mills. They had no trouble storming the barricade which had been erected behind the back entrance to the building. What happened next has been described by Kawamoto in the following words:

'I heard someone giving them an order in a sharp voice of command: "Forward!" We were standing in close formation, one beside the other, our arms linked, each of us gripping his neighbour's belt, and we were singing so loudly that you could hardly hear your own voice. They came towards us. Cries of "Robbers! Dogs!" were drawing closer and closer.

'I hid my union banner, but unfortunately I forgot to put away my fountain-pen, which was in the inside pocket of my coat. By now they had broken through the rank in front of us and we were face to face with the police. They struck at our arms with their truncheons, and poked us in the chest to make us let go of one another, but we only clung together all the tighter . . . Suddenly a detective snatched my fountain-pen from my pocket and shouted at me: "If you want it back, come and get it!" I simply shook my head, to let him see that I wasn't falling for a trick like that. So he deliberately broke my pen in two in front of my eyes, and threw the two halves with all his strength straight at my head.

'Fortunately while we were waiting I had stuffed my cap with grass. So I wasn't knocked unconscious, but only deafened. When I had quite come to myself again I hurried towards the entrance gate, where the fight was still going on. A majestic group of Himalayan cypresses stood there, gazing down with evident contempt upon the wild free-for-all that was taking place beneath their boughs. I threw myself into the next intact line of our people, to strengthen them. But this rank too was broken through.

'A gang of policemen knocked me down and trampled on me. I thought I must surely suffocate. Instinctively I grabbed for the leather strap of one of the policemen's helmets. He yelled at me: "That is resistance to the forces of public order!" But before he could hit me, two or three of my comrades had pushed him aside and had carried me out through the gate.

'Gradually it began to calm down all around us. The red flag that had waved from the top of the cypresses was crumbling in flames. A policeman had climbed up and set fire to it. We now all stood there, in silence, gazing up into the sky, until the last puff of smoke had blown away . . .

'I was wounded in the chest. Before going to the demonstration I had bought myself a little copper crucifix. When they hit me with their truncheons they bent the crucifix, which became embedded in my flesh.'

Kawamoto says that never before that morning of defeat had he felt such solidarity with his fellow-workers, nor been so aware of the need for common resistance. Nevertheless – or, as he would put it, precisely for that reason – he attended evensong in his church that evening, and attempted to explain to the other members of his congregation why the strikers' demands were justified. 'Then I prayed for the salvation of the workers,' Ichiro relates. 'But no other members of the congregation would join me in this prayer.'

6

Kawamoto was profoundly disappointed by the attitude of his Church. 'I continued to attend the religious services regularly, but I began to have doubts,' he has told me. 'For I was so terribly discouraged by the indifference of my fellow-Christians.'

This impression was reinforced by a second 'betrayal' on the part of his religious community – for so did it appear in Ichiro's eyes. This occurred when the released Japanese prisoners of war were passing through Hiroshima.

At this time the Russians were beginning to repatriate the survivors from their prison camps, Japanese soldiers captured during the last few days of the war. The members of the Matobacho Church had originally intended to provide refreshments for these men during the brief period that they would have to spend in Hiroshima station. But then the newspapers announced that these men, who had spent four years in Siberia behind barbed wire, had astonished everyone on landing in Japan by announcing that they had become Communists in the prison camps. On hearing this, the churches immediately lost all interest in the home-comers.

When, towards midnight, the train carrying the repatriated men steamed into Hiroshima station, the platform was covered with red flags. Despite the lateness of the hour hundreds had turned out, and now, together with the emaciated and obviously deeply-moved soldiers, they all sang the *International*.

Kawamoto was much impressed by this scene, and deeply regretted that the other members of his church were not there to see it with him.

'If you withdraw into your oyster shells,' he said to them bitterly, 'you'll never be able to share your love with others! The Church must never be solely for itself, but must always stand on the side of the oppressed. Why did you not preach the words of Christ to them? He was prepared to preach to robbers, after all!'

After this fresh disappointment Kawamoto began to wonder seriously, and for the first time, whether he should not himself become a Communist. For a long time they had been after him. Ichiro had come to the conclusion that the Communists he knew were superior as human beings to the Christians and the Socialists, because each of them was ready to sacrifice all his personal interests for the sake of their organized workers' movement. On the other hand their spiritual arrogance repelled him. They thought that they alone knew all the answers, and anyone who was not prepared, as were they, to follow absolutely a devious and constantly changing 'Party Line' they dismissed with indignation, or at best contempt.

These observations were enough to prevent Kawamoto from joining the Communists at his factory. He noted in his diary at this time the following conviction: 'The Communists cannot stand any criticism of Soviet Russia, just as is the case with the Christians and America.' A few days later Kawamoto had an experience which, after all his disappointments, filled him with new hope. This happened in July of 1949, during the celebrations that marked the passage of the law according to which Hiroshima would be declared the 'Mecca of Peace'.

These opened with the singing of the new 'Peace Song', which henceforth would be the official festival hymn and would be sung each year on 6 August. It was far too 'tame' for Kawamoto's taste, for the text never once included the word *genbaku* (atom bomb) and indeed 'consisted solely of pretty-sounding, poetical phrases'. The official speeches which followed were as long as they were boring.

Then suddenly a white-haired American woman was standing on the platform, stammering in broken Japanese remarks that had never before been publicly uttered in Hiroshima: for she announced to the survivors of the *Pikadon* that in her opinion the dropping of the atomic bomb had been a crime. As an American woman she must therefore beg their forgiveness for this evil deed.

This woman – she was called Mary Macmillan, and since the end of 1947 she had done a very great deal to help the poorest people of Hiroshima – was a Methodist missionary. Ichiro Kawamoto soon learned to know her personally. She restored his faith to him, by showing him that there were Christians who were not merely 'as clever as snakes', but who had the courage publicly to criticize the misuse of power.

7

A few weeks later another American arrived in Hiroshima, a man whose words and deeds were to make an unforgettable impression on the inhabitants of that city. He was a Quaker named Floyd Schmoe, Professor of Botany at the University of the State of Washington in Seattle, and he had had to wait two years before at last receiving permission to come to Hiroshima. The purpose of his visit was to build homes for a few of those whose houses had been destroyed by the atom bomb. It was highly unusual that a white man should wish to show his involvement in Hiroshima's fate not by means of a gift of money or of goods, but by the work of his own hands. He was large and powerful, despite his snow-white hair. The news of Hiroshima's destruction had had a deep and lasting effect, largely because during the war he had run an internment camp for American citizens of Japanese descent and had struck up many close friendships with the inmates.

At exactly the same time that tens of thousands of houses were being smashed or burned in Hiroshima, Floyd Schmoe was just completing the building of his own house on the outskirts of Seattle. Now he felt ashamed that he should be living in such comfort while the survivors of the atom bomb had only caves or holes in the ground into which to creep. So when he sent his friends Christmas cards he enclosed a note in which he suggested that a few private individuals should get together and collect money for the building of houses in Hiroshima.

But when the Professor approached the responsible authorities, he was rebuffed with the remark: 'If you insist on doing something for the Japanese, you had better work for L.A.R.A.' The 'Licensed Agencies for Relief in Asia' were a charitable 'trust' founded during the summer of 1946, when there was famine in Japan. They had unified all the multifarious agencies attempting to help that wretched country, and collected, and shipped across the Pacific, notable quantities of clothes, food, drugs, and other essentials. MacArthur's headquarters had not explicitly forbidden individual acts of philanthropy, but certainly they were not encouraged.

Schmoe told himself that he would be able to carry out his plan if only he could get to Tokyo, for he did not believe he would have any trouble convincing the American authorities on the spot. But it turned out to be almost impossible to get there at that time, for without a military movement order or a government appointment there were for all intents and purposes no berths to be had on ships bound for Japan. So Schmoe got himself taken on as shepherd and milkman with a herd of goats that were being shipped across as a gift for a Protestant charitable organization. After the energy that he had expended looking after a dozen seasick nanny-goats during the week's journey, the difficulties in getting to see the 'new Japanese Mikado', Generalissimo MacArthur, and in persuading him to grant permission for his plan, were child's play by comparison.

In any event, the Professor had reached his destination at last. He was accompanied by Andy, a young preacher from Seattle,

Ruth, a teacher from Tucson, and Pinkie, a cheerful coloured girl from South Carolina. They arrived in Hiroshima at the beginning of August 1949. A delegation led by Governor Kusunose and Mayor Hamai that went to Hiroshima station to meet them almost missed the new arrivals; for Schmoe and his co-workers were certainly the first foreigners since the war to travel from Tokyo to Hiroshima third class.

Having finally arrived, it was not long before Professor Schmoe learned that the most deeply-loved formula of the bureaucrats – 'That's impossible!' – enjoys world-wide currency and was as popular in Hiroshima as anywhere else. In a city where there were still thousands of homeless it should have been extremely easy to build a few houses for the purpose of giving them away. The responsible officials of the Welfare Department, however, had only one worry on their minds. 'The moment you give one of your houses to one family, you will automatically and immediately make at least four thousand other families jealous. The lucky family will be treated with distrust, even with hatred, by their neighbours. And another thing: the people really in great need will not be able to afford to live in the beautiful houses you're planning to build. They couldn't even afford the maintenance and the taxes.'

But the anxious fathers of Hiroshima were prepared to help the helpers from America. They had immediately submitted an alternative programme to them: instead of building houses, Schmoe and his friends should construct a Youth Library. This would then be designated as a 'Monument to American Generosity' and would be given a place of honour in the proposed new city centre of the City of Peace.

The Professor did not hide his disappointment. He admitted that such a collection of books would undoubtedly be of value to the younger generation. Perhaps it might even lead to a decline in the figures for juvenile delinquency. Would it be a milestone along the road to better understanding between the nations? That might well be true. But were there not at the moment tasks of more *immediate* importance waiting to be done?

'And what sort of books do you actually plan to put in the library?' Schmoe finally asked.

'That's settled. We've received 4,000 volumes as a gift,' was the reply.

Schmoe asked to see the books. And it transpired that these consisted entirely of duplicates from an American Army Library, and therefore, of course, were all in English. 'As far as we were concerned, the Children's Library was "out" from that point on,' Schmoe has said. 'So we came back to our problem of "houses to live in". We discovered that the city was building about 100 units for bombed-out families on city property. These would be owned and maintained by the city and rented to selected families at 700 yen per month (about $1.85). This was the solution. We would build four units in this programme and give them to the city to be managed as were the other houses. As usual, there was no "problem".'

During the following weeks and months the inhabitants of Hiroshima were treated to a curious spectacle. Professor Floyd Schmoe, one of the most distinguished citizens of that nation whose 'new weapon' had in a matter of seconds flattened their city, was to be seen, day after day, working inexhaustibly to rebuild what had been destroyed and personally to make good a tiny fraction of the disaster.

But what a contrast between the forces of destruction and those of construction! On the one hand the billion-dollar budget of the Manhattan Project, on the other hand a tiny fund, laboriously collected, a dollar here, two dollars there. Then the wartime teamwork of the most brilliant scientists and the most skilled engineers: now a handful of amateurs, men of goodwill, attempting to be house-builders. In order to bring 'Little Boy' – as the creators of the Hiroshima bomb significantly called their product – into the world, the most delicate and complicated machinery ever conceived by man was put in action : all that Floyd Schmoe and his co-workers had in the way of technical equipment was a single, small handcart. On it he transported the planks from which the houses would be built, single-handed, from the saw mills to the building site in the Minamimachi district. But when the *seizonisha* (the survivors) met this man in his fifties, engaged, day after day, on his task of carting wood, even as though he were one of them, they would bow low to him with genuine respect.

The houses were built in the Japanese style, each surrounded by its own little rock-garden. The Professor put them up with the help of a single local carpenter, his three American assistants, and a dozen Japanese volunteers. On 1 October 1949 a short ceremony took place to mark the handing over of the first four houses thus completed to the representatives of the city of Hiroshima. The scholarly builder gave a brief address, in which he said: 'What we felt four years ago, when first we learned of Hiroshima's tragedy, can only be expressed inadequately in mere words. That is why we came to you, as soon as ever we could, to build houses for the homeless.'

In the annual statistics concerning the reconstruction of the great city of Hiroshima for the year 1949, these four new houses make scarcely any impression. But in the hearts of the atomic victims that solitary man – *Dok Shumo*, as they call him – has even today a place of honour.

THE DEMOLITION MEN

1

AFTER his fight with the Australian N.C.O., Kazuo M. was for a long time without work. His reputation as a fighter had spread quickly and no employer was willing to give a job to a trouble-maker such as he.

Fortunately, his father, Setsuo M., had at last managed to re-open his little gramophone business. Apart from repairing machines, he now also bought and sold second-hand records, and his business was a flourishing one. All Japan was 'record crazy' at this time, and in the fourth year after the catastrophe this had assumed epidemic proportions in Hiroshima.

From early morning till late at night the entire city reverber-ated to the rhythm of hit tunes. Men hammered and shook in time. The barracks, the new green and white excursion buses, even the newest rebuilt square of the tourist-crammed 'City of Peace' re-echoed to the love moans of foreign singers and the muted saxophone of the 'Shopping Boogie'. Music was a *hiropon* now, at last available to all, and in as mixed and strange a dose as possible: a French popular song would follow a Schubert quintet, to be succeeded in its turn by a local Japanese hit that was followed by excerpts from the *Götterdämmerung*.

Kazuo hated this perpetual musical din, yet had himself become as much an addict as had all the others. Immediately after the catastrophe he had believed that only silence should be permitted to succeed the horror, a silence in which a new world, shattered and trembling, would come to birth. Instead of which the trom-bones whined, the guitars twanged, harps dispensed a mendacious gaiety, while the percussion tinkled and boomed. Anything rather than thought! Nothing should be taken seriously any more! The apocalypse was being smothered in syrup.

Kazuo's reputation as a wild man had attracted the attention of Mr Maruguma, the head of a small firm that for generations had engaged in the business of dismantling and transporting houses. The employees of this firm were traditionally young, strong, tough, and the boss usually recruited them among those recently discharged from corrective institutions or from prison. Since the end of the war he had experienced increasing difficulty in finding the sort of men he wanted, for the gangsters and the black market offered more attractive ways of earning a living to those young hooligans than did the dangerous work of house demolition.

Maruguma arranged that Kazuo be brought to his office, so that he might have a closer look at him. But when the applicant for a job entered the room, he found himself confronted not by the head of the demolition business, a man known to all in Hiroshima, but by a girl aged, apparently, about fourteen. She spoke to him at once, and with an ease of manner that was most unusual in a Japanese girl of that age. From the first moment of their conversation Kazuo felt a trust in this child in her schoolgirl's uniform such as no human being had inspired in him for a very long time. Yukiko reminded him of Sumiko, the girl who had died in his arms the day after the *Pikadon*, and he told her about all those anxieties that had been oppressing him for so long.

'Every word I uttered then', he later said, 'was an expression of my anger and my grief. But she listened attentively, occasionally nodding in agreement, at times even smiling, as I spewed out my disgust at everything and everybody in our post-war world.'

Finally, almost two hours later, the boss appeared. He gave an obviously doubtful glance at Kazuo's thin arms, but nevertheless with a certain hesitancy inquired whether he wished to join the Maruguma-gumi. So at last Kazuo had a job again. Yet as he made his way home he realized that the most important event of the day had not been finding work, but meeting the girl Yukiko. He was to discover on the following day that she was the second eldest daughter of his new employer.

Up to now Kazuo had only been accustomed to relatively light manual work. Now he had to use his whole strength. But the boss and his *shigotu-shi* (assistants) displayed great patience with the 'new boy'. They showed him how to drive the sharp end of the *tobi* into the wood, how to loosen an entire wall by a skilful tugging of the hook, and precisely when to jump aside in order to avoid being crushed by the fall. They warned him of the dangers that lurked beneath ruined houses, demolished by the bomb and now covered with undergrowth which must first be carefully cleared away, tough and heavy work.

After a few months Kazuo was indistinguishable from the other employees of the *gumi*. He had grown strong and agile and had developed a sixth sense for the danger of falling rubble. He could knock down house posts, lug heavy loads, and no longer felt sick when he stumbled over a desiccated corpse.

The passing of the law whereby Hiroshima was honoured with the title of 'City of Peace' inaugurated a period of boom for the demolition men. To begin it there had first to be fought a paper war between the city administration of Hiroshima and the Central Construction Office in Tokyo, as to how the special grant was to be spent; it was not at all clear what the community would finally be allowed to build with the millions at its disposal. Meanwhile, a beginning was made by clearing the city centre and the railway station district of those *barakku* and booths that had sprung out of the ground like mushrooms in the period immediately after the *Pikadon*.

Before the demolition men could get to work it was often necessary to call in the police to remove families of squatters. Some had submitted petitions requesting a temporary stay of the expulsion order. When these were refused they often offered physical resistance, and sometimes even attempted to murder the policeman who had come to evict them. To these desperate people even a prison sentence seemed preferable to the fear of being homeless once again.

Kazuo saw much unhappiness and much that disgusted him in those months. He did his best to conceal how deeply he was affected by it all, when he saw the pain, the anger, the impotence, and the defencelessness of the people being evicted from their temporary homes. As the ruins of a house demolished by himself and his comrades came roaring down about his ears, not all the music from all the gramophones could blot out, in his head, the sounds of voices from 'the past'. Memories of 'that day' quite simply refused to be silenced.

2

All the same these were the happiest months that Kazuo had known since 1945. Like most of the other demolition workers he had joined the Voluntary Fire Service, the I-gumi. He says about this: 'The men who joined it were, in fact, good-for-nothings to a man. They looked on their work with the Fire Service as a sort of voluntary expiation of their sins, as a gesture of compensation for their evil deeds. As the word "Voluntary" implies, nobody compelled us to do this work, and we received not a single yen by way of payment or subsistence. The members of the Service even had to pay for the fire-fighting equipment out of their own pockets, and when the alarm went we had to transport it ourselves to the scene of the fire. If one of us were hurt, or killed, there was no question of compensation.

'As soon as the bell rang we clambered into our protective clothing and hurried, as fast as ever we could, to the scene of the fire. We always fought it in imminent peril of death. But I thought to myself: "Even if I should die this way – I don't regret it." '

Kazuo could at last give vent to the aggressive side of his nature as a fireman, without running the danger of falling foul of his employer or of coming into conflict with the forces of the law. Indeed, this aspect of his character now won him admiration and respect. Membership of the Fire Service meant far more to him than to any of his comrades. He wrote about this:

'Our *gumi* has the designation of *Gi-yu*, which does not mean only "voluntary" but also has the meaning of "just" and "courageous". Our "City of Death" has been resurrected, and now – well, now it has an appearance such as none could have foreseen. I can certainly understand that the young men and girls should wish above all to dance and sing and enjoy themselves. But I myself feel a strong antipathy to all that, and deliberately cut myself off from that life, which indeed often fills me with emotions of disgust. I am giving expression to that disgust when I obey the orders inherent in the word *Gi-yu*, and hurl myself against the Demon of Fire. At least I can drive him out of the city!'

Immediately beneath this entry in his diary there is written, in a very small hand:

'This work is fun. Every day is a delight. And not just for that reason. I've got a girl-friend. She knows what she likes. Clever and full of fun. My comrades envy me. But they say: "You'll make a fine couple one day, you two."'

The girl about whom Kazuo wrote so enthusiastically was Yukiko, whom he had met on the very first day he joined the *gumi*.

A few months later an entry in his diary reads:

'Discovered that Y. has dimples. Told her so. She: "How rude! Did you only notice that today? I know where your birthmark is. On the lobe of your ear." And then her dimples showed all right . . .'

That all this must lead to something more seemed unavoidable, nor did they try to hide their emotions from anyone. But both families registered instant disapproval. Kazuo's mother maintained that they were both too young to marry, and Yukiko's elder sister based her disapproval of Kazuo upon the fact that he was their father's employee. In view of this, a marriage between the two would be inadmissible according to Japanese custom.

Almost exactly one year after Kazuo and Yukiko had first met, he wrote in his diary:

'The resistance from both sides is driving us wild. We won't be parted. On the contrary, we're not waiting. For no one can separate us any more.'

3

On 15 January 1950 a ceremony took place in Hiroshima which many citizens of that town greeted with more enthusiasm and delight than they felt on 6 August 1949, when their city was officially proclaimed a 'City of Peace'. This ceremony was the opening of the new baseball stadium and the simultaneous re-creation of what before the war had been a famous local baseball team, 'The Carps', so named after the Carp Castle which had been destroyed by the atom bomb.

Next to *sumo* wrestling the American game had, even before the war, been the most popular sport in Japan. And Hiroshima had had the reputation of being Japan's 'Baseball Capital'. As Mayor Hamai states in his memoirs, he had two good reasons for wishing to revive a sport that was so popular with the masses: the first was his desire to give the citizens 'something that they could enjoy and get excited about together': the other was his calculation that the city would profit from the gate receipts to the tune of several million yen per year. The second consideration proved mistaken, for just as the preparations were being completed for the re-creation of the Carp team, a tax reform was introduced in Japan according to which the profits of all sporting events would no longer accrue to the cities, but would be paid into the coffers of the provincial administrations. But Hamai's hope that the Carps would encourage a community spirit among the citizens was to be fulfilled. In the local patriotism of sport, the old and the new citizens of Hiroshima at last found something about which they could all be equally enthusiastic. It is true that the Carps lost almost all their games and were almost always to be found very near the bottom of the 'Central League'. It made no difference; the members of the team were henceforth the idols of the greater part of the population. Kazuo knew one of the sporting heroes, a man named Kakuda, well, for they had been at school together. He therefore frequently asked him out, even though the baseball star had only one unvarying topic of conversation, baseball.

Yukiko, who had played in her school soft-ball team, followed Kakuda's tales of epic heroism on the diamond with far greater attention than did Kazuo, who, if the truth be told, was frequently bored by them. She did not say much, even when the ball player was describing and analysing a recent game for the fourth or fifth time, but her eyes shone: it seemed to Kazuo then that they shone exactly as they had done on that occasion long ago when first he had told her about himself and his life.

Actually Kazuo's jealousy should have been aroused at once. But he showed patience; indeed he even continued to invite the sporting hero to go out with them, because for some time he had suspected that his girl-friend was beginning to find his own company somewhat boring. She was a typical example of the youth of post-war Japan, and loved hot music, wild dancing, and spectator sports for the masses. She read sexy novels for preference, and pseudo-scientific magazines such as *Liberal*, *Aka to Kuro* (Red and Black), or *Fuju-Seikatsu* (Married Life) in which 'sexual liberation' was discussed and extolled. Kazuo, on the other hand, felt increasingly remote from the 'modern youth', which was interested in nothing save the pursuit of pleasure and immediate satisfaction. He attempted in vain to excite Yukiko's interest in the ideals of old Japan.

Then one day a girl of his acquaintance whispered: 'Kazuo-san, haven't you noticed what's going on between Yukiko and Kakuda?' He dismissed this angrily, as the spiteful gossip of a woman scorned, for this girl had indicated more than once she would be pleased if Kazuo were to make a pass at her. But soon he was to hear similar remarks from other quarters, so he decided at last that he must have it out with his sweetheart.

'At first she said nothing,' Kazuo remembers. 'She hid her face in her hands. Then all of a sudden she burst into tears and admitted everything. She made no attempt to excuse herself. So I boxed her ears. I must have hit her two or three times. Then I thought: "What's the point in punishing a girl like this?" I saw that I had been blind and stupid, and I felt deeply ashamed of myself.... Now, at long last, it was all quite clear to me: I had lost, all along the line I had lost. The customs of the new generation had acquired greater strength than my principles. This was an unbearable discovery, and from it there grew at last a plan. I would commit suicide. I went to Yasuji's and Sumiko's grave, and there I swallowed a large quantity of poison. A strange thought occurred to me: Yasuji and Sumiko, who had died on "that day", had really been luckier than I. It was only because I had survived that I was compelled to go on living in a world that was rotten through and through.'

He was first conscious that the poison was beginning to work when he felt a burning pain in his stomach. But his mind remained perfectly clear. 'What will the people say?' he wondered. 'That I killed myself for unrequited love? No, not that. I refuse to die on account of a slut like her! They'll all sigh and murmur:

"Yes, yes, crossed in love!" But what I have done was done for quite different reasons.

'Because I just didn't want to have anything more to do with it all. I was frightened lest bit by bit I grow soiled and dirty myself. I have tried to live a clean and upright life. And now all my self-confidence is gone . . .!'

Suddenly the young man made a desperate decision. He must still perform some action which would prove to all the world, beyond a shadow of doubt, that he had not wished to die for silly reasons of jealousy. Yukiko's unfaithfulness was not as important as all that. But the way she had failed him had reopened the 'cheloid in his heart'. And tormented by his memories of 'that day' he asked himself: 'Why are people today incapable of replying to the greatness of past pain with the greatness of a better life?' It was because of this disappointment that he was about to vanish from the earth, and he was determined to tell them all, before he did so. Therefore with his last remaining strength Kazuo dragged himself home.

And then:

'My chest hurt, as if someone were crushing it with brute force. My head ached, as if it had been split open. There was noise, people far away. . . . They were coming closer . . . and right beside my ear a voice was crying "Kazuo!" I awoke and was fully conscious. The brightness before my eyes was blinding. As if I had buried my head in the sun. "Kazuo-san, you're saved!" My body lay on the operating table in the hospital. The faces of my father and mother, our neighbours, they were all crowded about me, one next to the other. . . . "It's all right now, he's saved," a doctor was saying. He was about forty years of age and spoke with self-satisfaction, as if he alone were responsible for having dragged me back from the jaws of death. Those words infuriated me.

'I shouted at the top of my voice, so loudly that even I was surprised by the noise: "Who says I wanted to be saved? Enough, finish me off, once and for all. Kill me, why don't you kill me?"'

THE MURDER

1

THE shiny little steel ball fell through a forest of steel pins, deflected now to the left now to the right, winding its way downwards. The player attempted to foresee what was scarcely foreseeable. Should the ball fall where he hoped, a bell rang, and a torrent of these small balls was disgorged at him. These he could either exchange for cheap prizes or he could play them again.

The player almost always lost. The owner of the pin-ball saloon could so arrange his machines that the chances of winning were very slender indeed. But each player persuaded himself that he was perhaps quick and skilful enough to beat the machine. And when he had just about decided he was not, and was on the point of giving up, the bell of a nearby machine would ring out, a win! If the fellow along the line could pull it off, why, so could he! Another go. . . . He would pull the lever, a new steel ball would appear above the horizon of the automaton's world . . . and . . . begin . . . to fall.

This game was called *pachinko*, and enjoyed an unrivalled popularity in post-war Japan. Thousands of *pachinko* parlours were opened, some with only ten machines, others with several hundred, and these remained open from early morning till late at night. A few of these establishments tried to increase their appeal by playing popular music or even by treating their customers to free striptease shows. But this did not really have the desired effect, for the players had no wish to be distracted from their game.

In Hiroshima too the *pachinko* parlours achieved a rapid popularity and were crammed at almost every hour of the day. The most popular one of all was located in a street on the outskirts of the business district called Hachobori Street: its name was *The Atomic Mushroom*. Kazuo M. was one of those who frequented this place in the days immediately after his unsuccessful suicide attempt. He had previously regarded the '*pachinko* mania' as yet another example of his compatriots' decadence. Now he too was to be seen standing for hours on end amidst the clatter of the machines, staring as if hypnotized at the metal balls as they rolled down the slope, now pulling the lever with an ingratiating gentleness, now giving it a brutal jerk, and then waiting – waiting sometimes for an entire afternoon for the moment of relief when at last one 'good' ball would have followed the proper path and a whole glittering cascade of them would pour forth into his cupped hands. The winning player received no money, but 'prizes' consisting of cigarettes, chocolate, or chewing-gum. All such prizes could quite easily be converted into cash in the black market that still flourished.

Just as Kazuo had suddenly become a *pachinko* addict, so he gave it up again with equal suddenness. While wandering about the entertainment district he had got to know a young electrical engineer by the name of Nakata whose house was the rendezvous for all those adolescents in search of excitement, sex, and easy money.

It was through Nakata, who had already served a prison sentence, that Kazuo first really came into contact with true 'bad ones', those girl juvenile delinquents whom the Japanese call *zube-ko*. 'They are women who no longer care about their reputation,' he explained to me in one of his letters from prison. 'Divorced women, waitresses, dancing girls, and emancipated girl students too . . . they all came to Nakata's. Morality, if such a thing exists, we completely ignored. We lived a life absolutely different from that of all the other people. It was really a wild business.'

Here – preserved in Kazuo's diary – is a typical conversation with one of these girls.

'Emi said to me: "Kazuo-san, I think I'm going to have a baby." Maybe it really is my child. But only two months ago she was still going with Nakata. Most of the *zube-ko* have several men at once.

'"Emi, are you quite sure it's mine? There's only one person can know for sure. You! And apart from you, maybe Mr Amen . . ."

'"Emi, don't give me that fish-eyed stare! Try and think how we can get rid of the kid. Because neither you nor I want one. If it's money you need, here you are ...!" I tossed a roll of bank-notes across to her. Enough for an abortion. Maybe she'll go ahead and get one. If a person chooses death, I'm not the one to hold them back ...'

A later entry:

'Heard that Emi's got a child. Others say she's got rid of it. All rumours, nothing definite.

'All that's known for sure is that she hangs out in Osaka these days. Also that she's still alive. And now I share my bed with another girl, equally crazy. She's called Chiyo, I think, and it's extraordinary how evenly she breathes when she's asleep.'

'And so I went from one to the next,' Kazuo wrote me. 'I be-came chucker-out in a night club, spent hours wandering the streets, and got into brawls whenever I could. The little swindlers and thieves admired me and called me Kazuo the Ryanko.* In April I stole some money from my parents and moved in with Nakata altogether. He was wanted by the police at that time. A couple of rich clients had got him to fiddle their electric meters, in exchange for a cut in the profits. When the business came out, he vanished. Nakata's wife and three children were living in abject poverty – because of course with him away there was no one to run his workshop. His assistants packed in one after another, and Mrs Nakata began to sell the furniture. I couldn't bear to see this, and I lent her more and more money.

'About two weeks after I'd moved in there, Toyoko – that was her name – walked into my bedroom one day and said: "There's nothing lonelier in this world than a woman who's been left. If you like, Kazuo-san, you can come into my bed."

'A married woman! That was what really sent me off the rails. I asked myself if I and I alone was solely responsible. And I decided that I was not. The guilt could not be mine alone. It was our broken-down society which was really responsible. It was the fault of the war, and of the atom bomb. . . . It had half ruined me already, I told myself. It might just as well ruin me altogether. It made more sense that way.'

* A romantic rebel of the Robin Hood variety.

2

Money, money, money . . . it became Kazuo's battle-cry. 'Every-thing in the world is money, money, money.' Such was the discovery that he believed he had made. 'Yukiko left me . . . because of money. Toyoko sleeps with me because of the money I bring in. I get it quite cold-bloodedly from blackmail. They say that a man who wants money shouldn't be squeamish about how he gets it. That's a sentiment which seems to be tailormade for me.'

But such small-scale business did not bring in much cash, because it was only little people who would be frightened by a solitary blackmailer such as he and who, under threats, would part with a few yen. It was while looking for a larger field in which to operate that Kazuo happened to stumble upon a money-changing firm. What happened was that Se-o, one of the electricians who was now out of work as a result of Nakata's flight, came to Kazuo and said:

'Listen here, there's a group of *nisei* [Americans of Japanese origin] tourists in town. One of them wants to change two hundred dollars on the black market.'

'How much does he want for it?'

'390 to 400 yen to the dollar.'

Kazuo set out to look for a man who would buy the 'black dollars'. He knew that in Hiroshima there were the proprietors of certain general stores who were always on the look-out for dollars: through relations or middlemen they could use them to buy goods in the States or in the American PX. Together with a 'specialist' in this line of business – the much-imprisoned Takemoto – Kazuo visited a number of these merchants. 'Sorry, the black-market price at present is between 375 and 380 yen per dollar,' they said, one after the other. 'If you've got dollars to sell at that price, we'll take ten times the amount you're offering us. On a cash basis, naturally.'

So this deal fell through because the price he could get for the *niseis'* dollars wasn't good enough. But Kazuo had made at least one important discovery. For he now knew how relatively large were the sums that changed hands when such secret and illegal transactions took place.

3

It was an unusually hot and heavy summer in Hiroshima, where the population had grown to 280,000 in the course of the last year. For the first time since 1946 the now overcrowded city suffered a water shortage. Day after day the sun burned down out of a cloudless sky on to the dusty city, which, save for an occasional green oasis here and there, was still treeless. When the wind rose, the streets were filled with the stench of decay. Some said that this came from the bottom of the swamps, now dried up, others that the dry river-bed was the cause. But there were rumours that the smell was the stink of corpses from 'that time'. Inhabitants of the modern community centre of Motomachi, which had been built close to the place where the mass graves had once been dug, dared not open their windows at all for days on end.

The social and internal political tensions which had first become apparent with the Nippon Steel Works riots went on. On fences and house walls placards were to be seen, with the poem, *Ikari no uta* (*The Day of Anger*), that Toge had written in honour of the steel strike. The Communists were no longer content to repeat their warlike slogans. Early in the year Moscow had accused them of adopting 'too conciliatory an attitude'. So now they embarked upon a campaign of 'direct action'. While some elements of the Party hesitated to embrace this formidable policy, which apparently did not even exclude political terrorism, in Hiroshima the radical 'international faction' (that is to say the Moscow-controlled elements) guided the Party's destiny.

Since the introduction of the 'Dodge Plan' the whole country had clearly been suffering from an economic recession. Unemployment rose, many small firms were forced out of business, while political scandals involving the bribery of officials were undermining the nation's faith in democracy.

Hiroshima too had its public scandals. Senior officials in the provincial administration were convicted of having pocketed funds publicly collected for charity through the so-called 'Red Feather' organization, and of having spent this money on themselves. For a time suspicion was even directed to Kusunose, the Provincial Governor, not merely for his failure to detect and prevent such peculation; some people said that he had himself profited from it. The Society of Hiroshima Hemp-thread Purveyors was accused of a swindle involving millions of yen. According to a subsequent analysis by the *Chugoku Press* in their issue of 12 December 1950, criminal activity during this year reached record levels. Of particular significance was the increase, sixty to eighty per cent, in cases of arson, the typical crime of vengeance and terrorization. The Family Court even felt obliged to publish a special report dealing with divorce and crime among members of the younger generation; the 'economic chaos' was stated to be principally to blame for the current state of affairs.

The news of the outbreak of the Korean War came as a great shock, and nowhere more so than in Hiroshima. Toge, the poet who had looked to a happier future, was so upset when he heard it that he had a heart attack. The statistics for suicide showed a sharp increase. While the inhabitants of other Japanese cities rapidly prepared to exploit the expected war-time boom to the full, the people of Hiroshima felt otherwise. In the atom-bombed city the memory of war's horror was too profoundly branded into their bones: to begin with they simply relapsed into a mood of the deepest hopelessness.

Ichiro Kawamoto recalls those summer days of the year 1950:

'From one moment to the next we had been thrown back into the past. With our own eyes we could watch the development of this new war by day and by night. . . . Open flatcars loaded with tanks, trucks and heavy artillery rolled through the city. Whole trainloads of white and black troops passed through on their way to their embarkation ports in Western Japan. And as dusk fell there came once again the roar of aeroplanes overhead. Quickly, as though driving the sun away, they were gone. Everything seemed to create an atmosphere in which a Third World War might break out at any minute . . .'

In October of 1949 the Soviets had announced that they too possessed nuclear weapons, and this had been the signal for a general acceleration of the atomic arms race. One result of this had been the founding in Hiroshima of a Peace Movement, consisting primarily of scientists, writers, and artists, and, to begin with, this had had no party political bias. Now, with the outbreak of the war in the neighbouring country of Korea, the Peace Movement became more active, issuing manifestoes and printing leaflets. When the press first indicated that atomic weapons might possibly be used in Korea, the city administration announced its intention of collecting eyewitness accounts of the destruction of Hiroshima: these would be translated into English and distributed throughout the world as a warning.

The gossips and scandalmongers worked overtime. It was said that the 'Hundred Metre Street' had, from the beginning, been laid out as it was in order that it might serve as a runway for jet fighters. It was also said that the promenade which was being built along the quays, as a place where the citizens of Hiroshima might take a pleasant evening stroll, had in fact a far more sinister purpose: it was intended to serve as an exit through which these citizens could flee in the event of Hiroshima being atom-bombed once again. And as it happened – though really for reasons quite other than these – those two items of the general reconstruction project were exceptionally far advanced. Had the city fathers received advance information of the coming war? And was it really pure coincidence that at this particular moment Mayor Hamai should happen to be travelling abroad?

4

In this strained and overheated atmosphere, at a moment when almost everyone was reckoning on the immediate and inevitable outbreak of a new world war, and when a second destruction of Hiroshima was seen in the writing on the wall, Kazuo M. made his own private plan of campaign for the war that he now proposed to wage against a society that he had come to hate. 'I wish to become a really evil man, a proper criminal. That will be my rebellion against "those others".' Those were the actual words which he wrote at the time, his own private mobilization order that he addressed to himself.

An 'enemy' was easily found. In the Inari Machi district there lived a certain black-market operator by the name of Yamaji who because of his greed and harshness had made himself particularly unpopular. If a would-be customer should find any of his goods too expensive, he would growl: 'Why should I worry if you don't earn enough money, woman? If you think my prices too high, don't take the goods.' If with heavy heart the customer should nevertheless decide to buy from him, Yamaji would then amuse himself by mocking her: 'No, no, I couldn't sleep at night if you were to think I'd robbed you. Go and buy your condensed milk somewhere else. Anyhow, you're not getting any from me, that I promise you.' Because he knew for a fact that at that time – thanks to a brother who worked for the Americans and who received illegal supplies regularly – he was the only person in Hiroshima who had canned milk to sell.

So Kazuo decided that Yamaji should be his victim, and he could and did tell himself that this choice exonerated him from acting purely for reasons of personal gain. For was not Yamaji a foul person, a menace to his society, who should be neutralized? Furthermore he did all sorts of dirty deals with those foreign soldiers whom Kazuo loathed so deeply. Another advantage was the fact that Takemoto, the same person with whom Kazuo had tried and failed to do the deal in black-market dollars, had been at school with Yamaji and thus enjoyed the merchant's complete confidence.

Kazuo's plan was as follows. He would offer, through Takemoto, to sell Yamaji two hundred dollars. When the black-marketeer arrived, with the equivalent in Japanese currency, Kazuo simply planned to hit him on the head from the back and run off with the money. Since he would never before have had any dealings with the man he proposed to rob, suspicion must inevitably fall on Takemoto, who had already been sent to prison three times for theft. ('A second menace to society neutralized,' Kazuo remarked to himself, with inner triumph.) Kazuo would then be in a position to set about planning his next campaign.

These calculations, however, were almost immediately proved wrong. Yamaji sent a message by the middleman Takemoto to say that he was not interested in 'small deals'. At the moment he needed at least $500, for which he was prepared to pay between 180,000 and 200,000 yen, depending on the black-market rate prevailing on the day.

Two hundred thousand yen. . . . Kazuo was like a drunken man when Takemoto gave him the figure. At a single stroke he would become the possessor of a small fortune. But at once another thought crossed his mind. Since this was a sum so much larger than he had anticipated, he could no longer reckon on Yamaji coming to the rendezvous unaccompanied. He would certainly bring one or more 'bodyguards' with him. 'How,' Kazuo wondered, 'can I bump off several men at the same time?'

The nineteen-year-old pondered for days on end how he could lure both Yamaji and his bodyguards into a trap. Then he read in the newspapers a report of the sensational trial known as the 'Teikoku Bank case', which had been going on for months in a Tokyo court and which was now approaching its end. One day in January 1948, shortly before the bank closed for the night, a painter named Hirasawa had appeared, disguised as an official of the Health Department, and had told the branch manager that he and his staff of fifteen must immediately drink some medicine which would act as a prophylactic against the various epidemics then raging. He had brought the medicine with him. The treatment was, needless to say, at the government expense. Since there were indeed epidemics rife at this time, sixteen persons immediately obeyed this order, which seemed quite reasonable, and swallowed the bitter draught. They had collapsed almost at once, whereupon the bank robber had calmly and quietly set about his real business.

As in this *cause célèbre*, so now Kazuo decided that potassium cyanide would be the logical solution. This poison was comparatively easy to come by. For Funabashi, a close friend of the M. family, had mentioned that in his work, which was the gilding of picture-frames and lacquer bowls, he used potassium cyanide. Indeed, one day when they were discussing the much publicized trial, he had said, by way of a joke, that he possessed enough potassium cyanide to dispose of every bank employee in the Province of Hiroshima.

When Kazuo entered his acquaintance's place of work he found him engaged in conversation with two customers. They were being told, in great detail, exactly how to use a ventilator which they had come to collect; Mr Funabashi repaired such objects, as a sideline. Kazuo had wished to appear entirely calm, but the delay had made him nervous. As a result, when he said to the family friend that he wanted 'some of that stuff for gilding things', his voice was so tremulous and excited that the craftsman hesitated for a moment. Then he warned Kazuo: 'If you were to swallow that much of it . . .' and he showed on his middle finger exactly how much he meant,'. . . it's "curtains" in sixty seconds.' Perhaps he had heard about Kazuo's attempted suicide and was afraid lest the boy be planning to try this again.

Now it was only a question of fixing on a meeting place. Such a big deal could obviously not take place in the street, nor would any sort of public house be suitable. Kazuo tried in vain to find a suitable room. Since there was none to be had Kazuo made an almost incredible decision: he asked Takemoto to bring Yamaji to his own home. 'Not Nakata's place. Bring him to Danbaracho, my parents' house.' And on the same day Kazuo packed up and left his mistress's house, to return to his parents. It is to be assumed – though he has refused to comment on this – that Kazuo wished to keep Mrs Nakata out of the business altogether, while he derived a certain grim satisfaction from turning his intensely respectable and strict father's house into 'the scene of the crime'.

5

'First birthday of the City of Peace.' 'Wire thieves electrocuted cutting live cable.' 'Printing of *Akahata* (*Red Flag*) and 229 other publications forbidden.' 'Water supply exhausted.' 'Hiroshima Tramway Company to dismiss 131. Lively protests expected.' 'Mayor Hamai presents an Atomic Cross at Caux Moral Rearmament Meeting.' 'Golden Temple in Kyoto burns. Arson?' 'New Zoo opens.' 'Six years penal servitude for spreader of anti-

American leaflets.' 'Truman requests two billion dollars for new A-bomb project.' 'Kenichi Yamamoto (19) stabs Hisao Dan (42) with carving knife.'

Kazuo read one old issue of the *Chugoku Shimbun* after another but the time till the meeting just would not pass. Then it was precisely eleven o'clock, and they should have arrived long ago. He began to read the serial, a novel called *The Poisoned Grass of the City*, instalment No. 147. The author, Taijiro Tamura, had made his reputation with a book entitled *Gate of Flesh*, and had simultaneously inaugurated the exciting 'Flesh Literature' school which was doing so well in post-war Japan.

Eleven-fifteen. . . . Now only the advertisements were left. At the Kokusai Cinema they were playing *Story of a Decline*. The advertisement was intended to make the reader's mouth water: 'The heroine of this film, based on the famous novel by Tatsuzo Ishikawa, commits one crime after another for love, until she goes to bits. An anthology of tears. . . .' In the Futabe Theatre, *I am Going to be Killed*, with Barbara Stanwyck.

They arrived at last, half an hour late. Kazuo has described what happened in the following words:

'As I'd imagined, Yamaji had brought two toughs with him, as his bodyguards. In addition to these three, Takemoto was there as well. I asked them to sit down and said: "Morita – an invented name, he was the person whom was supposed to be producing the dollars – hasn't come yet. Please be patient for a little while." That was how I calmed them down, blaming it all on my imaginary partner.

'Then I made sure that they'd got the whole sum with them, in cash. Yamaji showed me the wad of banknotes, two hundred thousand yen, in thousands. He'd wrapped them up in an old piece of newspaper.

'The hands on my watch showed twelve o'clock. "Mr Morita is very unpunctual." It was Yamaji who said this. There was probably no double-meaning to his words but I interpreted them as meaning: "There's something fishy about this whole business."

'I also began to suspect that his bodyguards were looking at me with mistrust. Those two had hardly said a word since they arrived, but kept staring at me in a most peculiar way, their heads down. "Must get this over and done with," I said to myself. And it seemed to me as though my watch were ticking away the seconds faster and faster.

'"Morita-san must certainly be turning up at any moment now," I said. "But while we're waiting I'll fetch us all a drink." I was glad to leave the room for a moment: the atmosphere in there was really becoming intolerable. Two or three doors down the street I found a little Ice-cream Parlour. I bought four bottles of lemonade, the sort called Calpis. Without anyone noticing, I slipped the cyanide I had ready into the lemonade.

'The moment I'd poured out the drinks all four of them took an enormous swallow of Calpis. Immediately one of the bodyguards began to heave, and ran out of the room, swearing. Then the others ran out into the street too, and I noticed how some of the liquid, which had been spilt, was bleaching a bright yellow patch upon the straw mat.

'"Listen, you. What's that drink you gave us?" I felt a tremendous grip. It was the tough who'd run out first. He was holding my shoulder in a grip of steel.

'"What do you mean? It was Calpis, of course. What's the matter?" I pretended to be completely surprised. But I realized as soon as I spoke that my voice was trembling.

'"The stuff had a horribly bitter taste,' he grumbled. "Must have gone off. Come on, let's complain to the shop."

'He picked up a bottle, with something still in it, and together we made our way to the Ice-cream Parlour.

'"Hey, you," I said to the man behind the counter. "That Calpis we just bought from you, it had a funny, bitter sort of taste."

'"Impossible. Only first-class goods sold here."

'"But it's bitter as hell. Really. Ask this man here."

'While this argument was going on, we suddenly heard a woman's voice screeching: "There ... over there ... a dead man!"

'We ran out. About ten yards away, in the middle of the street, a man had collapsed. It was Yamaji.

'We picked him up by his head and his feet and carried him back into the house. As we stepped over the doorway something fell out of his trouser pocket and landed at my feet. It was the bundle of banknotes, two hundred thousand yen. Almost automatically I picked it up and tucked it in my pocket. So now I'd got the 200,000 I'd wanted so much.

'But I didn't feel at all happy about it. Indeed I was horribly upset. "Murderer!" a voice kept shouting inside me: "Murderer!" I began to tremble, everything was swimming before my eyes, and yet when this got better I once again heard: "Murderer!" I tried to silence this inner voice by pressing my hands to my ears and closing my eyes tight. It was no good.

'"Send for the doctor!" I had suddenly sprung to my feet and was shouting for a doctor. No, not for myself. I wanted to save Yamaji's life. I was, quite simply, scared that I'd be branded as a murderer for all eternity.

'Some man, overcome with curiosity, was standing as if entranced beside Yamaji's stretched-out body, staring at him and not knowing what to do. This was the man I yelled at to get a doctor, and he ran off at once. Yamaji's face had turned bright red. He looked extremely ill, but he was breathing regularly. Perhaps he might still be saved. I got him some water, and even poured it into his mouth myself. He managed to swallow half a glass, but the second half he vomited up again. His bare chest had now also turned deep red. I laid a damp cloth over it, and prayed that he might yet live. The cloth very quickly became hot; when I went to change it I saw that his chest was now turning purple. Did this mean it was the end?

'I shook Yamaji's body with all my strength. At last the doctor came. He tried artificial respiration. Sat like a horseman astride the poisoned man. And inside my head a voice repeated, rhythmically: "Murderer . . . murderer . . . murderer."'

AUGUST THE SIXTH

1

It was generally known as the 'Calpis Murder', after the brand name of the popular lemonade into which Kazuo had poured the potassium cyanide, and the story excited much interest among Hiroshima's sensation-hungry newspaper readers. Here was a boy of nineteen who at his first examination admitted with brutal frankness that he had been prepared to murder four men, if necessary, simply in order to acquire 200,000 yen! Every reader could feel that, no matter how devious his own paths might be, he was a man of outstanding virtue in comparison with such a monster as this.

The black-marketeer Yamaji, who died twenty minutes after taking the poison, was not the only victim of the story. The ice cream salesman, Teraji, was only accidentally involved. Yet when Kazuo had complained of the bitter taste of the lemonade he had sold him, in his determination to show that he did not believe this he swallowed what was left in the half-empty bottle in a single draught. For days he hovered between life and death.

On the other hand the remaining three victims of the attempted poisoning only needed immediate first-aid treatment at the Yoshizaki Hospital, from which they were released that same day.

When the accused, Kazuo M., was arrested close to the scene of the crime, he gave the impression of having also been badly poisoned. He was lurching along, head down, occasionally reeling like a drunkard, without any apparent destination. The policeman who picked him up was called Okamoto, and had known Kazuo since childhood. The reason he brought him in was that he thought Kazuo must be suffering from food poisoning, and he therefore took him to the Health Department clinic.

The doctor on duty used the stomach pump on the boy and reported, significantly enough, that he had found traces of poison. In the days that followed, when the case was being given nation-wide press coverage, this story was confirmed. The popular theory was that in order to encourage the others to drink, Kazuo had himself sipped the cyanide lemonade.

In his own version of it all, Kazuo maintains that he, 'had not swallowed a single drop of the drink'. How did the doctor come to make such a statement? Apparently he wished to get into the limelight. Or so it seemed to Kazuo, as he lay on the doctor's table after having been given no less than twenty anti-toxin injections; and this seemed to the young man yet further proof that even those medical men who were honoured by society as incorruptible and devoted men were not honourable.

In fact it was another sort of poison that had entered into Kazuo, a poison undetectable in any test tube, but one that is always fatal and for which no antidote exists, the poison of memory. It had entered into him at the moment that he gave the black-marketeer a glass of water, fearing that this was too late. Years ago, after the *Pikadon*, he had knelt like this beside his dying friend, Sumiko, and had moistened her lips, had tried to wipe away the screams that had come from those lips during their walk through hell together.

Such a similarity in the faces of the two dying people . . .! Yamaji, whom he hated, and Sumiko, with whom he had felt so intimately linked. 'In truth isn't Yamaji also a victim of that same bomb?' Kazuo asked himself. During the hot days and nights that he spent in a cell reeking of ammonia, sour oil, and the lavatory in the corner, while he waited to be examined, the present and the past became strangely confounded.

Since the day it happened Kazuo had never dared to try and remember the exact details of that walk through the burning city. But now the time of reckoning had come; now he must judge himself; and so even what had been most unbearable now came flooding back. Perhaps it would enable him to understand or, better still, to shed his burden.

He wrote in his diary:

'Why didn't I run away while I could? I've committed a murder. Even now I find this hard to believe. You can't believe it? He's dead. What's so remarkable about that? On the day of the atom bomb you saw so many dead people, side by side, on top of one another. And you heard the sound of bones cracking as you climbed over them, and you weren't even particularly shaken. Extraordinary, all my feelings must have been dislocated at that time. If I'd shouted at myself then: "You've killed a man!", my answer would have been: "Really! That makes one more." For the rest – did I really need money so badly that I was prepared to kill for it? That can't be true . . . But what was it that sent my life off the rails? It was that day, that sixth of August. . . . And I'm not the only person for whom it must bear the guilt. Not just the flesh and bones, but the hearts and the souls of countless human beings were ruined by that day. Since then the whole structure of society has tottered. Small wonder that the weak should starve while the strong have become robbers. This Yamaji, a foul creature! He did his dirty deals almost publicly and got away with it, because he was well in with the police.

'It all boils down to this: in our dark city I tried, all alone, to follow the path of honour. As the old saying has it: "An honest man on his own is always in danger . . ." And now they all act as if they were astonished, their eyes almost pop out of their head, because a single black-market operator has been rubbed out! And me? I did a good job. Nevertheless – my tears flow. I cannot hold them back. Is it because I do not understand, or are my tears shed in pity for myself?'

2

At his first examination the officials treated Kazuo with their customary brutality. One hit him in the face. Another kicked him in the stomach. 'Spit it out!' they shouted. 'Confess, or you'll get more of the same. Don't imagine we're going to treat you soft, just because you're a kid. Anyhow we know all the facts already. Don't pretend to be ignorant.'

Then he was taken before a senior police official, whose tone was very different. This was the head of the Prefecture Police, a mild, elephantine man, who treated the prisoner with gentleness, even with a sort of sympathetic understanding. He scarcely referred to the crime. Instead he spent two hours encouraging Kazuo to talk about his past.

The reason for this unusually sympathetic attitude on the part of the senior official was that he had received a visitor on the previous day. A man named Setsuo M. had arrived at his office, claiming to be the father of the 'Calpis murderer' and urgently requesting an interview. 'The usual plea for clemency,' the police chief had thought and had prepared his customary reply, consoling but non-committal.

But the skinny little man seated on the far side of the desk had had quite another request to make, a plea such as had never before been made to the police official in his thirty years of service. For he requested that his errant son, who had caused so much suffering and brought so much dishonour on his family, should be condemned to death without fail. Only thus could the stain be washed away. The father had even gone so far as to offer his own life as well in expiation.

When Kazuo's interrogation by the police chief was over, and he was being led out of his office, he found himself face to face with a battery of cameras and flash bulbs. The fact that the most senior criminologist in the district had taken on the case assured him of even more publicity. Kazuo's prison warder told him: 'You wouldn't guess it to look at him, but he's a master of judo. He's reached the seventh grade, one grade higher than most judo teachers.'

Kazuo thought that in his present circumstances the police rank and judo grade of his interrogator were really matters of complete indifference to him; nevertheless, the awe in which his guards held the police chief was reflected, in a way, in their attitude towards himself. He was moved from the remand jail into the larger and much better equipped Yamaita prison. He was given a particularly spacious cell all to himself; usually several prisoners were lodged in it. He was allowed, indeed ordered, to write about his past. And so for the first time Kazuo committed to paper the most important event of his life, and one that he had been trying for five years to forget. He wrote down his recollections of 6 August 1945.

3

It was very difficult for him to do so. He had often recalled the past up to the moment when, coming back towards the town from the Mitsubishi Works, he had met the blinded, naked fugitives who had shouted: 'No further! Don't go into that hell!' He had hitherto always lacked the courage to summon up what had happened after that.

But now, now it had to be. From time to time he would have to break off for long periods. None the less, though constantly interrupting himself, he wrote in a trembling hand:

'The bridge was half destroyed, and hung in flames into the river. So I ran to the iron railway bridge, a hundred yards downstream. The wooden sleepers were burning here too, but I ran along the red-hot metal rails. On the far side crowds of maddened people were running like demented lemmings, trying to get across the river. They were screaming, and it sounded like one enormous voice. In the middle of the bridge lay four or five bodies, unrecognizable as human beings, but still moving. Their skin hung from them like strands of dark seaweed! Instead of noses, holes! Their ears and hands were so swollen as to be shapeless. One of them falls off the bridge! Now another! And then one after the other they tumble into the river, helplessly exhausted. They drowned, and made no attempt to save themselves. But there were still fifty or sixty clinging to the red-hot rails. In their terror of dying they clawed their way over one another, their eyes hanging from their sockets, pushing one another into the river, and screaming all the time.

'Somehow I got across the railway bridge, but on the far bank there were mountains of corpses blocking the way forward. These people must have been chased by the roaring tongues of flames that caught them here. They were still burning. I thought that they were all dead, but now they began to whimper. A woman was calling for her husband. A mother for her child. And the flames sprang to life again and gripped them pitilessly. My own eyebrows were singed, my hands and my face burning. My only thought

was that I must get out of here, somehow, anyhow. I must fight
my way through the corpses. I pushed them aside, pulling on a
head to clear a passage. "*Zuru, zuru*". . . . This contact with my
hands was loathsome. The skin on the face stuck to my palms.
Beneath the skin was something yellowish. I was trembling all
over, and I dropped the dead man's head, tried to push his hand
aside in order that I might get through . . . and that hand was
nothing but bones beneath charred flesh, and the skin off his face
still stuck to me.

'I climbed on top of a pile of corpses. Layer upon layer of them.
Some were still moving, still alive. I had to get over them. I had to
climb over. There was no way of getting through. I can still hear
the cracking of their bones. At last the mountain of the dead lay
behind me. One of my feet was aching horribly. Only now did I
notice that I had lost a shoe. My bare sole had been cut by glass
splinters and was bleeding. An open water tank, against air raids.
I buried my face in it. The water was boiling hot. I began to feel
faint. And thirst, such a thirst. There was no drop of sweat on my
desiccated body, but it was covered in blood and bits of strangers'
skin. I reeled and wanted to vomit. I took hold of myself and
automatically picked out the little stones that had got into the
wounds on my feet. Now the wounds began to bleed again from
horrible, black gashes. And the little stones were in them again.
There was no sense in taking them out. Up to then I had at
least been able to breathe and moan and shout. But now my
throat was so parched that I could scarcely utter a sound. When
I tried to shout it was as though my throat was pierced by a
thousand needles being driven into an open wound. I mustn't
think about the pain! I must run, run, run, that was all – run for
my life.

'What purpose did all this misery serve? I remembered someone
who always used to say: "This is an unjust war." Could this be a
divine punishment, because Japan had wanted to win an Empire?
Be that as it may, this was no time to wonder about the past! Any
second could decide my future. . . . My body was expanding, as
if it would burst at any moment. Then, suddenly, something
gigantic, something black, was collapsing on me. With an
instinctive twist of my body I had slipped out of the way in the

nick of time. It was the second storey of a house, entirely wrapped in twisting, red flames. The evil spirits wanted to go on playing with my life a bit longer. . . .

'So tired that I thought I must die, I staggered on, step by step, through this labyrinth of fire. I thought: "If I stop here now, it's all up with me." Then there was somebody, close by, calling: "Kazuo-san, please help me!" Whoever it was knew my name, so it must be somebody I knew. But who? Who was this thing? A girl? Her hair was burned off. Quite naked. Only the rubber belt that had held up her trousers still hung ridiculously about her hips. The lower part of her body, which was smeared with blood and filth, was badly cut, a deep wound. In such a condition I should not have even recognized my own sister.

'I asked: "Who are you?"

'"I'm Sumiko."

'Then I knew. Sumiko! She lived just near us. But this couldn't be she! Sumiko! She had been so beautiful a child that we had nicknamed her "the white lily". I asked: "Is that really who you are? The little Sumi-chan? Don't be scared. I'll see you get home. Courage! Come along!"

'She was already so weak that she couldn't even take a single step. I tore off my shirt so that she might at least hide her breasts and her shame. Only then did I try to rub away the blood that had poured from her wound. The cut was deeper even than I had first thought, but it was not bleeding too badly. Only a thin trickle of fresh, bright red was making its way down her trembling thigh.

'I tried to support Sumiko, but each step was so painful for her that she cried aloud.

'"Sumi-chan, I know how it hurts. Please hold out."

'We struggled for a further ten yards, then stopped to rest beside an open water tank, and wetted ourselves from head to foot. But the heat from the flames was so great that we were dry again instantly. It had been hard enough for me to get through on my own; with the two of us it was now almost impossible. Once again whole walls of dying people blocked our path. They'd collapsed in the middle of the street. We tried to creep between them and became entangled in electric wires. When the poles burned or collapsed these wires had fallen everywhere. Like metal snakes . . .

'I was at times close to giving in myself. Maybe I'd have done so. But by telling Sumiko over and over again to keep her courage up, I kept up my own. It was only because I had to save her that I was able to save myself. And so at last we reached Dobashi.*

'The dead here were all schoolgirls. From the First Middle School, the Shudo Middle School, the Methodist Middle School. They were all there. Almost without exception. And a few peasants, too. They'd come in with carts, horses, and oxen to help with the evacuation of the girls' schools, which should have been done long before.

'We stumbled on, often falling now. The smoke was here growing so thick and biting that we could go no further. With a heavy heart I said: "Sumi-chan, we can't go on this way. We'll have to turn back and flee to Yogokawa."

'So we had to give up our attempt to go home, to our parents. A hard decision to take. But we had no choice. Bit by bit now the road was growing wider and less cluttered. But again and again we met parents calling for their children, or babies crying for their mothers. And then a detachment of soldiers from the Second Western Regiment. All dead. But still drawn up with military precision. At their head, his uniform tunic still recognizable, was their officer. He still held his drawn sword in his hand, but the whole lower part of his body was – white bones.

'We stumbled across Yokogawa Bridge and then headed north, till we reached the river bank near Misasa. Here at last there was no longer any trace of burning, and everything that happened to us in this externally undamaged quarter was like a nightmare at midday. . . . We sat down beside some bamboos on the river's edge. A few other refugees were already lying there. How many hours had passed since I had left the factory building in Furue? Five? Ten? Or was it yesterday? For the first time I was conscious of hunger.

'From a nearby clump I heard a voice crying: "Hi, you there! Medicine for burns. Anyone who can still walk, come and get it." They were crawling towards a man who was shaking a thick

* A square not far from the epicentre of the bomb's explosion.

liquid out of a petrol can. I let him pour some of it into the palms of my hands. It was vegetable oil. I rubbed it all over Sumiko's body, while she whimpered with pain. Then I wiped my greasy hands on my own body. After which we fell asleep, a sleep so deep that we might have been unconscious.

'As dusk fell, the bamboo thicket came to life.

'"Water, water ... please ... give me water ... *itai, itai** ... Mother! Kill me! Anything to stop this pain."

'More and more screams and groans filled the darkness. "The devils! Water ... Just one drop...." A woman jumped to her feet and collapsed. Another began to cry insanely: "He ... ha ... ha ... Mitchan.... Look, there's my Mitchan.... She's running away.... Come here, Mitchiko.... Come here and I'll give you milk." The young woman clutched at her shrunken breasts and thrust them upwards, towards the sky. She laughed as she did so, and her loosened hair tossed about her head. Now she fell upon the bamboo stems, thrusting them aside and shaking them, dementedly, as though from somewhere among their leaves the child whom she had lost might come tumbling down at her feet. But all that fluttered down were the leaves. They shone in the light of the fires that were Hiroshima burning. The darker it became, the more brilliantly did the flames flicker across to us.

'How many can have found refuge in this place? And how many of them were to die here, before dawn broke? Maybe, among them, Sumiko, who had pillowed her head upon my chest. We put our arms around each other and waited for the new day.

'Somehow – I still cannot say precisely what happened – we at last made our way to the spot where my home had been. It was now nothing but a heap of blackened rubble. Of my room, which I had loved so much, and of the little veranda which had stood in front of it, there was nothing to be seen whatever. And there was no trace of mother, father, my sister. I stood there, feeling nothing, incapable of making any movement. If they were dead I must set about immediately searching for their mortal remains in order to cremate them. I dug in the place where the kitchen had been, then where I thought the sitting-room had stood. The

* A Japanese cry of pain.

wounds on my hands opened again, but I dug on and on. The only thing of Father's that I could find was his cigarette tin, and of Mother's possessions nothing save her wrist-watch.

'This I put in my pocket as a memento . . .

'We went on to Sumiko's house.

'"Water, water!" she whispered. "Please, Kazuo-san, please, just a few drops!" But in this district there was nothing except cinders and ashes.

'"Kazuo-san . . . I . . . can't . . . go . . . on. It's all up with me. . . . Thank you . . . thank you for all you've done. . . . You must go back . . . and look . . . for your mother. . . ."

'She had folded her hands as in prayer, but I interrupted her sobbing.

'"Have you gone mad? Get up! Don't you want to see your parents again? If you give in now it'll have been all in vain. Do you understand me? You must not die. *You must not*." I had taken her by the shoulders and was shaking her.

'An old woman passed close by.

'"*Obasan*,"* I shouted rudely, "where's there water in these parts?"

'She made it plain by her expression that my bad manners displeased her, but at last she waved her hand and pointed angrily: "Over that way."

'"Thank you," I cried after her, and to Sumiko I said: "Sumi-chan, did you hear? Water, drinking water, just here. Sumi-chan . . .!" She smiled feebly. When I came back with the water she was motionless. She already felt cold. "Sumiko!" I cried, "Sumi-chan! Wake up! You've got to live." I threw my arms about her and sprinkled water over her face which was now smiling and relaxed. The drops ran across her lips. The water she had longed for now trickled uselessly down her chin.'

4

While Kazuo in prison was recalling the events that had followed the dropping of the atom bomb – events that for more than four

* Old woman.

years he had deliberately blotted out of his memory – in the world
beyond his prison walls the celebrations to mark the anniversary
of that bombing on 6 August were, for the first time, forbidden by
the authorities. For the Occupying Powers and the Office for
Public Security feared lest these celebrations become the pretext
for a mass demonstration of protest against the Korean War.

Every sort of public assembly was at this time strictly forbidden.
Only the howling of the recently re-installed air-raid sirens at the
precise hour of eight-fifteen was allowed as a reminder of 'that
day'. In order to ensure 'the security of public order', police were
drafted into Hiroshima from all the surrounding districts. On that
hot, sunny morning of 6 August, Hiroshima resembled one huge
army camp.

Despite all the precautionary measures taken by the police,
several columns of demonstrators did set out to march through
the city, while from the roof of the rebuilt Fukuya department
store thousands of leaflets fluttered down on the city.

Among those whom the police, using their batons, forced to
disperse was Seichiro Tage. Pale and scarcely recovered from his
haemorrhage, he had left his sanatorium in order to demonstrate
for peace in the 'City of Death'.

He has described his experiences on this day in a poem which
was later to be read and recited throughout the length and breadth
of Japan. This is what he has to say about 6 August 1950, in
Hiroshima, the 'City of Peace'.

> They drive at us,
> Drive at us
> From here
> From there,
> Pistol on hip,
> The Police drive at us:
> August the sixth nineteen fifty . . .
>
> At the Deadmen's Tower on the bald-burned spot
> The outflood of the citizens,
> The flowers which they brought
> Torn headless in the milling whirlpool,
> When those with sweat-stained chinstraps
> Let fly into the crowd. . . .

Let the doves fly high,
Let the peace bell ring
And the mayor's peace messages
Twisted in the wind,
The feast of freedom,
Blown to naught
Like fireworks. . . .

STRAW SANDALS

1

'... and so I request that I be sentenced to death.' In interrogation after interrogation Kazuo M. begged the officials who were preparing the case against him to include this – his sole and last wish – in the protocol.

The stubbornness with which M. insisted on this unusual request gave the legal officials cause to think. From the prison warders' reports they were already well aware that the moment he was left alone the prisoner Kazuo M. would begin to pace nervously up and down his cell; that he tossed and turned and talked in his sleep: briefly, that he showed all the normal, visible symptoms of fear to be expected of a man faced with death. But no sooner was he seated in the state attorney's office than he began to act the part of a hard-boiled criminal, who even underlined the fact that he killed merely out of a vulgar lust for money. Had he had any other motive? No, none.

This picture that he drew of himself did not in any way correspond to that drawn by those witnesses who had known Kazuo at all well. Something must therefore be wrong, and the state attorney* was determined to find why this particular criminal, unlike all the others whom he had ever cross-examined, was so anxious to heap such guilt upon himself.

He therefore had Kazuo brought to his office once again, and came straight to the point:

'You're hiding something from us. I've been told that you were a volunteer in the Fire Service. I've also been told about how you came to blows with the foreign soldiers. Somebody has said that you used often to go to the cemetery of the unknown victims of the atomic bomb, on Hijiyama Hill, and that you used to talk to yourself there, and cry. I have a feeling that all these are

* In Japanese law the accused is examined by the state attorney before the trial.

significant facts, which are somehow connected with what you did. . . .'

Kazuo remained stubbornly silent and gazed out of the window behind the attorney's chair, as if all this were no concern of his.

'It's also obviously no mere accident that your victim should have been a black-market operator. Listen to me, Kazuo, the state attorney is not always and automatically the enemy of the accused. So say what's on your mind! Well . . .? Open your heart to me . . . tell me everything. You'll feel much better and easier in yourself once you've done that. . . .'

There was still no word from Kazuo, nor so much as the flicker of an expression to show that he had even heard what the other man was saying. Now the state attorney spoke sharply:

'If you stick to the statements you've been making, there can only be one outcome for you: the death sentence. But if you want to save your life, you've got to come clean and lay your cards on the table.'

As Kazuo said to me at a later date:

'For a moment I felt that I ought to tell the man everything. But when he said "if you want to save your life" I became furiously angry. So he thought I was scared of dying! I most certainly was not, and this I was determined to show him.'

And Kazuo reacted accordingly. He asked the state attorney:

'Is it certain that my written statement will be accepted by the court as it now stands, if I don't change it in any way . . .?'

'Quite certain,' the official replied. He was utterly dumbfounded. He looked hard at Kazuo, for he knew that if Kazuo were to sign his statement as it now stood it was tantamount to his signing his own death warrant.

He was determined to try once more. He therefore said to Kazuo:

'There's one piece of advice I'd like to give you. I have here before me a plea for clemency on your behalf. If everything that it contains is true, it's obvious that you're no ordinary criminal. As a child you were a keen painter. You were a bookworm. You were said to be a gentle, dreamy character. After the war you suddenly became an altogether different person. In this plea for clemency it is stated that it's scarcely possible to believe a person such as yourself could have committed so brutal a murder. It doesn't make any sense to me either, now that I've got to know you. I've heard that you were very popular with your schoolmates. I've also heard that when you met friends from your schooldays you would protest, with tears in your eyes, against the frivolity and immorality of the youth of today.

'I simply cannot believe that you should have lost your passion and admiration for what is clean and fine. . . . The crime of which you are accused certainly cannot be wiped out; it happened, and that's that. But you must understand that my job is to expose and to hold up to execration the crime itself, and not necessarily the person who committed it . . . So please regard me as your friend . . . I should like to treat you as a human being. Can you not understand this even now?'

But Kazuo remained silent. Yet, as he later told me, these words had moved him deeply. But he followed the dictates of his 'stubborn heart'. He insisted on putting his 'signature' – a finger-print – beneath these statements he had made, and in them he had drawn his own portrait as a calculating and brutal murderer who killed solely for money.

2

The examining judge had come close to the truth when he guessed that Kazuo M. wished to use the State's institution for justice for his own purpose, which was to commit suicide. He had already thought of suicide when he had destroyed his reading primer, and he had spoken of it in the *Rain Poem* that he had written in the weeks immediately after the *Pikadon*. A failed suicide attempt had been his answer to Yukiko's infidelity.

The frivolity and absence of planning that had characterized Kazuo's crime, the fact that when he had actually got the stolen money in his pocket he made no attempt to get away, and finally his behaviour during the examination of his case, all led to the conclusion that it was the death wish that had brought him to commit murder. It was himself, not Yamaji, who was the real victim, whom he had wished to hound to death, and now the point had been reached. . . .

According to the Japanese system the accused and the witnesses do not all appear together to give their evidence at a single trial. The procedure is one of several weeks 'or even months' duration, during which time the various aspects of the case are dealt with in individual sessions. From October 1950 until August 1951 Kazuo M. had to appear at no less than six such 'open hearings'. Meanwhile he spent a large part of the time between these hearings writing his diary, in which he expressed his bitter struggles and fears:

'X Day, X Month, 1950. Light rain. Looking at me: eyes filled with curiosity, eyes filled with hatred, eyes filled with pity. (Who has ever asked you to feel pity for me?) The flashlights of the newspapermen stab into my body. Look at me. I have no fear of being condemned to death. You can be sure of that. I bare my teeth at you all. And you stare back at me in horror. I feel fine. Listen, all of you! Do you know that the shaft of the axe is hewn from that same oak tree that the axe lays low? I wanted to smash everything. . . . Yes, everything. . . . Including my own life. . . . And I've done it. . . . Precisely that. . . . Yes, precisely that. . . .

'X Day, X Month, 1950. Father, father, I long for my father. How they all stared at me again today. And they all think I'm a great criminal. And I act as if I were, as if I didn't care what they think. But when the end comes I'll surely weaken. For in reality I'm no sort of iron man. I would like so very much to draw closer to my fellow-men, to love and be loved, but they have all avoided me. The more I tried to draw closer to them, the further they moved away from me. I was always alone. Entirely alone with myself. If the truth were told, I don't want to die at all. I want to live, to live. . . .'

3

One night when he was turning sleeplessly on his plank bed, the warder rattled his door:

'You in there – a visitor!'

Kazuo jumped up, pulled on his trousers, and was about to buckle his belt when he remembered that his belt had been taken from him long ago. The ridiculous way in which he had to clutch his trousers to him whenever he stood up or took a few steps was for Kazuo the severest humiliation that he had had to endure during this long period in prison.

There, in a corner of the examination room, huddled on a chair with sunken head, was the visitor whom he had longed for all these months, but who, he had long ago decided, would never come to see him – his father.

They looked at one another. In Setsuo M.'s eyes there was an expression of sorrow and despair, that expression which was to be seen on those rare occasions when he dropped his pose of rigid self-control and admitted: 'My wife's family are decent people. But me? I'm a good-for-nothing.'

'Kazuo, what have you done?' he said. 'I'm ashamed before our forefathers and our fellow-men. . . . I have even tried to take my own life. As expiation, as atonement. But . . . I couldn't even succeed in that.'

His voice took on a forced note of self-consciousness as he went on:

'I shall make good your crime. I shall work and slave for the community. Even if it kills me.'

Kazuo would have liked to throw his arms about his father, but even now he dared not do so. Setsuo M. handed his son a small parcel. 'I worked at it all night long. It is the last present I shall ever give you. . . . But there is something more that I wish to say to you: all this is not in fact your fault. I and your mother – it is we who are to blame. Forgive your mother. She tried her best to bring you up to be a decent human being. . . . But me, your father, well may you curse me. . . . Do you understand, Kazuo? Enough, Kazuo. Only one last request: don't be a weakling, my son.'

When his father had gone Kazuo was allowed to undo the little parcel wrapped in newspaper, under the supervision of the warder. He hesitated, for this was a precious moment. Never before had his father given him a present. But the warder was growing impatient, and told him to get on with it. Slowly Kazuo undid the parcel. It contained a pair of straw sandals with black and white straps.

Kazuo saw the expression of horror on the warder's face. It was a moment or two before he realized what he had not understood when first he opened his father's present. These were sandals of the type that are tied to the feet of corpses, before the funeral.

'Sandals for the dead.' The phrase re-echoed through Kazuo's brain. 'Sandals for the dead. So he wanted to show me that it is essential I should die, that is the sort of man my father has always been. Preferring to talk in hints and riddles rather than come out and say clearly what he meant or what it was that he wanted done. A man who can say to his own son: die! So he wishes his son to vanish from this earth. To flee into nothingness. Any other father would have driven the world mad with his cries of "Save my son!" But not my father, not mine.'

In his diary, when he came to write of this decisive incident, Kazuo said:

'Last night I slept with the sandals in my arms, the sandals my father brought me. . . . When I awoke they were wet with my tears. It is so long since I met my mother or my sister in my dreams. Father, I'm wearing them already, your sandals. Sometimes I rub them on the floor, or knead them with my hands in order that they may be entirely smooth and may fit my feet to perfection. . . . I shall stand beneath the guillotine and shall wear the sandals proudly. For they are the only expression of love that my father has ever given me. . . .'

4

When my colleague, Kaoru Ogura, and I, after hunting through the voluminous archives in the Judicial Department of the Hiroshima district administration finally found the volume that contained the court record of the Kazuo M. Case, we read of an event to which Kazuo himself had made no reference either in his conversations with me or in his own notes. But this event was to decide the fate of the accused.

On 20 July 1950, Kazuo had been interrogated by the prosecutor, and had said among other things:

'On January 2nd of this year I fell off a ladder and broke both my arms as well as several ribs. Also after the fall I suspected that I had damaged my skull. From then on I was nervous and some people even said I was hysterical. Although I had fallen so badly that I may well have slightly fractured my skull, I never lost consciousness. But when I was discharged from hospital I could only move my arms with difficulty, and as a result I lost all my will to live. On February 14th I drank rat poison in an attempt to commit suicide. But by early March my arms and also my ribs were completely cured. Yet since my suicide attempt I had been frightened of looking for work of any sort. . . .'

At this point the officially appointed counsel for the defence, Daikichi Honma, had intervened. It should be very easy to obtain corroborative evidence to prove the truth of what Kazuo M. had said about his accident, for it had taken place in the presence of a large number of witnesses. On 6 January of each year a great public display by the Fire Service takes place in most Japanese cities. This is called the Dezome Shiki, and the bravest and most skilful firemen perform hair-raising feats of balancing. The high point of these displays, which take place in the open air, is always a demonstration of acrobatics on bamboo ladders. Standing on one leg or hanging by one foot, the firemen swing back and forth, high in the sky, while unfurling brightly coloured banners or twirling painted umbrellas made of paper.

Already in December Kazuo had had a fall while practising for the display. This was his first practice, and the fall had been a nasty one, but he had survived it unscathed. Since then he had lacked assurance, and four days before the display he had fallen again with the serious results already referred to. The lawyer for the defence could produce evidence from relations and friends, all of whom commented on Kazuo's 'peculiar behaviour' since this fall. He also obtained a relevant affidavit from the medical authorities. The expert evidence supplied by Dr Takashi Fujiwara of Okayama University could hardly fail to carry weight; the neurologist declared that it was entirely possible that during the six months following his accident, in consequence of the shock to his brain, the accused might well have shown 'certain changes to his mentality'.

In the hearing, neither M. nor his lawyer ever referred to the deeper emotional background behind the crime. Not a single word was devoted to the spiritual shock he had suffered at the time of the *Pikadon*, nor to Kazuo's post-war experiences, though these might well have been regarded as mitigating circumstances.

The accused kept silent on this score because for him the verdict had already been pronounced – his father had spoken; while his lawyer did not wish to make use of such psychological arguments. For he was bound to see that the judges were highly unlikely to accept such a plea; were they to do so, the other survivors of the atom bomb might well advance similar arguments and claim freedom to take the law into their own hands in any moment of personal crisis.

State Attorney Kataoka had meanwhile taken over the case for the prosecution from the official whose saving hand Kazuo M. refused to take. On 16 August 1951 he demanded the death sentence for the accused. The accused, he said, had prepared his crime in cold blood. By his own admission he had been ready, purely for motives of financial gain, to kill not one but several human beings: his was a sad example of unstable behaviour among the younger generation. Attorney Honma pleaded 'diminished powers of judgement' and had some surprising further evidence to produce in support of this plea: it had recently come to light that in the months before the murder Kazuo M. had made two further suicide attempts hitherto undisclosed. Once he had stuck his head for hours on end into a gully-hole, while on another occasion he had been found lying on the railway lines. This was further proof that since his two falls from the Fire Service ladders he had been temporarily living in a state of mental aberration.

5

It was announced that the sentence on the 'Calpis murderer' would be promulgated on 8 September 1951. Even before the court was opened – it was Courtroom No. 2 in the new District Courthouse which had been rebuilt since the atomic bomb – the corridors were crowded. Yet the proceedings could not be begun on time, for another case was being heard in Courtroom No. 2 and had not yet been completed.

Among those who waited was Kazuo's father. He stood with

his face to the wall and tried to avoid recognition by the crowd that pressed about him.

When he heard somebody speaking to him he jumped nervously; he had hoped to be left alone with his shame and his sorrow.

'I believe you're the young murderer's father?'

He looked up and saw an elderly woman standing before him. He had never seen her before.

'I have come here to give him courage,' the old woman said. 'I have heard that he is an *oya-koko-musuko*, a young man who looks after his parents. I do not believe he is a criminal.'

These words had a profound effect upon Setsuo M., but before he could thank the unknown woman the doors of the courtroom had been thrown open and he had lost her in the rush. Nor did he ever see her again.

'As always during the open hearing, I felt myself surrounded by countless eyes on every side,' Kazuo M. has said. 'And my heart revolted against those eyes. All right, stare at me, all of you, here I am, yes me, the killer. Have a good look, don't mind about me, you damned fools! You would never be able to understand even one hundredth part of what has happened within me.

'And then the verdict. Hundreds of eyes fixed upon my back, eager and tense. It's: LIFE IMPRISONMENT.*

'Was I "happy". . . .? No, certainly not. . . . "Unhappy"? No, nor that. "The wrong solution" – that is closer to what I felt. For what did "life imprisonment" mean except "go on living"? When a man has lived in such close proximity to death for as long as I had, when he has said to himself day after day: "It's that much nearer, the net is drawing closer," it's hard for him to take a different line. . . .

'The whole courtroom was buzzing with voices now. As I left the Courthouse my feelings were tending cautiously towards relief, even happiness. But mingled with this happiness there was a sort of indescribable sadness . . . I know now: I did it wrong. . . . Everything.'

* Kazuo has recently been let out on parole.

4

The Survivors
(1952–7)

THE FISHCAKE PALACE

1

THE 'Peace City' of Hiroshima only really began to recover and to flourish when a new war, or, as it was euphemistically called, 'the Korean Incident', came to refill the city's chronically empty coffers. Prime Minister Yoshida described as 'manna from heaven' the large contracts for military supplies that were placed with Japanese industry on behalf of the United Nations forces fighting in Korea; up to then the Japanese industries had been starved by the austerity programme of the American financial adviser Dodge. Hiroshima, as a former centre of the armament industry, did particularly well out of all this. Since the end of the war the atom-bombed city's old munition plants had been engaged on the making of passenger ships, railway lines, and motor-vehicle transporters; at times it had been extremely difficult to sell these. Now they reverted to repairing jeeps, making spare parts for machine-guns, assembling pontoon bridges, and renovating old Second World War assault landing craft, which had been rusting away since 1945 and which were now urgently required for operations in the new war.

All the statistics for the years 1950 to 1952 reveal how rapid was the rate of recovery of Hiroshima's economy. A great deal of money was earned and spent. The city shot upwards, the entertainment quarter sported fine neon advertisements, and the bars and brothels flourished as they had not done since the 'great days'. A soldier in Korea, should he find the time to examine the markings of the many olive-drab vehicles that serviced the United Nations forces fighting the Reds, would surely have been surprised to see, in white paint, a name that only five years ago had been regarded as the final and last word marking the end of war: HIROSHIMA. For it was customary to mark each reconditioned item of military equipment with the name of the place where it had been reborn and re-equipped for its new baptism of fire.

If Hiroshima in the years immediately following the *Pikadon* had recalled some gold-mining town of the Wild West, now the city centre, with its new flat-fronted, flat-topped buildings of few or many storeys, its omnipresent electric wires, and its strident advertisements, came more and more to resemble any Californian 'Main Street'. Even the covered shopping streets which before the war had been confused, tumultuous oriental bazaars were now more like the elegant arcades of some western metropolis. Before the war Hiroshima had been a typical provincial city with the element of intimacy and cosiness that characterizes such places. In the rest of Japan this west coast garrison city was regarded as a rather sleepy place, but not without a particular charm all its own. Therefore in those days officials had found it an outstandingly pleasant spot to retire to. When, before 1940, the Japanese spoke of the 'Hiroshima atmosphere' they meant a relaxed and agreeable way of life.

Now that was all over and done with. The charm that had marked the terrace restaurants beside the Ohta, the famous geisha houses, the idyllic private gardens, and the narrow twisting streets could not be 'planned' anew. And when nowadays the other Japanese spoke of Hiroshima, they often referred to it as a 'second Chicago'. For it did resemble the second city of America as they had seen it in countless films. Furthermore, the inhabitants of Hiroshima themselves seemed to encourage this idea, in that for years on end they regaled the readers of the yellow press with a long-drawn-out gangster war between the 'Oka Gang' and the 'Murakami Gang' – something that had never before happened in Japan. It was not until December 1952, when a battle between the two gangs was fought out in the streets, that the police seriously intervened; even so the influence of the underworld to be felt throughout all local political life was scarcely affected.

The years immediately after the war had been characterized by large quantities of temporary, rapidly-knocked-up booths; with the beginning of prosperity more and more permanent buildings were rising towards the sky: banks, shops, radio stations, newspaper buildings, office blocks. In 1950 the Catholics laid the foundation stone of a magnificent 'Cathedral of Peace'; the Buddhists announced the construction of a 'Temple of Peace';

and Government authorities in Tokyo began to build a complex of administrative buildings which, Hiroshima learned with pride, would only be surpassed in size by the administrative buildings in the capital itself. Even the university could at last repair its own severely damaged edifice, and plant a 'Garden of Peace', for which it requested trees and shrubs from all the other centres of learning throughout the world.

With their coffers bulging as a result of the war boom, the various ministries were now able to produce the first payments of the grant that they had been obligated to give Hiroshima ever since the passing of the 'Reconstruction Act of the City for Peace' in 1949. Needless to say there were countless conditions and restrictions as to how this money might be spent. Mayor Hamai would have liked to use the State funds available to him for the building, in the first place, of schools, homes, and for a reorganization of the sewage system. But this he was not allowed to do. According to the Finance and Reconstruction Ministries this special grant was to be spent exclusively on projects that specifically commemorated 6 August 1945, that is to say primarily monuments and theatres.

As the masterpiece and spiritual hub of the 'City of Peace', a 'Garden of Peace' was to be laid out on an island encircled by two arms of the Ohta. Here there were to be a memorial to those who had died in the *Pikadon*, an atomic museum to hold Professor Nagaoka's collection, which had hitherto been lodged in an old barracks, and a 'Trade Fair Exhibition Hall'. A new 'Bridge of Peace' would enable the visitor to reach this island of memory. A design for this hub of the 'New Hiroshima' was drawn up by Professor Tange, an architect in the Corbusier tradition; but when this was submitted to the authorities in Tokyo, they immediately declared that the proposal was both too ambitious and too expensive. Mayor Hamai was not the man to be discouraged by such rebuffs; he announced that the city would itself contribute to the cost of the project in its original form, even though this must mean a certain delay in its completion.

The Government authorities made further difficulties when they learned that the proposed burial ground for the atomic victims would contain the ashes of tens of thousands who had thus died.

T – C.O.H. – H

They dug up an ancient law according to which it was forbidden to have graves in a public park. So beneath the smooth grey stone of the Cenotaph all that might be buried was a list of names of those who had been killed or reported missing.

But the land where the future 'Park of Peace' was to be already contained one small mass grave; in this were interred the remains of the boys who had attended a Middle School and who had died in the *Pikadon*. Technically this grave should have been removed before work on the park was begun. But the authorities were tactful enough to turn a blind eye and not to take official cognizance of its existence. The relatives of the dead boys wished to embellish this grave with a small memorial of their own; they were advised that they might only erect this on a Sunday. For on that day the officials, being off duty, could ignore this 'illegal action'.

The great Memorial to the Atomic Victims, a beautiful, simple roof structure in the style of old Japanese houses and made of grey granite, was dedicated in August 1952. The inscription carved into the stone reads: *Rest in peace. The mistake shall never be made again.* This led to an immediate protest, for a section of Hiroshima's population maintained that this could be interpreted as admitting that the victims were at least in part responsible for their fate. One infuriated mother even requested that the name of her three-year-old son be removed from the list of victims' names to be buried beneath the memorial; he had certainly been guilty of no 'mistake', were it made again or not.

2

As Hiroshima became more and more just another large city, so the gulf that separated the survivors of the bomb (the *higaisha*) from the world in which they lived grew wider and wider. The houses and streets might be rebuilt, but they remained ruins, human ruins, falling ever more into decay with each day that passed.

During 1947 and 1948 it had once again seemed that those persons suffering from the radiation sickness would recover after all. The number of miscarriages declined; semen examination showed that some men rendered temporarily sterile were so no longer; cheloids were disappearing; and the blood of those suffering from anaemia and allied weaknesses was evidently returning to normal. Not only did the official spokesmen of the Occupying Powers draw attention to this general improvement, but also certain Japanese doctors felt free to publish prematurely optimistic reports. At that time the illusion spread throughout the world that the dropping of the atomic bombs on Japan had produced only negligible long-term effects.

This false diagnosis of the development of the disease had been encouraged by the censorship policy of the Allied authorities ever since 1945. For not only were all references to the atom bomb censored in the press, on the radio, and in books, but publications by Japanese scientists dealing with the subject were also strictly controlled.

The rigid enforcement of a policy of secrecy (which incidentally was applied in the United States as well) had had certain results as early as 14 October 1945; on that day a special unit of the United States Army, commanded by a Colonel Mason and stationed at Ujina, close to Hiroshima, had closed a 'Japanese Army Hospital for the Study and Treatment of the Atomic Sickness' which had only recently been opened in a former textile factory: all the research material on which this special unit could lay its hands was requisitioned. The Japanese doctors, who had opened this clinic which specialized in radiation sickness – the first of its kind in all the world – scarcely a month before, were ordered to return to Tokyo forthwith. They were able to save most of their papers. For the next few weeks they collaborated at Hakone Spa with the staff doctors, and compiled an exclusive report in which they gave the results of the observations that they had made in Hiroshima. They set and printed their report themselves, on a small hand-press. So on 30 November the first textbook ever to deal with the medical results of atomic bombardment was published. That is to say it was circulated only in the medical faculties and among specialists, who passed it from hand to hand as if it were an illegal political pamphlet. Perhaps that is why there is no reference to this book in the otherwise exhaustive bibliography put out by the American 'Atomic Bomb Casualty Commission'.

Throughout October and November 1945 such special teams suddenly appeared in all the hospitals and university medical faculties where the after-effects of the 'new bomb' had been a subject of study since the previous August. They not only confiscated anatomical specimens which certain scientists had removed from the corpses of the atomic victims, but even seized a scientific training film which showed Professor Tamagawa dissecting corpses in a Hiroshima hospital mortuary, as well as portraits that the painter Moya had made from life of some twenty victims of the radiation sickness. Tamagawa recalls that he was instructed not to discuss his work even with Americans unless these were provided with a special authorization.

These manoeuvres were a particularly severe blow to Japanese scientists for, during the period when the Japanese Army had been supreme, Japanese scientists had regarded the freedom of research that prevailed in the West as a model to be imitated, and with the collapse of Japan they had hoped that they too might now enjoy similar rights and freedom. Instead of which a number of them were forbidden either to undertake research or to publish their findings, and this prohibition was far more rigidly enforced than had been any such regulations during the period of the Army's rule. After a special meeting at the Education Ministry in 1946 the world-famous atomic scientist Nishina, who had studied and worked with Niels Bohr, had turned to the two representatives of General MacArthur who were present, and had said:

'We have no wish to research into how the atom bomb is made and used, but simply into the results that atomic bombardment produces. This would be a contribution to science generally.'

The radiation expert, Professor Tsuzuki, used stronger language:

'At this very moment, while I am talking to you, men and women in Hiroshima and Nagasaki are dying of a new disease, the "atom-bomb sickness". We have not yet solved its riddles. So long as we may not carry out our research and get at the root of the problem, we shall not know how this disease should be treated.

From the point of view of humanity it is inexcusable that research and publication concerning scientific matters of a medical nature should be forbidden.'

In the months and years that followed, this strict policy of security concerning the work being done by Japanese scientists in biological and medical fields was, it is true, somewhat relaxed, yet research scientists whose work had led them to pessimistic conclusions even then did not dare publish these results. For example, Professor Zan Watanabe of Hiroshima University, who had carried out a major study on a group of atomic victims, has stated that he did not publish his report until after the end of the Occupation because the Americans had said to him: 'We do not forbid any sort of scientific publication, but if we should get the impression that by publishing you might cause harm to the Occupying Power, you would be court-martialled at once. You must reckon on this.'

That was why until the end of the Occupation in 1951 and 1952 no exact reports on the nature of the chronic radiation sickness were available even in Hiroshima; it was not known for certain, or even with any high degree of probability, what delayed aftereffects could be ascribed to the atomic bomb. As a result of this thousands went on living with the after-effects of the *Pikadon* at work within their organisms. In only a few cases – not the majority – could one perceive from the beginning a clear-cut picture of some recognizable malady. They would suffer from leukaemia, internal haemorrhages, or damage to the eyes – all of which could be ascribed with more or less certainty to the effects of radioactivity.

Far greater was the number of those survivors whose sufferings assumed a less easily defined form. They often suffered from giddiness, headaches, retching, tiredness. With them the most harmless maladies, normally over and done with in a few days, became chronic. For example, if they caught cold it took them far longer to get back to health than other people: if they cut themselves the wound took longer to heal. It seemed as though the 70,000-odd people who had been within the two-mile radius about the bomb's epicentre on 6 August 1945, and who had nevertheless survived the catastrophe, had thereby been deprived of a considerable portion of their living strength and of their recuperative powers.

Mr Uematsu, 'Miss Woodstick's' father, had been the prey to such ill-defined aches and pains ever since the *Pikadon*, nor could he shake them off.

When the former factory owner, robbed of his small means of livelihood, as of his health, by the atomic bomb, finally took to his bed, it was the seventeen-year-old Tokie who had to set about becoming the bread-winner for the family.

She reports:

'One day (it was snowing heavily) I set off for the Unemployment Office. . . . While I waited there, I prayed silently: I don't want to be a pampered youngest daughter any more. The first firm that interviewed me: nothing doing. The second: "We're not taking on any cripples." The third: "References? Previous experience? Nothing? Sorry!"

'I had begun with a tailor not far from our home, near Hiroshima Station. Later I hobbled all the way to Koi, between two and a half and three miles. My bad foot had lost all feeling. This was my sixth interview. If I weren't taken here, I'd decided to give up my plan of becoming a seamstress. The proprietor was a gentle, friendly man. I had almost forgotten that such people could still exist! I would be earning money and at the same time learning how to sew. It would be very hard work. Dear God, thank you!

'The roof of the shop in which I worked with six other girls was full of holes and we could see the sky. Sometimes it was blue, but sometimes when the weather turned bad there'd be such a draught from the roof and through the floor that my feet would be like blocks of ice; and sitting for such long hours at my sewing-machine gave me a backache, so that I could scarcely move for the pain. But what I was really afraid of was that they might say: "You can't sew properly anyhow, on account of being a cripple." So I didn't complain. I sewed on and on for just as long as my nerves could stand it.

'In the workroom the atmosphere was one of superficial comradeship. The girls sang pop songs, and laughed and giggled for no reason. I myself could no longer even manage to smile. Each day I was exhausted, nor could I ever recover from the exhaustion of the day before. Besides, I was constantly haunted by my terror of being sacked.

'I usually only reached home from my work at one or two o'clock in the morning. My parents waited up for me, and they'd have hot tea or something of the sort ready. I was incapable of telling them about the unbearable or even the merely irritating incidents of my day's work, because I had no wish to worry them. So for them I remained even now their little girl who knew how to behave properly, and we smiled at one another just as we used to do. . . .

'The money that my sister and I brought into the home amounted in all to some 8,000 yen per month (approximately £8 or $22). This was not enough to secure proper medical attention for Father. Lying in bed – that was all the medical treatment that he could afford.

'When Father had rested in this way for half a year he announced one day that he was feeling better and got up. On one occasion I overheard him saying to Mother: "It's terrible for me that the children should have to work so hard." On rare and exceptional occasions when I managed to get home early, at seven or eight in the evening, I was able to do some work for myself, sewing children's clothes. For these I got 16 yen (4d. or 5 cents) a garment, but I was often so tired that I simply could not bring myself to start work again. Then I would just collapse on to my bed exhausted and massage my leg.

'One hot summer's day Father took out a handcart and pulled it through the streets. He had loaded the few tools that remained to him from his old smithy on to the cart. I wondered anxiously what he was planning to do. Evening came. We were all worried, because he had not yet come home. At last he arrived. He looked very tired, and he sat down without a word. Only bit by bit did we learn that he had spent the entire day dragging his handcart through the town, repairing the pots and pans that strangers brought him.

'I could imagine how hard it was for him to do his work in the street, like a tinker. For he had always been so proud of his skill as a steelsmith. When we girls were tiny he had often told us the story of his life. He had once worked in Kamchatka and had lived with the natives there; he had with his own hands helped to build the famous iron landing-stage at Miyajima.

'When we saw him as he now was, his face so deathly white and covered in sweat, we sisters swore that we would work even harder than before. But struggle as we might, our wages could not keep up with the rising prices. So I tried to swallow my pride and visited the office that gives assistance to the poor. Yet the official in the City Welfare Office refused to take my visit seriously. "But I ask you," he said, after referring to our former prosperity, "a family such as yours cannot . . ."

'Every day now Father set out with his heavy handcart. When he had to repair gutters Mother went with him. But the work was too much for him, and in the autumn of 1952 he had to take to his bed again. . . . His condition grew worse from day to day. My sisters and I worked longer and longer overtime. Often my feet would go entirely numb from working the treadle of my sewing machine. Now my work went on each day till midnight, and often till one in the morning, and at home they were afraid that I too would collapse. . . . So my sister made a confidential complaint to the Employment Office. The owner of the garment factory – he was my second employer; the first had gone bankrupt – was sent for by the Employment Office and given a stiff warning. With what result? He submitted false books, and, from then on, black curtains were hung over the windows, so that the people outside should not be able to see that we were compelled to work at night. For the rest, there was no change.

'On the last day of the year 1952 I set off for work in really good spirits because I was so pleased about our New Year's Day bonus. I had promised Father a pair of new *getas* [wooden sandals], and I planned to pay Mother's debts in the market. My sister, in anticipation, had already got credit to the extent of 3,000 yen. With this we had bought rice and promised to pay the rent. With anything that might be left over we planned to celebrate the New Year.

'But instead of the bonus I expected, I found that I had been dismissed, and all I got was the back pay due to me, 2,500 yen. The reason given for my dismissal was that I was no good at my work. This upset me horribly, because I knew that I had done my work well and carefully. How could I go home with this ridiculously small sum of money? I was absolutely determined to stand up for my rights.

'Even Father, who had always advised me to keep my mouth shut and never to complain, was incensed now. He shouted "Your Father will go there himself, and speak to these people!" But the excitement was too much for him. On that New Year's Day he suffered a severe relapse.'

3

For how many of the 100,000-odd people who had survived the atom bomb in Hiroshima was post-war life more or less that of the Uematsu family? It will never be known for sure, for most of the *seizonsha* (survivors) took care that their suffering should remain hidden from all save their closest relatives. At the beginning, those who had lived through 'that day' often talked to one another of the horrors that they had passed through in common, and indeed would even boast about this on occasions. But now they kept silent. For almost imperceptibly the attitude of the rest of their society towards the survivors had changed. What yesterday had counted as a distinction was today regarded as a blemish.

Public bathing establishments refused entry to men and women whose bodies were disfigured by large, ugly cheloids; there was an entirely unjustified rumour current that these scars could be the source of infection. Matrimonial bureaux, which arrange most of the marriages in Japan, informed applicants from Hiroshima and Nagasaki that survivors of the *Pikadon* were not acceptable as brides or grooms; it was feared that they might father, or give birth to, deformed children.

Most employees among the survivors, with the exception of persons employed by the authorities, whose positions were guaranteed by law, lost their jobs, for their ability to work declined markedly. They usually suffered from giddiness, defective memory, bad nerves, and a general disinclination for work. Once they were out of a job it was difficult, indeed wellnigh impossible, for them to find another; nobody wished to employ 'atomic cripples'.

So those who were still in work did their uttermost to hide any manifestation of tiredness, or of feeling sick, for as long as they could. For fear that while today they might be pitied tomorrow they would be out on the street, those people did not even dare any longer to complain of having a headache or a cold. Even such of these as possessed the means dared not go to the doctor, for they feared lest a rumour be spread that they were suffering from the 'atomic sickness'. There were occasions when not even the closest relatives of the breadwinner were aware that he was growing sicker, until he suddenly collapsed; only then would a doctor be summoned, and by that time it was usually too late.

Thousands tried to hide this new cause for shame, that they were survivors of the *Pikadon*, by moving away, to Tokyo, Osaka, Kobe, or some other city. But this was of little help to them. Every Japanese is followed by his papers, in particular by his Family Book, wherever he may go, and thus by the story of his past.

The most complete lack of understanding for those victims of the atomic bomb who sickened years later was to be encountered among the people who lived in the country outside Hiroshima. There was, for example, the newly-married peasant girl who came into the city to be examined because she was suffering from precisely those symptoms which usually marked the onset of the radiation sickness: a humming in the ears, fainting, a tendency to tiredness, a general weakening of the constitution. 'A young woman who only eats and who can't work – that's a real misfortune.' That is what they had been dinning into her ears for months on end. At first her young husband had protected her against the rest of his family, but when the village doctor had announced that, so far as he could diagnose, she was suffering from no known complaint, he too began to turn against her. The girl was not sick enough to be admitted to hospital: on the other hand she dared not return to her home. In vain she begged: 'Please don't send me back. Please keep me here.' But the doctors could not agree to this. The few public hospitals in Hiroshima had not even sufficient beds for persons who were seriously ill. No part of the reconstruction subsidy had been ear-marked for the hospitals. The erection of splendid, silent housefronts calculated to impress seemed to the post-war generation a more urgent task than caring for the sick who were suffering from a malady that was as yet neither understood nor even recognized.

In the summer of 1949 Norman Cousins, the publisher of the American periodical, the *Saturday Review of Literature*, had been taken on a conducted tour of Hiroshima's hospitals by Mayor Hamai. He was shocked by what he then saw, and a little later he wrote:

'You saw beds held together with slabs of wood; nowhere did you see sheets or pillows; you saw dirty bandages and littered floors and rooms not much larger than closets with four or five patients huddled together. You thought back to what you saw in the D.P. camps in Germany. You looked in on an operating room that seemed little better than a crude abattoir. . . . You saw all this with unbelieving eyes and then you had some idea of what Mayor Hamai meant when he said that Hiroshima needed America's help to take care of its sick.'

4

Only eighteen months after this visit of Norman Cousins, in January 1951, the Americans opened a clinic on the top of Hiji-yama Hill, which commands a wide view over the new city of Hiroshima that was then arising from the ashes. This was the most modern and most perfectly equipped clinic in all East Asia. The wide, smoothly asphalted road that ran through the park to the aluminium and glass buildings, silvery in the sunlight, had alone cost several million yen. Those persons who had been politely invited to undergo a medical examination were carried along this road in brand new American cars or in fast jeeps. For many of them – and particularly for the women and children – this was often their first automobile ride.

Mayor Hamai had once warned the American officers who insisted on building this institute on the sanctified ground of the

Hijiyama Military Cemetery that the populace of Hiroshima would never accept this. But the joy that at last a special hospital for 'atomic illnesses' had been opened succeeded, for the time being, in silencing any angry comments on that score. Even so, many a pious patient was offended at the sight of the broken and overturned tombstones lying around the new buildings, and a certain comparison inevitably came to mind. For not far away there was a small graveyard where were buried those members of the French military forces who had died of yellow fever in Hiroshima at the time of the Boxer Rising. All through the Second World War, even when the French were the enemies of the Japanese, an elderly Japanese woman had at all times cared for and looked after these graves.

The new complex of buildings, which overlooked the new Hiroshima like some feudal castle, soon got a half-friendly, half-ironic nickname. They called it the Fishcake Palace. And indeed its half-rounded, two-storeyed buildings, resembling Quonset huts in style, did recall those sausage-shaped fish pasties so beloved of the Japanese.

A patient would here be thoroughly examined for a whole day by the most outstanding specialists and in the most perfectly hygienic conditions, and it would not cost him a single yen. Indeed, the patient was even driven home and deposited at his own front door without charge. It was like something out of a fairy tale. There was only one snag: though the patient's sufferings were diagnosed with the most extreme thoroughness, nothing was done to cure them. If a sick man should bring himself to ask: 'What do you advise, Doctor? What can I do to get well again?' the doctor's reply was always the same: 'This is not a therapeutic establishment but a scientific institute, founded in collaboration with the Japanese health authorities, with the exclusive object of carrying out research. For treatment you must go to your own doctors.'

5

As a result of the stir caused by the reports of two military medical missions, the A.B.C.C. had been founded in 1947. The American

Defence Secretary, James Forrestal, had been impressed by the arguments of specialists returning to the U.S.A. from Hiroshima and Nagasaki, and on 18 November 1946 he had written a letter to the President in which he spoke of 'this unique opportunity for examining the medical and biological effects of radiation'. Such a study, the Secretary of Defence insisted, 'would be of the highest significance for the United States'.

The 'unique opportunity' of which Forrestal had spoken was used as effectively as was possible in view of the money and technical personnel available. In the two years immediately after the bomb, what research had been done into radiation effects had been of an unsystematic nature. Now this was all to be changed. In the two years that started in 1948 two large-scale research projects were inaugurated, one into the hereditary effects of radiation and the other into its effect on children. During the following five years some 75,000 young people in Hiroshima and Nagasaki were examined. By checking the lists held by the rationing authorities – and in particular by compiling a list of pregnant women, who received subsidiary rations – the research teams were able to 'follow up' pregnant women from the fifth month on. By cooperation with the midwives – who received a cash payment for each birth notified – the proportion of babies born dead and the progress of those born alive could be established with a high degree of accuracy.

There was, for example, Project PE–18. Some 2,500 children aged five, six, eight, and from ten to nineteen, who had been exposed to radiation, were examined periodically: the results were compared with those of similar examinations carried out on 2,500 children of identical ages – 'Control Children' they were called – whose parents had only recently moved to Hiroshima or Nagasaki and who had therefore not been subject to the effects of atomic radiation at all. Then, as from July 1950, Project PE–52 was started. The object of research here were the so-called 'First Trimester Children', that is to say those whose mothers had been in one or other of the 'laboratory cities', Hiroshima or Nagasaki, and had been less than three months pregnant when the bombs were dropped. Finally there was Project PE–49. This involved the so-called 'Thousand Metre Children' or children who had been less than one kilometre from the epicentre when the bomb exploded on 6 August 1945.

It was not until January 1951, when the A.B.C.C. had moved from its temporary headquarters (the Hall of Triumph in the waterfront district of Ujina) to its fine new home, that the Adult Medical Programme which had been started during the previous September could really get going in a big way. Within the framework of this Project ME–55, it was planned to examine, so far as this was possible, all those who had survived from the 'Thousand Metre Zone', as well as a 'representative cross-section' of those who had been within a radius of one to one-and-a-half thousand metres, and to repeat this examination annually. This group would amount in all to some 2,500 persons and these too were to be compared with a similar group of 'control persons not exposed to radiation'. In addition to these major projects there was a considerable number of specialist teams engaged on other tasks. These were sensibly camouflaged behind code letters and numbers. For example there was HE–39 (research into leukaemia); OG–31 (sterility and infertility); OG–35 (therapeutic abortion); ME–47 (research into eye-damage caused by radiation); SU–59 (burn scars). Behind these letters and numbers were concealed all those agonies that the atomic bomb had inflicted upon the people of Hiroshima and Nagasaki.

6

There were hundreds of such studies carried out, for the list given above is only a minute fraction of them all. If one examines the result of the research work carried out by the A.B.C.C. one cannot but be impressed. During years of mass examinations in Hiroshima and Nagasaki valuable discoveries were made, and simultaneously new methods of examining the health of large quantities of human beings were developed. It was not only those men who specialized in the young science of radiation biology who profited from this massive research project; other branches on the tree of science are also sure to derive great benefits from it for many years to come. Never before in medical history has so impressive a number of human beings – both sick and well – been so thorough-ly examined in so short a space of time in so limited an area with a definite purpose in view.

This same undertaking assumes a very different colour when it is examined within the social, political, and psychological frame-work in which it took place. Dark shadows are then cast across the brilliant picture. Divorced from the circumstances in which it was inaugurated and carried out, this seems a great act of human magnanimity: if the background and circumstances are taken into account, however, it must be regarded as a grossly callous, indeed an inhuman performance.

The trouble began with the fact that the A.B.C.C. Clinic was run by the Americans and almost entirely financed by the U.S. Atomic Energy Commission, an agency which was primarily and ultimately interested in the perfection of nuclear weapons. The citizens of the same country that had dropped the atomic bomb were now determined to find out at all costs what the biological after-effects of this act had turned out to be. This struck Japanese public opinion in the main as tactless in the extreme. It also led to the disastrous conclusion, a conclusion as erroneous as it was insulting, that cause and effect linked the first act (the dropping of the bomb) with the second (the scientific research into the bomb's after-effects). People began to wonder whether in truth the citizens of Hiroshima had been the victims of a strategically justifiable act of war. Might it not be that they had suffered in the interests of some outsize American scientific experiment? This supposition appeared to be reinforced by certain highly unfortunate reports that were published in some sectors of the American press con-cerning the A.B.C.C. For example, it was said by these journalists that Hiroshima, Nagasaki, and the 'Control City' of Kure were the Commission's 'three laboratories'.

This research was obviously of great importance to humanity for even in peace-time the danger of radiation was bound to in-crease. The fact that this was carried out by Americans, however, and with money supplied by the Atomic Energy Commission, was aggravated by the researchers' reluctance to treat – and if this were possible to cure – the bomb's victims. This served to emphasize and increase the victims' hostility to the whole project.

The creators of the A.B.C.C. had assumed that it was possible simply to *observe* the people living on this patch of sorely-tried and still inhabited land which the Japanese called 'The Place of Suffering'. They imagined that, in a place where patients could get no medical treatment from their own doctors, they could simply examine these 'interesting cases' and, after establishing the fact that thousands of such cases were suffering from this or that agony, just send them home again without treatment or even the hope of treatment. This surely showed a truly terrifying short-sightedness.*

Thus could it happen that the Hiroshima 'atomic clinic' became a greater source of hatred than the bomb itself. Whereas many citizens of the victimized city might have strong views about the iniquity of the new weapon but yet be prepared to excuse its use as a military act committed in war-time, they regarded the 'purely scientific' activities of the A.B.C.C. as simply inexcusable.

As early as 1949, when the A.B.C.C. was still functioning in comparative obscurity on the outskirts of the city with a limited staff and limited objectives, the American, Norman Cousins, had already recognized that the situation was one that would lead to a crisis. After having visited the wretched public hospitals of Hiroshima he felt compelled to publish the following in the *Saturday Review of Literature*:

. . . I thought of the millions of dollars being spent by the United States in Hiroshima in the work of the Atomic Bomb Casualty Commission – excellent work and important work, for it can tell what happens to people in atomic warfare. Nothing of those millions goes to treat the victims of the atomic bomb. The Casualty Commission only examines patients; it doesn't treat them. And you had the strange spectacle of a man suffering from radioactive sickness getting thousands of dollars' worth of analysis but not one cent of treatment from the Commission.

Back in New York after his visit to Hiroshima, this warm-hearted journalist devoted a great deal of his energy to helping the victims of Hiroshima. He did his best to see that a hospital for the treatment of radiation diseases should be built with privately

---

* The explanation and excuses as given by official American sources will be found later in this book on pages 264–8.

collected funds. It was to be in the middle of a 'Hiroshima Peace Centre' dedicated to World Peace: Protestant pastor Kiyoshi Tanimoto, who enjoyed a world-wide fame as the result of Hersey's great piece of reporting, *Hiroshima*, had first suggested that this 'Centre' be created.

As early as August 1949, that is to say while Cousins was still in Hiroshima, the foundation stone of such a 'Peace Centre' had already been laid – on the site of the old feudal castle where the lords of Hiroshima once had lived, and which had been destroyed by the *Pikadon*. But the undertaking was too grandiose to be completed solely with funds collected privately. The building site reserved for the project remained open ground.

Cousins had greater success with the project whereby 'atom orphans' were to be 'spiritually adopted' by American foster-parents. (Owing to the Oriental Exclusion Act, which formed part of the American immigration laws, actual adoption was for the time being unfortunately impossible.) A few hundred orphans received financial assistance from these 'foster-parents' in the United States, and some of them even took the name of their American sponsors, men and women whom they had never seen.

THE HELPERS

1

THROUGHOUT almost all the years 1951 to 1953 the pains and the sickness that resulted from the long-term effects of the atomic bomb were particularly in evidence in Hiroshima. As could be subsequently established from the statistical evidence, this was the period of crisis for many of the illnesses induced by radiation, such as leukaemia. It was common, too, for so-called 'cataracts' now to appear in the eyes of the survivors: small, black spots, of which an exceptionally large number were to be found in the eye's crystalline lens.

The discovery of these 'radiation cataracts' was among the first important results of the research being carried out by the A.B.C.C. One day while the doctors were sitting in their cafeteria, one of the waitresses told them about a kitchen maid who couldn't see properly. 'She was hurt in the *Pikadon* but she recovered again completely. Recently something's gone wrong with her eyes.' A doctor examined the girl and even with his pocket ophthalmo-scope he detected an unusual black spot. 'The most important discovery in the history of post-war Hiroshima had been made,' according to a report in *Life*. The journalist, whose style recalled that of a war correspondent reporting from the front, went on to say: 'Here, suddenly and unexpectedly, it happened that Hatsue became an eminent figure in the history of atomic warfare.'

Hermann J. Muller, the father of modern genetics, has com-mented on this phenomenon of 'radiation cataract' in the following words:

'In the people that were bombed a long time ago at Hiroshima you can see a lot of little opaque points in many of them in the lens of the eye where evidently cells have been badly damaged. That damage did not appear until much later, when the cell probably undertook to divide. The reason you can see it there is because the lens is a transparent tissue. I think there is reason to believe that this happens in all the tissues of the body that contain cells subject to division. These tissues would, therefore, be weakened. It is true that other undamaged cells would tend to replenish the damaged places. But that replenishment or regeneration, it is to be expected, will not be complete and perfect. Therefore, there is a certain amount of damage left. That damage you can see would be a generalized damage all over the body, wherever there are these dividing tissues. Therefore, it would be expressed as a weakening of resistance to disease and infirmities of all kinds, somewhat like what occurs in ageing. . . .'

So it was really neither hypochondria nor the expression of an 'atomic neurosis' – as their fellow-citizens maintained – when the survivors complained repeatedly that 'they felt unwell in every part of their bodies', that 'the devil's claws had left their traces in each and every organ'. What upset them almost more than their actual sufferings was the fact that nobody seemed to know for sure what these sufferings were caused by; indeed the very existence of these pains was even now not recognized – and neither in Japan nor abroad was any public authority prepared to help them.

Ichiro Kawamoto now attempted, with the totally inadequate resources at his disposal, to fill this gap as and when he could. He did not first demand 'scientific proof' that these people were suffering. He simply did what he could to help, without asking too many questions.

Years after the *Pikadon*, Ichiro himself began to feel the after-effects of the digging that he had done when the city was still infected by the bomb. But he always forced himself to get up from his sick-bed, for there were others who needed him, men and women more sick and more lonely than himself. He would take one a little boiled fish to eat; to another he would give a blanket; a third he would visit solely to encourage and divert him with his conversation. Today he would set about finding a place in an orphanage for a little girl who was living all alone in a house inhabited by gangsters and prostitutes; tomorrow he would visit a family which had recently lost one of its members as a 'delayed-action' victim of the atom bomb, and would do his best to console them.

There was nothing planned or systematic about these innumerable small acts of neighbourly love. Sometimes Ichiro would forget all about one of his charges for days on end, because at the moment another would seem to him more important. Then he would suddenly remember, as he walked along, and would change direction and would hurry to make good his neglect. Once, so he told me, he arrived too late. A young man by the name of I. had sickened a few weeks earlier with leukaemia. By the time Kawamoto remembered about him and went to see him, it was too late. The young man had been taken off to hospital, where he had died.

To people of our age the impression made by a man such as Ichiro Kawamoto may be old-fashioned, ridiculous, even downright suspicious. Many people in Hiroshima, too, tried to dismiss him in such terms. If a man is so anxious to help others, does it not mean that in his own life and profession he is a failure? Is he not simply anxious to assert his own personality? Is he not motivated by some guilt sensation? Men – and not only those living in Hiroshima – are nowadays always ready with an explanation which will diminish, and even denigrate, the good deeds of others; thus do they cleverly disguise their shame at their own failure to do likewise. The 'spirit of the age' appears to be incapable of recognizing human decency and selflessness unconditionally.

But, as it happens, this highly improbable figure, Ichiro Kawamoto, does in fact exist. Year after year his long, worried face is to be seen in the barrack-like working-class quarter of Hiroshima where the 'atom pariahs' live, and he gives not a hoot for what people may say about him. If only he could cheer them up a bit! He usually dresses up as Father Christmas for the orphans of Shinsei Gakuen. Inevitably his fancy dress made of red paper gets torn to shreds, and from behind it there appears the very ordinary figure of a casual labourer whose working trousers are not always immaculately clean. The little children laugh, and clap their hands, and throw their arms about their old friend. 'He's the only grown-up who's never frightened me . . .' one such parentless child once said.

2

Kawamoto was also one of the founders of the Genbaku Higaisha No Kai (Association of Atomic Victims). Owing to the initiative of the authoress Tomoé Yamashiro, fifteen *higaisha* had first met together in August 1952. To begin with they held their meetings in Pastor Tanimoto's church, but some of them began to suspect that the pastor wished to convert them to Christianity; so they preferred to go to the shop of the souvenir salesman, Kikkawa, where, without any sensation of shame and without any feeling that they must excuse their condition to those who had had the good fortune to be spared, they discussed those problems that concerned them all. But from the general exchange of anecdotes concerning 'that day' something more gradually emerged, which eventually took the form of a plan to inform public opinion about the fate of 'atomic victims' and to bring pressure to bear on the public authorities in an attempt that something be done at last for those who now suffered through no fault of their own.

A travelling theatrical company, the *Shinkyo* Dramatic Group, donated all the takings of their performances in Hiroshima to the 'Association', which was thus enabled to open a small office where all those who had suffered as a result of the bombing might come for advice. The first secretary of the Association of Atomic Victims was Kawamoto's friend Tokie Uematsu. Her salary came out of the monthly contribution that the Association was now getting from certain charitable business houses in Hiroshima.

Little 'Miss Woodstick' had long ceased to be the delicate, over-sensitive being whom Ichiro had first learned to know a few years back when they were both studying English at the church school. Her experience in the struggle to survive, her unspeakably hard years as a seamstress when Kawamoto had scarcely ever managed to see her, and finally her father's serious illness, had turned her into a determined, even a stubborn, young woman, filled with energy and at times positively masterful. Now every morning Tokie hobbled from her parents' home in the Nishi Kaniyacho quarter to the gasworks at the far end of town where the office of the 'Association' was located; for she lacked the money to take a tram. If it got very late, or the weather were exceptionally bad, she would not return home at all, but would make a bed for herself out of two chairs in the office.

Tokie received a theoretical salary of 4,500 yen per month. But it was almost never paid to her, for the finances of the 'Association' were always in a bad way, particularly since the rumour had got about that its members were Communists. And when she got home her sister would ask her: 'Tokie-chan, did you get paid today?'

'No, but tomorrow I'll insist.'

But she knew very well that that was the one thing she would never do. Nor would there have been any point in insisting. So she had to pawn her overcoat after all, in order to get the money to pay the rent. For she was determined to hang on to this job just as long as she possibly could. Her work as a seamstress had come to seem futile and senseless to her; whereas here she had the feeling that she was really doing something important. This helped her to put up with all the pain and penury.

'When Dr Mitsuo Taketani came to Hiroshima in 1952 and explained scientifically the damage that can be caused by radioactivity, I was astonished,' Tokie has said. 'If the people among whom we lived cared nothing for us, if so many atomic victims did not even take their condition seriously themselves, the explanation was that the facts were not known. Only now did we begin to suspect how horribly protracted the sufferings inflicted on us by that inhuman bomb must be. Until I attended his lectures, I myself had had only a somewhat vague inkling of the "frightfulness"; now I began to understand more clearly.

'The victims now met in our office, a room that was let to us by an "atom widow", who lived there with her deaf mother and her three children. The old woman, who had lost her hearing in the *Pikadon*, was particularly anxious to look after us. It was then that I learned to talk with my hands, my eyes, and even, when the occasion arose, with my feet. We, the survivors, did our best to console one another mutually. Nevertheless, we heard over and over again such defeatist remarks as: "It's all quite pointless," or "It's senseless even to open our mouths." But I wasn't going to be put off as easily as that. "If we don't speak out now," I said, "we'll have missed our last chance."

'I had to repeat this three or four times. We had to be patient. After much hesitancy other "victims" began to speak out. To begin with they were paralysed, as it were, by the fact that each of them was entirely preoccupied with his own predicament. Now one or another of them would occasionally say to me: "You look frozen. Come and warm your hands at the stove!" This was already a good sign. And when a letter came from one of them saying that our meetings were for him the happiest moments he had known since the *Pikadon*, we even forgot our tiredness, our hunger, our lack of money. . . .'

Towards the end of the winter of 1953, when the peach trees were just coming into blossom, Father Uematsu's illness took a sudden and decisive turn for the worse. 'He was almost never conscious now,' Tokie recalls. 'Day after day and night after night we listened to his groans and watched his strength ebbing away.

'Four days before Father's death a man came from the Electricity Company and threatened to switch off the current if we did not pay our bill at once. Father could hardly speak any more, but with tears in his eyes he stammered to the man: "I much regret that I should have caused you such inconvenience . . ."

'And that is how he died, in the most abject poverty. If only he had gone to a doctor in time! Perhaps he might have been saved. But he worked and worked, until he had reached the end of his tether.

'The atom bomb had begun by robbing Father of his livelihood. It ended by taking his life as well.

'On the day of the funeral, which was 9 March, a jeep came from the A.B.C.C. The man asked if they might carry out a postmortem on Father's body. They said it was of importance to humanity, and that Father would certainly not have objected.

'It was they who had dropped the atom bomb which made the last years of his life one long misery. They were guilty that he had had to work until he was completely finished and done for. And now they came to our house and even demanded that we hand over his poor, dead body.'

'I shall not hand my dead father over to you.' Tokie Uematsu's anger was under control, but so great was it that her voice was scarcely audible. That was what she said to the men called 'contactors' who studied the announcements of deaths in the papers and who, as a routine matter, visited every family in which the dead person might be suspected of having had the 'atomic sickness'. The 'contactors' expressed their sympathy in uncommonly courteous fashion, and on the form that they had brought with them they wrote the word *Ref.*, which was their abbreviation for 'refusal'. As the passive resistance against the A.B.C.C. increased in strength, the file containing the 'refusals' grew and grew. The statisticians of the A.B.C.C. would now add to this file the name of Uematsu-san. He was one of those who 'owing to the prejudice of his family' must be regarded as lost to science.

3

The first person outside her immediate family to whom Tokie told the news that her father had breathed his last was Ichiro Kawamoto. During the past two years they had frequently not met for days on end, and nowadays they never discussed their relationship. This visit in the early hours of the morning was, in fact, Tokie's first open declaration of love for Ichiro. Thenceforth they both knew that they belonged to one another.

Ichiro had taken it upon himself to provide the money needed for the funeral. And he succeeded in borrowing from his friends, a few yen here and a few there, while the Uematsu family's neighbours also contributed what they could. So a considerable sum was eventually collected and the unfortunate Uematsu-san did not after all have to be buried in a pauper's grave.

On the day of the funeral Ichiro suddenly fainted while travelling by tram. That same evening he heard that at precisely the hour on which he had lost consciousness the poet Sankichi Toge had died on the operating table. The nurses in his sanatorium had disobeyed instructions concerning their authority to give blood to patients, in the hope that by so doing they might save their patient, who had lost such a very great deal of blood. The postmortem later carried out produced extremely surprising results. It was not merely his old lung malady that had led to Toge's death but also radiation damage caused by the *Pikadon*. Though he more than anyone else had devoted the last years of his life to the struggle against the atomic danger, it had never occurred to him that he too was suffering from the weird malady that afflicted so many of the survivors of 6 August 1945.

Kawamoto had first met Toge at the première of a Japanese anti-war film in 1950. In the discussion that followed the performance Ichiro had also spoken, and had said that in our age the promise of peace offered by Christianity was of the greatest importance – even though the so-called 'Christian nations' did not seem to take their religion seriously. These remarks had interested Toge, who had then sought out Ichiro.

Since then they had been very closely linked. Now that Toge had gone, it became plain to Kawamoto that it was his duty to continue his dead friend's work, even though he lacked skill, charm, and education, while Toge had been a highly literate, noble, and famous man. That work was the enlightenment of public opinion concerning the fate of the atomic victims, who were themselves forced to keep silent, starve, and die.

Thus a new period began in the life of Ichiro Kawamoto. The silent helper became an outspoken publicist, the Samaritan a propagandist. The climate of the age was conducive to this. Since the end of the Occupation a powerful 'Peace Movement' had come into existence in Hiroshima. But more important than this, in the other cities of Japan people now began to be preoccupied with Hiroshima. In August of 1952, a few months after the Peace Treaty with the United States was ratified, the large Japanese magazine called *Asahi Graphic* had published a special number containing pictures which the censorship of the Occupying Powers had previously banned. These were technically imperfect and often blurred or scratched snapshots taken immediately after the bomb had been dropped. Nevertheless the impression created by these pictures of hell was truly enormous. They let loose a wave of horror throughout Japan and aroused great sympathy for the victims of the *Pikadon*. Now, in rapid succession, there appeared articles, eyewitness accounts, novels, and finally films dealing with the subject.

In late May 1953 the scriptwriter, director, and producer of the film called *Hiroshima*, which was to cause such a tremendous stir, visited the *Pikadon* city. They wished to reconstruct the scene of the atomic disaster on the spot, in order to obtain the maximum realism. Kawamoto immediately got in touch with these film people and offered his services as technical adviser.

'On the following day I had my head shaved, so that I might – without pay, I may say – be one of the many extras,' he says. 'My friends at the Saka Electricity Works and the children all laughed at my shaven priest's head, which must have looked very funny. I dug out the helmet which we had had to take to work during the war, and collected all the old rags that might come in useful, and I took all these over to the headquarters of the film people.

'The first scene was supposed to show the crowds fleeing towards Hijiyama Hill. Together with a woman who worked at the Shudoin Orphanage and six of her orphans I went to the Labour Office. When we got there, we found that a number of actors made up like "atom ghosts" had already arrived. Even I was horrified by their make-up. At the sight of them the little children were absolutely terrified and began to tremble all over. "Let's go, please let's go. I'm frightened," they began to scream through their tears. I had to calm down the little ones, and kept saying to them, "But it's only a game. . . . We're playing at ghosts." Then I bought them all some caramel candies and they quietened down. Finally they were even quite happy to let the make-up men disguise them as the children of these "ghosts", as the children of that frightful day. We tore into rags the clothes that had been collected from the Women's Association and from the schools. We even half burned them and smeared them with rust and wood ashes. We painted our bodies brown and black, and I rubbed ash on to my priestly pate.

'Finally we all set off for the location, in Hijiyama. The wood that had been made ready was set alight. . . . In front of an air-raid shelter the film people poured out a black fluid. A "corpse" was to fall on top of other "corpses". Then the great crowd had to stumble past, with heads and arms hanging, and they had to keep on doing this, again and again, until they got it quite right and the scene could finally be "shot".

'To begin with, it was all just a game. People would laugh at the rags and make-up of the others. Many of the extras had only come here for the fun of the thing. But with people who really had suffered on that day, then it was quite another story. Suddenly the horror, the immeasurable agony, of "that day" was rekindled. We ran as if our lives really were again in peril. Some began to scream their anguish aloud at the top of their voices, others to tremble all over with fury and shake their fists at the sky. We stumbled, fell over one another, and women and children on their backs were trampled underfoot in front of the air-raid shelter. One actress's clothes caught fire. . . .

'All in all over one hundred thousand people acted as extras, without pay, in the making of that film.'

4

'We sold the *tatami* from our rooms. We sold the furniture to buy rice. Finally we even ripped up the floorboards and burned them in order to keep warm.' Thus does Tokie describe the poverty that prevailed in the Uematsu household after the expense of her father's funeral had swallowed all that was left of their savings. 'I simply couldn't bear to look at Mother's lined, grey face any more. And the day was drawing closer when there would be nothing whatsoever left to sell or to burn.' So Tokie was forced at last to decide that she must give up her job as secretary of the Association of Atomic Victims and find work for which she would receive regular pay.

'At the next street corner there was an extremely noisy establishment,' she says. 'People were shouting one another down in there and in addition there was dance music blaring out from early morning till late at night. It was a new *pachinko* saloon, only recently opened. The owner told me at once that he had no use for anyone with a crippled leg because, in the sort of jobs he had to offer, his employees were standing or walking about all day long. But I begged him, and so desperately, that at last he agreed to take me on.

'All the other girls who had to work there dreaded the daylight, either because the debt-collectors were after them, or because they had such hideous burn-scars as a result of the *Pikadon* that they could only hope to get the sort of job where no one ever saw their faces. We worked on the far side of a wall behind the pinball machines. There was a narrow passage, not more than eighteen inches wide. Each of us had to look after twenty of these one-armed bandits, which growled, clattered, and spat as if they really were alive. We had to feed them with new ammunition, those little silvery balls that cost 2 yen apiece. These balls were packed in cartons of five hundred, and the girls had to fetch them down from an upper floor, where they were cleaned and polished, to our row of machines. When I heard this I was terrified, because the weight of such a carton would be far too great for me to carry – and another thing, with my bad right leg I could scarcely even manage the stairs. Did this mean I'd have to give up the job at once? They all laughed at me, but one girl was sorry for me and from then on she lugged the heavy cartons down to my place of work for me every day. I shall never forget that girl.

'We were woken at half past six each morning and just had time to wash our faces before the day's work began. By the time we had distributed the little steel balls among the machines – and we had to make absolutely sure that each one got exactly the same number of balls – we were already bathed in sweat. At seven o'clock sharp the "saloon" was opened and many gamblers came pouring in at once, even at that early hour. They had obviously been standing about outside, waiting for the doors to open.

'At ten o'clock we were given time off for breakfast, and at three in the afternoon we got our dinner, and our evening meal was at eight. We never closed before eleven o'clock at night. . . . During the sixteen hours that the "saloon" was open, we got only two hours off, in all. Our living and sleeping quarters were in the attic. The ceiling there was so low that not even a small person could stand upright anywhere. The sun beat down on the tiled roof, and the attic was always hot and stuffy. There were only small windows, facing west and east, and these gave so little light that it was impossible either to see or to read up there, even at midday.

'In this place, which had room for six human beings at the most, twelve "*pachinko* girls" slept. Our mattresses were on the floor and we had to clamber over one another to reach them. None of us even possessed a locker. We were kept up there as if we were in prison. If one of us wanted to go out, to buy something, she had first to get permission. Anyone wishing to post a letter was not even allowed to put it in the letterbox herself.

'At first I could not understand why we were deprived of our freedom in this way. But bit by bit I began to see why. We simply were not trusted. It could happen that one of us might come to a secret arrangement with one of the gamblers and pass him balls which, when exchanged at the counter against "prizes", were as good as cash.* Each of us was told to spy on the other girls. There was even an arrangement whereby, if one girl should report another for doing anything wrong, the stool-pigeon would receive half the other girl's monthly pay.

'Most of the girls had no religion, nor did they give any thought to their lives or to the world around them. Obviously all that they were capable of thinking about was food and about what they would eventually buy with the money they were saving. Their favourite topic of conversation was what clothes they would wear and what sort of jewellery and so on they would bedeck themselves with. When Ichiro sent me a claret-coloured ribbon, which I sewed on to my white pullover that was far too tight for me, they all copied me and managed to get hold of identical ribbons, in the identical colour. When they talked to one another their conversation consisted almost exclusively of spiteful and nasty remarks about the other girls who were not present. The only thing that impressed them was being well dressed. Those girls whose bodies were scarred by a cheloid or some other mark left by the *Pikadon* were not even allowed to hang their laundry up to dry near the other girls' clothes, and the plates off which they ate were kept away from the rest and were washed up separately. But when I told these ill-treated and despised girls that they ought to join the Association of Atomic Victims they simply made a bored face.

'Once the gambling machines had been cleaned and the floor washed, that is to say at about midnight, we were allowed to go to

* It was against the law for the gambling saloons to hand out cash as *pachinko* prizes. The buying in of the prizes that they did distribute became a profitable subsidiary racket for the criminal gangs active in Hiroshima (the *Oka-gumi* and the *Murakami-gumi*). They would sell back these prizes to the gambling saloons, at a considerable profit needless to say.

the public baths. That was the best time of the day. By the time
we had walked "home" from the baths it was usually about two
o'clock in the morning. Our conversation revolved around an
unending theme: when would we be able to shake the dust of this
place from our feet? This was a subject of which we could never
have enough.

'Every three days I got a letter from Ichiro. He wrote me about
the Higaisha No Kai, about the friends we had in common, about
life outside. Three times I had to change my job and find work in
another *pachinko*. Once because I advised a man who had already
lost a thousand yen to stop playing. The boss happened to be
standing close by and heard this. He summoned me into his
office and accused me of damaging his business. When I defended
myself he hit me in the face as hard as he could. So I decided then
and there that in future I'd keep my mouth shut. But I could only
keep that up for a short time. I began to hate myself. I simply
could not bear not saying what had to be said, what I thought.

'But at long last the time came when I was able to escape from
this abyss, up into the sunshine once again. One of the girls I
worked with had got the sack, and she told me that she planned to
try her luck as a seamstress, working on her own. If she should
succeed in making a go of it, she'd get in touch with me. And in
fact one day I got a letter from her. She said: "You can risk it.
Come on."

'But when I had stopped working in the *pachinko* saloon I was
far too exhausted at first to do anything at all. For ten whole days
I thought of nothing, read nothing, but simply slept and slept
and slept. And when at last I began to stop feeling so totally
exhausted, I started to think about the life I'd been leading up to
now and about what my future way should be. "From now on
I'm going to be cleverer than the others," I said to myself. But
who was I, to talk like this? Was I somehow better than the
other girls? I was a poor deluded fool.'

5

In November of the year 1953 Ichiro Kawamoto made up his
mind to take a decisive step. He gave up the job he had held for

so many years with the Saka Electricity Works because he wanted
to be able to devote more time and energy to his other activities,
activities which had come to seem increasingly important to him
and which he now described to himself as his 'services to society'.

Such a decision in over-populated Japan, where unemployment is a chronic and perpetual scourge, had far more significance
than would a similar decision taken in any other country. Here a
man who has been apprenticed in a sound concern, and has
proved himself as a good worker, will normally be content to be
employed by that firm until his working days are over, for though
his wages may be small they will at least be secure; because even
in times of crisis a Japanese businessman, in order to 'save face',
will do everything in his power to avoid dismissing his regular
employees. But a man who, having secured such a lifelong job,
should then give it up or otherwise lose it will have a very hard
time ever obtaining another secure niche in the social framework.

His workmates and finally even his department head visited
Kawamoto in his home and did their best to persuade him to give
up this 'crazy idea'. Even his friends, the people who relied on
him for help, and the sick, warned him. An established job with
a good firm, steady wages, gradual promotion – that was what
they were all longing for, in vain. How could any man deliberately throw away such good luck and let himself fall into the state
of terrible insecurity which was all that the swamplands at the
base of society had to offer?

Ichiro promised his advisers that he would think it all out
carefully once again. On 29 November 1953 he shut himself up in
his room and thought about it all through the night. 'Will I have
the courage to live in poverty and insecurity?' he asked himself.
'As a casual labourer I shall have to do work for which I am
physically far too weak.'

Now he recalled the conversations that he had had with Mary
Macmillan in recent years. This was the white-haired missionary
whose public acceptance of America's guilt for the atrocity of 6
August had moved him so deeply in 1949, at the very time when he
was beginning to despair of Christianity. Since then she had become his closest friend, apart from Tokie. In the course of his
visits to this good, active, invariably cheerful woman in her

modest home, Kawamoto had come to the conclusion that the reason why the promises given in the Gospels had not been fulfilled was solely due to the fact that not enough people were really prepared to live their lives according to the Christian doctrine. Did it not say: 'Be like the lilies of the field'?

Kawamoto prayed until it was bright daylight, and with an ardour such as he had never felt before. Then he told his friends that his decision was now irrevocable. That was what he had decided, and that was how it was going to be. Later Ichiro was to receive offers of employment from various Christian organizations, welfare institutions, and also from the financially sound 'Anti-Atom Bomb Movement'. He turned them all down because he did not wish his 'service' to be degraded to a bread-winning job.

During the course of that night Ichiro had made another major decision. But it took him over a week before he could put this one into action.

'On 30 November I finally resigned my job,' he says. 'And on or about 8 December I won a human heart – I asked Miss Uematsu to become my wife.'

Since Mr Uematsu's death Kawamoto had not always had an easy time with his girl-friend. She was going through a phase of doubt, of weariness with living, of contempt for human beings, which resembled in some respects a similar phase through which Kazuo M. had passed in the course of his life. Looking back on this period today, Tokie remembers:

'At that time I was filled with hatred, rage, and a longing for revenge. What I hated above all was that country which had dropped the bomb and which was even now making new ones. I had truly attempted to believe in God, but now the divine message was no longer reaching me. That at least is the way it was during that period of my life. I threw my Bible into the garbage can.'

But, unlike Kazuo, Tokie had a human being at her side ready to catch her when she fell. 'In those days Ichiro was worried, and kept giving me sidelong looks,' she recalls. 'He wouldn't let it all confuse him, though, and he continued to follow steadily along the path he knew to be the right one. I envied Ichiro-san his certainty, and even hated him for it at times. And I did the craziest things, simply in order to try and give him a jolt. But whatever I did or said, Ichiro always forgave me. And that was how his love for me saved me from really going to pieces. If he had lost patience with me at that time, I don't know what would have become of me.'

Maybe Kawamoto proposed marriage to his girl-friend in order to give her that feeling of being protected and cared for which she had lacked ever since her father's death. It made her happy, and she accepted at once. And so the two of them began to make plans, discussing their future life together for hours on end. Another thing they had to work out was how they should break the news to Tokie's mother.

'I tried to practise the traditional formalities in which it is customary for a suitor to request the parents for a girl's hand,' Kawamoto says. 'But when I spoke them aloud to myself a few times I kept getting them wrong, falling over my words and having to start from the beginning all over again. Finally I'd got it pretty well by heart, and I hurried to the Uematsu family's home.

'My heart was pounding.

'"Please do it properly," Uematsu-san whispered to me. Then she acted as though her only interest in all the world was the rice that she was busily cooking on the stove.

'When I pushed back the paper sliding door, I found her mother seated beside the *hibachi* [charcoal stove]. I stammered: "Oh . . . I'm here, to make a friendly request of you . . ."

'"What is it?"

'"Oh, er . . . Toki-chan, Toki-chan . . ."

'"Yes, what about her?"

'"Toki-chan . . . I want very much . . ."

'"You mean you want to have Toki-chan? Well, since it's you, if you want her . . . all you have to do is come and take her . . ."

'"Yes, yes, that's it. Thank you, thank you!"

'I had hardly finished stammering my thanks before I ran off, into the next room, to tell Uematsu-san how it had gone. We were filled with happiness, and we took one another by the hand, both hands.'

COLD HEARTS

1

AT dawn on 1 March 1954 an accident took place thousands of miles from Hiroshima which was nevertheless to be of the greatest consequence for the 'survivors' living in that city. The Japanese fishing boat *Daigo Fukuryu Maru* (*Lucky Dragon No. 5*) was in the midst of the Pacific when it found itself caught in a highly unusual 'snow storm'. It was not until several days later, when the ship had returned to its home port of Yaizu, that the truth about this 'snow storm' came out. It had been radioactive, the 'fall-out' from the most powerful hydrogen bomb so far detonated by the Americans on the Bikini Atoll.

The fate of the *Lucky Dragon*'s twenty-three crew members excited Japanese public opinion more than any other event since the end of the war. For more than six months the newspapers, magazines, radio, and television services devoted more attention to the so-called *shi no hai* (death ashes) and their after-effects as these became gradually apparent, and to the first victims of the H-bomb now lying in two Tokyo hospitals, than to any other single subject. The progress of these men suffering from radio-active infection was reported in the greatest detail as it went through its various phases. Public opinion was kept fully informed. When the condition of one member of the crew, the wireless operator Kuboyama, grew so serious that it was feared he would not survive, the public became so absorbed by his story that millions of people wished to know several times each day what his blood-count now was and how fast his pulse was beating.

For the survivors of Hiroshima and Nagasaki alone there was nothing new in the reports from the hospitals concerning the crew of the *Lucky Dragon*. They had had to endure the agonies and surprises of the 'radiation sickness' in their own bodies ever since 1945. Hitherto public opinion had not really taken their stories seriously. The few *higaisha* who had not been prepared to suffer in silence, or to hide, were described as 'people suffering from imaginary complaints', or even as 'professional patients', whose only motive was to make themselves appear interesting by putting on long faces or, what was worse, to extract money from the pockets of sympathetic persons. Indeed there was even a phrase current at the time for such behaviour: 'selling the atom bomb'.

'Now at last they'll believe us,' the atom-bomb victims of Hiroshima and Nagasaki said with a sigh of relief as they read the reports about the *Lucky Dragon* and its crew. They wrote encouraging letters to the twenty-three crew members in their hospitals, and two *seizonshas* even compiled a sort of brochure for them, giving practical advice and entitled: *How to Survive the Atom Bomb*. But such sympathy was not altogether unalloyed with envy, as was perhaps inevitable. Not a tithe of the attention being now bestowed upon the men of the *Lucky Dragon* had ever been given to them, the 'atomic victims' of 1945, although many of them had been far sicker and far more in need of help than the sailors 'fortunate in their misfortune'. And they quoted the old saying: 'The first crow flew off ahead but the second crow gobbled up all the food'.

Once again the voices of those who had survived the *Pikadon* were raised in anguish: 'Help us, please! For almost ten years now we have been suffering from this weird sickness. . . . We are an entirely new category of war-wounded, and we ask that we be given our rights. We want help!' However, only a tiny minority dared advance such claims. The answer they received was a slander that had become common throughout the whole world since the beginning of the cold war; here, as everywhere else, it was used as a psychological weapon to silence every sort of social protest. For it was rumoured that, behind these revived protests by the atom-sick, sinister wire-pullers were at work: Communist agitators and nothing more. And this invention was, naturally, quite susceptible to subsequent 'proof'. People in Moscow and Peking had more sensitive ears than those of Tokyo and Washington; they hearkened to those appeals. As a result the Communist Governments immediately exploited the new situation by making a gesture which must make a great impression throughout all Asia. They gave seven and a half million yen for the treatment and

cure of the Japanese atomic victims – a sum of money, incidentally, which must appear negligible in the total propaganda budget
of a great power, for at that time this amounted to some $21,000,
or about £7,500. This became the basis of a charitable fund which
at long last was created in order that something might be done for
the survivors.

2

Public opinion in Japan was aroused by the accident to the *Lucky
Dragon*. The emotions thus let loose were whipped up and the
storm that had long threatened now burst upon the Atomic Bomb
Casualty Commission in open fury. From the spring of 1954 until
the autumn of that year the press thundered against it, and a hail
of manifestoes and protests descended upon the 'Fishcake Palace'.

The immediate cause of this outburst was a gesture on the part
of the Americans which was in reality both kindly and well meant,
but which was described by the American anthropologist and
sociologist Herbert Passin, then resident in Tokyo, as 'the worst
mistake of all'. What actually happened? Dr John S. Morton,
Director of the A.B.C.C., offered to take in the twenty-three unfortunate atomic victims from the *Lucky Dragon* and to give
them treatment in the clinic on Hijiyama Hill overlooking Hiroshima. 'Such an offer,' Passin has said, 'could only be made by a
man who totally misunderstood the feelings of the Japanese. For
years the American Government had been using all its resources
in the field of public relations to tell the Japanese that the
A.B.C.C. had not been set up in order to cure people, that it had
no facilities for giving treatment, and that this was how it had to
be. The argument was that the long-term results of objective
scientific research would in the end be as advantageous to the
Japanese people as simple medical treatment, and probably more
so. Nevertheless, the Japanese had never quite got over their
suspicions that they were being used as guinea-pigs by the
A.B.C.C. Therefore one of two conclusions must be drawn from
the A.B.C.C.'s offer: either the Commission's previous statements that it was incapable of giving medical treatment were a

lie; or else the Americans wished to make use of this latest catastrophe for their own research purposes. Neither of these conclusions was flattering for us. When Dr Morton of the A.B.C.C. visited the University Hospital in Tokyo, it did not occur to the Japanese that he might have done so in order to express his regrets or to offer his help. On the contrary, it was assumed that his motive was to study some of the symptoms resultant upon exposure to H-bomb radioactivity. Dozens of articles appeared in the press, all with the theme: "We won't be treated like guineapigs."

The directing staff of the A.B.C.C. has admitted that as a result of this press campaign more and more of those invited to Hijiyama Hill for examination were now refusing to come.

This threatened the statistical validity of the results obtained. Something had to be done urgently to counteract the 'attrition of patient-material' which had by then reached thirty-nine per cent. Such was the phraseology used by the author of the A.B.C.C.'s semi-annual report; it is not purely accidental that his language should have resembled that used by staff officers writing a military dispatch.

As early as 1952, Y. Scott Matsumoto, the head of the 'contactors', had written a critical study of the difficulties and misunderstandings that faced the A.B.C.C. in its dealings with the patients and the public generally. This he had entitled *Patient Rapport in a Foreign Country*, and it was so outspoken that eventually only a bowdlerized and abbreviated version was allowed to be published.

The work of this American sociologist of Japanese origin is of general interest principally because it shows in exact detail the frictions that must be created when a modern Western organization attempts to function within the framework of a foreign, ancient culture and fails to take into account the external and internal conditions inspired by that culture. The reproach is frequently levelled at Albert Schweitzer that he has deliberately kept his jungle clinic in a primitive state: it is said that he has refused to equip it with all the most modern medical and technical devices out of a sort of 'stubbornness'. The experience of the A.B.C.C., with all its ultra-modern equipment, shows that Schweitzer is correct when he maintains that those who would bring help to others must, by behaviour, approach those whom they would help. According to Dr Matsumoto the new A.B.C.C. Clinic was regarded by the Japanese as being altogether too magnificent and elegant. Many women did not dare go there without having first visited a beauty parlour and got out their very best clothes. Poor people such as casual labourers borrowed clothes from their neighbours in order to make a 'decent' appearance.

When the patients first came into the entrance hall, which was entirely occidental in style, they showed evidence of 'confusion and discomfort'. Many immediately began to skid in their wooden sandals upon the smooth and polished floor. In the waiting-room American magazines were laid out for their entertainment, and in most cases they could not so much as read the print. Similarly the signs on all the doors were in English, so that the patients were frequently incapable of finding their way to the room they had been told to go to. The receptionists were almost exclusively *niseis* (Americans of Japanese extraction), whose behaviour, according to Dr Matsumoto, was in some cases 'unnecessarily abrupt, rude, or curt'. According to the sociologist 'the drivers who fetched the patients and drove them home again were more concerned with looking after their cars than worried about the well-being of their passengers'.

The Japanese are accustomed to being examined by a single doctor. It therefore seemed to them strange and even shocking that after having undressed and put on an unusual garment without a back they should be treated as 'something on a factory belt' and passed from one specialist to the next; these would take specimens of their blood, semen, bone marrow, skin tissue; they would be thumped, have lights shone in their eyes, be photographed, and pumped full of serum; and none of these specialists ever explained why or with what purpose all this was being done for them. In order to examine and compare the condition of children exposed to radiation, they would be examined in the nude, a procedure to which the young girls often objected, principally because the tactful handling promised in such cases was not always observed as it should have been.

In a word, the lack of skill and the tactlessness manifested by the A.B.C.C. derived from a defective imagination and an inability to anticipate the emotions of others. This in its turn led to rumours, and finally the Hiroshima clinic won the unenviable reputation of being a sort of modern torture chamber.

Dr Matsumoto's 'interviewers' collected all these rumours and did their best to scotch them as and when they arose. One result of their labours was that examinations now frequently ended with a so-called 'exit interview', at which the patient was asked in private and by a single individual 'what impressions his experience with the Commission had made on him'. From these interviews it transpired that the two procedures which the American doctors had thought must arouse the greatest resentment – the extraction of the bone marrow and the collection of semen specimens – did not in fact shock the person's being used as research material at all.

One of the major complaints noted by Scott Matsumoto was that patients repeatedly examined over a period of a year were not given a prompt diagnosis of their case at an early stage, and often only received such a diagnosis after a long delay. In his own words: 'Many patients report that two or three months after being examined they received letters in which was written : "You are in excellent physical condition," and that these letters arrived when they were actually ill in bed. One said that he had received such an examination report on his mother one week after her death.'

3

Even before the public crisis of the spring of 1954 the A.B.C.C., on the basis of the Matsumoto Report, was already attempting to dispel the misunderstanding of some of the patients. The floors were no longer waxed till they were dangerously slippery; the staff were ordered to be cheerful and polite at all times, with the result that their manners did improve somewhat. There were now Japanese periodicals as well in the waiting-room, and the inscriptions on the doors were in two languages. And those patients who could afford a private doctor now also knew that he would be given a complete and full report of the results revealed by the A.B.C.C. examination.

All these changes and improvements had, however, failed to dispel the atmosphere of distrust which, growing ever worse, now quite enveloped the clinic in the minds of the people of Hiroshima. An autobiographical novel with the title *The Devil's Seed* is proof of this. It deals almost exclusively with the effects of the A.B.C.C. and it was intensively discussed throughout Japan. The author, himself a Hiroshima man with the name of Hiroyuki Agawa, described the experiences of a newspaperman who visits his native city Hiroshima eight years after the *Pikadon* with the purpose of collecting material for a series of newspaper articles. There he experiences the havoc that the 'atom death' works, in his own family: a little nephew must suddenly take to his bed because he does not feel quite well. Soon his pains are diagnosed as being caused by leukaemia, the result of radiation; the child slowly grows sicker, dies, and is the object of an autopsy. Of all the accusations levelled against the A.B.C.C. in this novel none is perhaps more monstrous than the allegation that the Americans were quite uninterested in treating and curing the sick because only by letting the illness run its course could they examine the full progress of the malady, undisturbed.

There is another accusation that Agawa makes against the A.B.C.C., and one that has been constantly repeated ever since. He says that though they allege that the results of their research are available for public examination, in fact their most important scientific discoveries are kept secret and that this is done so that in the event of an atomic war the United States would be defensively in a stronger position than the enemy.

The Japanese author was not able to produce conclusive proof of the allegations made in his novel. Nevertheless, general credence was given to what he had to say. The stubbornness with which, despite all criticism, the Americans continued to refuse medical treatment to the survivors of Hiroshima and Nagasaki repeatedly and inevitably led to these and similar attacks being levelled at the A.B.C.C. Did they fear that by treating and curing the victims they would reveal a secret therapy now known only to themselves, which they therefore regarded as a 'secret weapon' in the event of another atomic war?

The arguments with which the A.B.C.C. sought to defend

itself when attacked for its refusal to treat the atomic sick were of
too formal a nature to convince. Dr Matsumoto, for example, had
recommended that this principal cause of resentment should be
answered as follows: 'The physicians on the Commission's professional staff have no local licence whereby they may practice in
Japan. The treatment of patients is the prerogative and work of
the Hiroshima physician, a sphere into which the Commission
feels it should not intrude or compete.'

This statement immediately provided the basis for further
questions. In the first place the Americans had requested and obtained from the Japanese Government an unusual permission to
examine Japanese nationals. Had they at the same time seriously
requested permission to treat those who were sick? If they had
done so, surely such an authorization would not have been with-
held? In the second place the Americans had spent billions of yen
on having their military weapons and equipment repaired by
Japanese technicians and workmen during the Korean War. Why
could they not produce a fraction of this sum for the 'repair' of
the victims of the atom bombs by Japanese doctors – if a cure
was in fact feasible at all? Why did they not set up a hospital for
the atomic sick, to be staffed by Japanese nationals? Why did they
not create a special insurance fund to cover the cost of treatment
for the survivors?

4

No convincing reply was ever given to these last reproaches. However, in that part of his report which was not allowed to be
published Dr Matsumoto does at least indicate one of the real
reasons behind the American Commission's stubborn refusal to
give medical treatment to the atomic victims.

For in the Matsumoto Report it is more than once explicitly
stated: 'No air of atonement is to be suggested in any way by the
Commission.' The observance of this basic attitude was so strict
that, according to Matsumoto, the original plan whereby 'atomic
victims' were to be taken on the payroll as 'contactors' – with
the job of getting in contact with those sick persons whom the
clinic's doctors wished to examine – was dropped because even

so minute an action of recompense on the part of the A.B.C.C. might have added an air of atonement to the A.B.C.C. project.

American official policy, from the very beginning up to the present day, has been adamant on one point: any special treatment for the atom-bombed cities and any right to special treatment for persons damaged by the atom bombs have been absolutely denied. For they have feared that even this would be interpreted as admitting the special nature of the atomic bomb. And this would inevitably pose a question of principle. In some respects the radioactive rays disseminated by the bomb could be practically equated with the effects of poison gas. Therefore, was the employment of a weapon which emitted such rays in accordance with the principles of international law, or did this not rather constitute a war crime? Here surely lies the more profound reason for the fact that certain American authorites have shown a constant and obvious tendency to minimize and understate the long-term effects of atom bombing: they have closed their eyes to them, in the hope that other people would then not see the brand mark of their guilt.

However, certain members of the A.B.C.C. either would not or could not obey their instructions whereby, in conversation with the survivors of the *Pikadon*, they were supposed to show no traces of pity, regret, or readiness to accept guilt. I was assured in Hiroshima that there were, in fact, certain American doctors who secretly visited their patients in their homes in order to help them; others went out of their way to display their feelings of friendliness towards the native inhabitants of the city.

For example, the anatomist, Dr R., took pleasure in entertaining Japanese guests in his living quarters up on 'The Hill'. When his chief, Dr Holmes, forbade this – on the grounds that racial segregation was ordered even in the clinic's cafeteria – Dr R. thenceforth spent almost all his free time in the homes of his Japanese friends, took to wearing Japanese clothing whenever he was off duty, and finally even became a Buddhist. Dr M. – without informing the then Director of the A.B.C.C. Clinic – married a Japanese girl, but was subjected to so many petty annoyances as a result that he finally had to leave Hiroshima.

Dr Earle Reynolds was one of the anthropologists employed

by the A.B.C.C. in Hiroshima. He spent years examining children suffering from atomic damage. He was so deeply moved by this experience that he later attempted to sail a 'protest ship' into the atomic-bomb testing zone.

Particularly impressive was the case of the American staff doctor, Dr H., a specialist in internal maladies. After his first examination of people suffering from the atomic sickness, he could not restrain himself from saying to his colleagues in the cafeteria: 'It's really abominable what we did here!' He was sent for by Dr Robert Holmes, a former army doctor who was at that time head of the A.B.C.C. Clinic, and was not only sharply reprimanded for having given utterance to his emotions in this way, but also henceforth forbidden all contact with the atomic victims. The alleged reason for this was that his 'emotional outburst' offered enough evidence to justify a supposition that he was not sufficiently 'emotionally stable' for such work, and that he must therefore immediately undergo psychiatric treatment in the neighbouring town of Kure.

The doctor who was being disciplined in this fashion decided, however, to put up a fight and insisted on his democratic rights as a citizen. He would not simply accept the Director's verdict. Through the National Research Council in Washington he began a campaign to ensure his reinstatement in the normal activities of the clinic. After fighting a paper-war for one whole year, he finally won his rights. Dr H. was thus enabled to carry out some interesting research work in Hiroshima, particularly in the cardio-logical field, without being compelled to leave his right to human feelings on the steps outside the clinic each time he entered its doors.

But the pressure of public opinion was becoming too strong even for the Director of the A.B.C.C. In his semi-annual report for the second half of 1954 even he finally felt compelled to advise the authorities in Washington for whom he worked that the A.B.C.C. should at long last be authorized to treat its patients. It is worth noting what were the arguments that he now advanced in favour of such a reform. The text runs as follows: 'With an increased effort to study more patients more thoroughly, and judiciously offer them more therapy, there should be a marked increase in the rapport between the families and the A.B.C.C. Then in the eventuality of some patients' death, it would be possible to have more worth while autopsies.'*

Thus, in the forefront of this proposal – which was presented to the public as a humanitarian measure – we see once again that the motive was not one of curing the sick, but was a hope that better oiled 'human relations' would lead to the obtaining of more productive 'research material'.

Furthermore, even these arguments, free though they were of any trace of human feeling, did not suffice to produce the hoped-for special credits needed if therapy were to be done.

The clinic was simply authorized to maintain the 'diagnostic ward' with ten beds which had been first set up in 1953, even though protests had then been lodged that the principle of non-treatment was being broken. But only particularly 'interesting cases' were taken into this 'diagnostic ward'. Attempted treatments or successful cures in this tiny ward were never referred to in the semi-annual reports; on the other hand, in a single brief reference to this ward, the text of the semi-annual report previously quoted contains the following passage: 'A considerable number of patients admitted to the diagnostic ward were found to have diseases which sooner or later would prove fatal. The diagnostic ward and the opportunities it presents furnish yet another most necessary part of A.B.C.C.'s programme, viz. the possibility of furnishing the Department of Pathology with carefully and well-studied clinical material. This is most necessary to Pathology, and certainly not less so for the Department of Internal Medicine. Unfortunately, the number of cases coming to autopsy at A.B.C.C. which previously had been studied at A.B.C.C. – even as out-patients – is less than half a dozen during the corresponding number of months.'

Kikkawa, one of the founders of the Association of Atomic Victims, has therefore maintained that it was principally only hopeless cases that were selected for the little diagnostic ward. This ward could then be quite correctly described as a 'corpse-production factory'.

* Page 9, *Semi-Annual Report*, A.B.C.C. Headquarters, Hiroshima, Japan, 1 July – 3 December 1954. (For official use only.)

5

I have already referred to Herbert Passin's analysis of the American-Japanese misunderstanding that followed the *Lucky Dragon* accident.* He describes the difference of attitude of the two nations in their reactions to the problems created by nuclear weapons, and he characterizes these as follows:

'Neither of the two parties was capable either of understanding or of acknowledging the sincerity of the other. Whatever the Americans said sounded like an insult to the Japanese, for their arguments were invariably of a purely technical and rational nature, while emotion and anxiety appeared to be ruled out as irrelevant.' Referring to the mistakes the Americans had made in their dealings with the Japanese, he therefore warns his own countrymen against reliance on exclusively technical and rational arguments when dealing with other nations.

As a positive counter-force to an official policy which won for the Americans in Japan a reputation for 'coldness and inhumanity' he quoted a number of 'warm, personal gestures' such as the invitation of the so-called 'Atomic Maidens' of Hiroshima who were given a free trip through the United States. It is only when viewed against the background portrayed above – the cold-hearted attitude of the American atomic victims commission known as the A.B.C.C. – that one can see why this private action created so deep and surprising an impression in Japan.

This idea – like the idea of some years before that Americans should 'spiritually adopt atomic orphans' – had originated with the inexhaustible Norman Cousins. Despite the greatest financial and bureaucratic difficulties, he succeeded at last in realizing this new project.

In view of all that had happened the Japanese had become extremely distrustful. When Cousins arrived at Hiroshima in the spring of 1955 to make the final arrangements for the voyage of the twenty-five girls who had suffered from the atomic bomb,

* 'Japan and the H-bomb', in the *Bulletin of the Atomic Scientists*, Chicago, October 1955.

almost everybody assumed that his motive was solely one of self-interest. The Japanese journalists were determined to find out what lay behind it all. Whose money was it? Was it true that it was all being secretly financed by the United States Government, as was said, in order to counteract the bad impression made by the *Lucky Dragon* affair? How about the story that the girls were to be used in a sort of travelling freak-show, moving back and forth across the United States and on show against the purchase of an expensive ticket? After all that had happened it seemed highly unlikely to the Japanese that the citizens of America could feel any emotion such as pity, or even fellow-feeling, of the victims of the atomic bomb.

It was in 1953, in the Reverend Kiyoshi Tanimoto's church, that Norman Cousins had first met some of these girls, disfigured by exceptionally large burn-scars. Because of their deformed appearance they no longer dared to mix with their fellow-creatures in the normal way. Cousins had wondered at the time if plastic surgery might not help them.

Back in the United States, he succeeded in obtaining the support of numerous clergymen, doctors, and private individuals for his plan.

By collecting money, obtaining sponsors, and the promise of free hospitalization by persuading the surgeons who would operate to waive their fees and relevant expense, the material bases for the journey were at last established.

He failed, however, in his attempts to make a similar arrangement with the airplane companies that would fly the girls and their companions from Japan and across the United States. It was now that the only 'government agency' to be involved in the business offered its services: the United States Air Force General J. E. Hull, of the Far East Command, offered a long-range transport to take the girls to New York. This particular arrangement was soon to prove its importance – and in a way that nobody had foreseen. For scarcely had the Skymaster C-54 left Japan with the 'Atomic Maidens' on board, than a radio message arrived signed by Walter Robinson, the head of the Far Eastern Desk in the State Department, ordering that the whole journey be cancelled forthwith. It can be safely assumed that the attention of this senior

Civil Servant had only been drawn to the project at this late hour, and that he was now trying to cancel it at the very last moment.

For a while it looked as though all the labours of the past two years would be rendered null and void by the stroke of a bureaucrat's pen. However, the pilot of the plane had seen, before they took off, how filled with hope and joy were the girls whose faces the bomb had clawed and disfigured. He did not hesitate for long. He radioed back that he could only accept orders from his military superior, General MacNaughton. Until he received a countermanding order from the General, therefore, he would continue to fly the arranged course, with destination the United States. The order to turn about did not come, though these were anxious hours for the few persons on board who were aware of what was going on. For 'normal channels' between the State Department and the commanders of the United States Air Force are fortunately longer and slower than the flight from Japan to Mitchell Field, New York. And to send back the girls without explanation after they had received their first, unusually friendly welcome in America – that was something even the stoniest-hearted politician dared not risk.

6

The attempt to do something for the 'Atomic Maidens' aroused, to begin with, less popular enthusiasm in Hiroshima than anywhere else. Pastor Tanimoto had played the chief part in deciding which girls should have the good luck to visit the United States. This outstanding man, who appears as one of the principal personalities in John Hersey's report called *Hiroshima*, was admired throughout all the world by the millions who had read that book; yet in his own home-town, in Hiroshima itself, he had made himself noticeably unpopular. It may be, as some said, that his fame had really gone to his head a bit, and that he had never learned when to open his mouth and when to keep it closed. Yet this was not enough to explain the many reproaches levelled at him by his fellow-citizens. The real answer is that he had become an object of envy.

And now, once again, Tanimoto became the target for countless unproved and unprovable slanders. It was said that he only thought up this visit of the girls to America in order to win publicity for himself. Would it not have been both cheaper and better to operate on the cheloids here in Japan, instead of organizing this sensational flight across the Pacific? It was also said that Tanimoto had only selected girls belonging to his own church, and that the Americans for their part had insisted that only such girls be sent as were not too hideously scarred, for they simply dared not show their compatriots the grimace of atomic war in all its full horror.

Yet such petty criticism was silenced by the press reports which had begun to arrive from the United States. These spoke of the extremely cordial reception that was being given the twenty-five 'young ladies from Hiroshima'. Also the letters that the girls themselves wrote home were so obviously enthusiastic that bit by bit the sneers and slanders died away.

On the other hand a question that had been debated ever since the accident to the crew of the *Lucky Dragon* came more and more to the fore in Japan, and was discussed with ever greater heat. This question was: 'What exactly are we Japanese doing for the survivors of the atom bomb?' And the answer, as provided by newspapermen visiting Hiroshima and Nagasaki, became less and less ambiguous: 'To all intents and purposes, nothing whatsoever.' And so now, at long last the Japanese began to think less about the 'cold-hearted Americans' and more about their own failure to do anything to ameliorate the suffering of the *hibakusha*.

For example, it now became generally known for the first time that the professors and students of the Hiroshima Medical Postgraduate School had long ago offered to treat the atomic victims for nothing, but that their offer had then been turned down as the result of an intrigue organized by a few influential doctors in private practice. Had not perhaps those same doctors continued their intrigue in Tokyo and arranged that the Japanese Ministry of Health refuse permission to the Americans – should they ask it – that they be allowed to give medical treatment to the victims of atomic radiation? Nor could it remain hidden any longer that Mayor Hamai, in his attempts to secure further help for Hiroshima from the Japanese State, had failed principally because the

Government party had insisted that the much-loved Mayor of Hiroshima must first join their political organization. Hamai had felt compelled to regard such 'horse-trading' as a betrayal of his electors, for he had twice been voted into office as an 'Independent'.

After his futile visit to Tokyo in an attempt to raise funds for his city in 1953, he had tried to arrange a bank loan for Hiroshima in the United States. This, however, was as unsuccessful as were the efforts of the well-known public relations firm, Harold Oram, to organize collections for Hiroshima on a national scale.

Oram had had to inform Mayor Hamai in June 1954 that unfortunately, and against all his expectations, he had not succeeded in founding a Hiroshima Supporting Society, as planned. The reason was that the 'influential and exceptional personalities' whom he had hoped would give their names as sponsors of this society had regretfully declined. (One of these was Dr Milton Eisenhower, the President's brother.) He blamed this on 'the new international situation and a noticeable change of attitude on the part of prominent personalities'.

It was principally owing to his failure to secure credits that Hamai's political career was now interrupted. It was said of the Mayor that he had no influential friends who could help Hiroshima. The result was this: when the man who more than any other individual was responsible for Hiroshima's reconstruction, ran for office for the third time, he was defeated at the polls.

Yet now at last, after ten long years, Japanese public opinion began to demand that something be done for the victims of the *Pikadon*. Special surcharge postage stamps were put on sale for the new year throughout all Japan. These brought in billions of yen immediately, enough to finance the building of a special hospital in Hiroshima for the treatment of patients suffering from the radiation sickness. In the Japanese Diet efforts began to be made to introduce a bill whereby the atomic sick would receive free medical treatment for the rest of their lives. Thus, after all, the action inaugurated in 1951 by a handful of determined individuals in the martyred city of Hiroshima to help the survivors of the atom bomb was now at last understood and carried forward by the weight of opinion of all the people.

TWO AGAINST DISASTER

1

IT had actually been Kawamoto's intention to marry shortly after Tokie had accepted him. With the severance pay that Ichiro had received when he ceased to be employed by the Saka Electricity Works he bought a few sticks of cheap furniture and found a place to live in a house in the railway quarter.

A little later, at Christmas time, their friend and brother-in-baptism, Fujita, also became engaged to be married. It was he who had first taken Ichiro to the language class, six long years ago, where he had got to know Tokie. They thought of arranging a double wedding. Fujita's marriage took place, but Tokie and Ichiro were only there as guests.

'Unfortunately we must wait a little longer,' Kawamoto explained. 'My severance pay hasn't been enough to buy everything we need. We don't even possess any decent bedding. I'm a day labourer now, and Tokie has to look after her mother.'

But to a few close friends he was more explicit:

'Our relationship is not a normal one. We've come together because we want to work together, to fill the gap where our society has failed, to help other people.' And as if by way of further explanation, he added, blushing slightly: 'When I've spent the whole day looking after the sick and the needy, by the time I get home I simply am not able to embrace Tokie-chan. At such moments I cannot get rid of the thought: what right have we to enjoy domestic happiness?'

Yet even this explanation did not give the whole truth. Many years ago Ichiro, when talking to the orphans of 'Sunflower Castle', had said that he intended never to marry, for he was afraid of bringing children into the world who would be incapable of living a normal life. That is to say, he shared the most profound anxiety that afflicted all the youthful survivors of the atomic catastrophe: the fear that their progeny would show traces of atomic damage, would be morons or monsters.

Since 'that day' dozens of midwives' tales had circulated throughout Hiroshima, stories about miscarriages and misbirths of grotesquely malproportioned babies, many of which were scarcely recognizable as human beings at all. Many of these abnormal children were allegedly disposed of quietly by the midwives or by their mothers; the few who remained alive were put into institutions.

There was an age-old story current in Japan that certain persons were, through their heredity, 'possessed by foxes', and that such people must abstain from marriage when they reached the suitable age. Thus this modern version of an ancient superstition was easily believed and spread quickly.

In fact the 'midwives' fairy tales' that circulated in Hiroshima and Nagasaki did contain an element of truth. It was correct that one in every five or six of the pregnant women who had lived through the *Pikadon* in either of the two Japanese cities did produce offspring which had been mutated by radioactivity. In 1945 and 1946 there was an exceptionally high number of misbirths. Some children were not only born with unusually small heads, but also showed signs of mutation in their rate of growth and of development. It was even found necessary to open a special home for mentally retarded atomic orphans, which was called the Roppo Gakuen. Finally it is true that in 1945 and 1946 statistics show that Hiroshima had a rate of miscarriages higher than the average for all Japan.

Yet none of this applied to children who were only conceived after the disaster, even when one or both their parents were themselves atomic victims. There was hardly any other field of study to which the A.B.C.C. devoted greater attention than to this: what, if any, hereditary effects were traceable to radioactive exposure? Laboratory research on fruit-flies, mice, and rats had shown that hereditary damage to these creatures' offspring and descendants was considerable owing to the mutations effected within the genes: it was now a matter of supreme interest to discover whether a similar process were detectable in human beings. The results were – at least so far as the first generation went – negative. However, by the time these good tidings were handed down from Hijiyama Hill, the people of Japan had long decided that the A.B.C.C. did not publish the whole truth. The reassuring news was therefore not believed at all in Hiroshima.*

Even if these pronouncements by the A.B.C.C. were not a deliberate attempt to conceal the truth, the question still remained open whether hereditary damage caused by radioactivity might not yet make its appearance in subsequent generations. In any event that was what Kawamoto feared, and shortly after his engagement he explained to his fiancée why, in his opinion, they ought not to get married. Originally his emotions had overwhelmed him, but now he had been able to think over quietly where his duties and responsibility lay; he was therefore prepared to give Tokie back her freedom.

But when Kawamoto pressed her in this fashion to break off her engagement, Tokie told him a secret which the Uematsu family had until now kept hidden from all the world: 'A few months after "that day" my older sister gave birth to just such a . . . child. Ever since then I've been frightened, exactly as you have been. Maybe we shouldn't really get married. But can we not at least remain together?'

2

So they remained together. They had originally hoped to pass the New Year holiday on their honeymoon. Instead they 'acted as replacements in the Shudoin Orphanage, so that the good sisters might at least enjoy one holiday a year'. Then back to normal life. Tokie had once again to work in a *pachinko* saloon. Ichiro, however, had become a proper *nikoyon*,† and he spent his days,

---

* Referring to this research work and to the optimistic conclusions that have so frequently been drawn therefrom, H. J. Muller, the 'father of modern genetics', has said: 'I think that it is very unfortunate to cite lack of results from one study, as indicating that there is no effect. . . . We need not feel at all secure or relieved that no effects were found.' Page 1084, *The Nature of Radioactive Fallout and its Effect on Man*, Congressional Hearings, 4–7 June, 1957, Washington D.C.

† The word *nikoyon*, which describes those unemployed men and women who are found work by the Unemployment Officer, first came into use in 1951. The daily pay of 240 yen (or approximately 6s. 3d. or 50 cents) per day

shovelling earth, building the new road that was to run over the Tenjinyama Hill.

They told some people, including Tokie's employers, that they were brother and sister; they did not correct others who assumed that they had got married quietly a long time ago. But they could not pretend to Mary Macmillan, the American missionary who was their close friend. And it was for her sake that they once again changed their minds and decided to get married after all.

Early in February, that is to say just one month before the date that they had fixed for their wedding, a Mr Kamikuri, the Director of the Shinsei Orphanage, came to see Ichiro Kawamoto. He had a question he wished to ask him, and it was this: would Kawamoto and Tokie take an atomic orphan into their home? The boy in question was at present still in jail, serving a sentence for theft, but he would be discharged at once provided a family could be found willing to look after him.

While Ichiro and Tokie had made up their minds that it would be wrong for them to produce children of their own, they had decided that they would look after young strangers who had no homes instead. Here was the first opportunity to put this plan into practice. But at this particular time, that is to say just before their marriage, Kamikuri's proposal was extremely inconvenient. Would they not now have to devote the savings they had so painfully collected to buying food for their guest? When he noticed Ichiro's hesitancy, the orphanage director explained at once that the ward in question was nineteen years old, and that he would work on the road-building along with Ichiro. He would thus earn some money and be able to contribute to the household expenses.

'When I told Tokie all about it,' Kawamoto has said, 'she did not take it as a particularly pleasant surprise. But at last she agreed, and said: "Very well then, I'll cook for you."'

'I went to see Mr Kamikuri with the purpose of meeting young Mr So-and-so, whom I'll call A. He looked intelligent. I hadn't expected that. It was marvellous to see the happy expression on Director Kamikuri's face as he gave A. the new suit he'd bought for

---

is exceptionally low, even by Japanese standards. *Ni* means two, *yon* four. Another word for these day-labourers is *anko*, a fish with a big belly which lies motionless, its mouth open, waiting for its prey to swim into its jaws.

him. After spending two or three more days in the orphanage, A. came to us. It was difficult for Tokie to make our home as pleasant a place to live in as it used to be, because A. was rather conceited and did nothing but talk about himself. He would tell us over and over again about his life in prison. "One thing's for sure, Kawamoto Niisan [elder brother] hasn't seen as much of the world as I have." He was forever repeating this, and really the way he talked to me was more as if he was the elder of us two.

'One day Tokie-chan asked me: "Have you any idea what's happened to that piece of black silk?"

'She almost whispered as she said this, though A. was out at the time.

'"No idea at all. What are you talking about?"

'"I can't find the piece of material. A customer brought it to me only yesterday."

'"Have you really looked everywhere?"

'"Absolutely everywhere. Even in the trunk."

'"Maybe you left it at your mother's house?"

'"I'm certain I didn't."

'The room I had rented for us was only nine feet by six. It contained one small cupboard. Was it possible that A. . . .? No, that was certainly not the explanation. Tokie had had the same thought. She was deeply upset, and finally she lost patience: "I don't know what to say. I don't even know what I'm trying to do. And I've had enough of acting as cook for you two. I'm giving notice here and now. I'm going back home."'

Later Tokie explained why she had run away from Ichiro at that time:

'I simply couldn't bear to see how Kawamoto kept on trying to excuse that ex-jailbird. Certainly his generosity touched me. But I was forced to say to myself that such goodness of heart was simply too much for me.'

When A. came home Kawamoto tried to question him. But no sooner had he asked him cautiously whether he had any idea where the piece of black silk might have vanished to than the other shouted in Hiroshima dialect and using prison slang: 'What are you getting at? You think I swiped it?'

Next day Kawamoto gave some pretext for not going to work

and instead turned the entire room upside down. At last he found the piece of stuff in an old box which had seldom been opened in years. This box was his sole inheritance from his mother. Here too he kept the many hundreds of letters that Tokie had written him.

Ichiro took the box and immediately ran with it to his wife's parents' house. There was still an expression of anger on his face as he pushed open the rickety front door and shouted in a rough voice that no one had ever heard before: 'Hullo! Where's Tokie-chan?'

The mother, sister, and the sister's friend, a certain Mr Sigiura, came running out. Kawamoto did not even see them, and pushed open the next door. In the middle of the room sat Tokie, white as a sheet. She was sewing and she did not look up.

He dumped the box on the floor, ripped open the lid, and said in a voice almost incoherent with rage:

'There you are! Just look inside that. And just look at what you've done, simply because you couldn't search for anything properly. You've deeply offended A. You've thrown him off the rails, just when he was beginning to live a proper, decent life again. Do you remember what we'd planned to do, you and I? We wanted to do small acts of kindness, quietly, to help our fellow-men. And you've left them in the lurch, and me too.'

'Please, please!' The mother and Mr Sigiura were now trying to intervene. 'Anybody can make a mistake. You must forgive her.'

Kawamoto would not be calmed down. Nowadays when he recalls this scene, it is always the water pot that first comes to his mind:

'This pot, filled almost to the brim with water, was standing on the kitchen hearth. I took the bundles of letters from Tokie out of the box. They were tied up with lengths of string, arranged according to their dates. I broke the string and then began to tear up the letters, one by one. I threw all the scraps of paper on the fire, under the water pot. Only then did I begin to realize for the first time how very many letters Tokie had written me. She stood beside me, as if she had been beaten, and could not bring herself to utter a single word: "No, I want to forget her absolutely," I shouted. "Not a single one of these letters will be kept . . ." And after twenty minutes it was done. The water in the pot had begun to boil furiously. "There – and now, good-bye!" I walked out of the house with the empty box in my hand. Behind me I could hear the pot bubbling away. . . .'

When Kawamoto got back to his room he heard a loud quarrel going on upstairs, on the second floor. A childless married couple lived up there. They were complaining to the landlord that while they were out somebody had broken into their room, which they kept locked. Nothing of this sort had ever happened in this house before the arrival of A.

Thus Kawamoto too began to have doubts about his guest. And when Tokie came to see him a few days later, to ask for his forgiveness, he gave it to her at once.

But it was not until several weeks later, when Ichiro and Tokie had already moved out and had given A. their room, that their suspicions were to be proved justified beyond the shadow of a doubt. Someone had visited the different people for whom Kawamoto was in the habit of doing his 'little kindnesses' and had begged for money and food, on the pretext that these were needed for 'poor Kawamoto, who had suddenly fallen sick'. In every case the description tallied exactly with A.

What is more, he had made a good haul, for each one of the people he approached was delighted with this opportunity to show, as best he could, his feelings of gratitude to the helper Ichiro.

3

On the day that Tokie and Ichiro moved into their new home with the Yamagata family, Mary Macmillan sailed for America. As a farewell present and memento they had got her a long rice spoon, which they took in a parcel to the station for her. Only as the train was pulling out of the station did it occur to them that they had planned to marry without fail before their friend's departure. And once again it had come to nothing. Sadly they made their way back to their new home.

Notwithstanding the way their guest had let them down, Ichiro and Tokie continued to offer the hospitality of their little home in the Sendamachi district to other young people. They shared all their possessions with them; indeed they even gave their guests the room with the straw mats, while they themselves slept on the bare and draughty floor in the kitchen. They finally had so many people staying with them that Ichiro had to nail a large letterbox to his front door, with the names of the inhabitants of his little flat written on it.

Many of their 'children' gave them much delight. There was, for example, C. with his hilarious talent for mimicry – his master-piece was to imitate a female *samisen* player (a Japanese guitar). Then there was little Miss Yamada, who was so happy that her brother Goro, who had been hard of hearing ever since the *Pika-don*, had at last been able to leave the orphanage and become a member of this somewhat unusual 'family'. Goro himself, how-ever, was convinced that he had drawn a dud in choosing those particular foster-parents. 'Give me rice!' he would growl twice a day when the dish of porridge was set before him for his midday and his evening meal. 'We got this filthy muck in the institute, too. It's about time I got a proper "silver dish" [Japanese expres-sion for rice] to eat!'

It was not only in the narrow circle of his wards that Ichiro was subject to repeated disappointments. In his work for the Anti-Atom Bomb Movement he was confronted only by intrigues, jealousy, conceit, and ingratitude. It often seemed an almost hopeless undertaking to attempt to mediate between the many different groups of 'atomic victims'. For the friends of peace fought one another with a positively bellicose ferocity.

He was sometimes afflicted with profound doubts nowadays: were not all their protests against the testing of atomic weapons a pure waste of time? Had the collections of signatures against such testing and the demonstrations against Japanese remilitarization any purpose whatsoever? Would the Governments concerned be in any way impressed by such actions? In the years from 1954 to 1956 it certainly did not seem likely that they would.

All the same – had not the atomic victims been saying among themselves for years that they would not have any hope of obtaining support from the State?

Yet now, in Hiroshima, the foundation stone had been laid for a new hospital to care for the atomic sick. (Incidentally, not a single *hibakusha* had been invited to attend this ceremony.) And now it was said that next year the Japanese Diet in Tokyo would pass a law whereby those suffering from radiation sickness would be given free medical treatment. So there was, after all, some purpose in fighting for a just cause! Eventually the day must dawn when even the deaf would open their ears to the truth. Provided that those who knew what the truth was did not grow discouraged and fall silent!

When Ichiro, alone or with Tokie's help, sat up late at night writing letters or painting slogans on banners; when he attended yet another of the congresses that now took place more and more frequently in Hiroshima, and listened yet again to the endless speeches: when he marched in demonstration after demonstration and spoke until he was close to physical collapse about the new disaster that threatened them all, to an audience consisting of children and old people, of women, casual labourers, and beggars: on such occasions he often found new strength to withstand his exhaustion by glancing at his little *dharma* doll. These are small figures of a man, lacquered red, on a rounded base which, when knocked over, immediately stands up again; they are to be found in many a Japanese household. Once, in the summer of 1955 during the great collection of signatures against the atom-bomb tests, Ichiro had called on a famous team of *sumo* wrestlers which was paying a visit to Hiroshima. He had gone to their dressing-room to obtain their signatures. It was then that the star of the team, the huge, good-tempered Tochinishiki, had given him the *dharma* doll and – as was the custom – had written his most ardent desire on the blank space where the doll's right eye should have been. What he had written was: 'Let there be peace at last!'

It was said of these *dharma* dolls: '*Nana – korobi – ya – oki.*' ('If you are knocked down seven times, you'll get up eight.') 'I no longer possess my resilient little man,' Kawamoto tells me. 'Because a child once begged me to give it him. But he has become my model and I have sworn to myself: "Whatever they may do to us, I shall spring to my feet again – no matter how often they knock me down . . ."'

4

It happened nowadays over and over again that one of the atomic victims whom Ichiro and Tokie had known well and even cared for would, all these years after the *Pikadon*, die as a result of the radiation sickness. And each time it was for them as if a relative had died. But none of these deaths moved them as deeply as that of Sadako Sasaki, a twelve-year-old girl whom Kawamoto had known for many years, for her father's little barber's shop was next door to the Y.M.C.A. building, and Ichiro had therefore met the child almost every day. A few days before she suddenly fell ill, she and Masahiro had themselves joined the Y.W.C.A. and had taken part in a bicycle ride from Tokyo to Hiroshima.

There is a Japanese belief that a sick person who, even on his deathbed, can fold a thousand paper cranes will be out of danger. As Sadako's leukaemia grew worse she bravely set about this task, and soon above her hospital bed there arose a web of strings on which the little cranes fluttered. But when the sick girl had just made her six hundredth little paper creation, her strength began to ebb away, and with No. 644 she was forced to give up. Her last words were: 'Please do not cry, Mother and Father.'

This death came as a particularly violent shock to the people of Hiroshima, because only a few days earlier another 'atomic child', a boy of fifteen named Norie Hirota, had died of the same sickness. That grown-ups should die as a result of the atom-bomb such a long time after the end of the war was shocking enough. But that children who at the end of the war were only a few months or years old should now also have to pay the war guilt of an older generation – this seemed to everyone particularly gruesome and unjust.

After the death of his little friend, Sadako Sasaki, an idea occurred to Kawamoto: a statue should be erected to commemorate the children killed by the atomic bomb, and beneath its shadow the young people should launch an appeal to all parents throughout the world. This idea was almost immediately greeted with approval throughout Japan. Schoolboys and schoolgirls in the whole country contributed something from their pocket money, and thus a large sum was collected.

The schoolteachers soon took control of this action, and Kawamoto was pushed into the background. But he worked on, in a subordinate capacity and without any trace of bitterness, for the Thousand Crane Movement which he had himself thought up ; it soon outgrew its original purpose and developed into a non-political Youth Movement for Peace.

However, as a result of this action, Ichiro and Tokie began to be known outside the immediate circle of the 'survivors'. One day an unusual visitor came to call on them in their wretched dwelling into which they had just moved, nor far from the Atom Dome.

'It was, I think, early in March or towards the end of February 1956,' Kawamoto remembers. 'The man came to see us unannounced. But I soon realized that he knew many of my friends. He was about thirty-five years old, on the short side, with big, round eyes and a swarthy complexion. This *Asaguro-shi* ["Mr Darkskin"], as we called him, was extremely polite. Indeed he made every effort to flatter us and to show us how extremely well-disposed he was.

'Finally I asked him outright: "What is it you actually want from us?"

'"I should like to know what this Peace Movement is really all about!"

'"Who are you, and where do you come from?"

'He mentioned some name or other, assured us once again that he wished to be our friend, and when he went away he left a little package as a present for us. When we opened this we found that it contained candy.

'Four days later he was back. This time he spoke quite openly: "I'm from the police and I've been told that you're an active and enthusiastic member of the Peace Movement. Would you please tell me about this?"

'"Why do you ask me? You must know a great deal about it already."

'"No. In fact I know almost nothing at all."

'"Then why don't you attend a few of our meetings? After all, a great many policemen were also killed by the atom bomb."

'When he went away he once again tried to leave a box of sweets behind. But this time we refused to accept his present.

'From then on he often visited us. He was always friendly, in an ingratiating sort of way, spoke the Hiroshima dialect, and was particularly interested in pamphlets or leaflets. If ever he saw any lying about, he always took them away with him.

'"Please give them to me!" he would say.

'"But they're publicly distributed!"

'Tokie-chan and I thought that he took these pamphlets away with him so that he might show them to his superiors and thus prove that he really was "working" on our case. He tried to get us to tell him the names of the men on the "Council against the Atom and Hydrogen Bombs" and of the leaders of the Teachers' Union; he also wanted to know what we talked about at our discussion groups. But he didn't get anything out of us.

'Finally he made us a proposition: our life was obviously a very hard one, and he would like to do something for us. How would we like a nice secure job? He could recommend us to various of his friends. For example in the Municipal Education Department, or some other branch of the Civil Service. But that sort of thing didn't interest us at all.

'When he arrived at our front door, he always asked softly: "*Gomen kudasai?*" [May I come in?] and when we answered: "Who's there?" he would say: "It's me!" By that time, however, he was inside our room. In fact he behaved as if he and we were confederates in some sort of a conspiracy.

'It occurred to me that the Communists and my friends in the Peace Movement might now perhaps be thinking that Kawamoto was a police spy. But "Mr Darkskin" must really have imagined that I was a proper Communist.

'Tokie and I had to laugh. In fact I've never been a Communist or a police spy. Why can't they ever see that?'

5

Until early 1957 countless signatures were being collected throughout the entire world of those who demanded an end to the testing of atomic weapons. In Japan alone the total number of those who signed the protest reached thirty-three millions. In the Hiroshima district the proportion of those signing was even higher. A million men and women of all political views from the extreme right to the extreme left, who normally had no single point of agreement, had here taken up an attitude opposed to the tests. In this question the mutual antipathy of the political parties was non-existent. For here in Hiroshima the people thought that they knew better than anyone else anywhere in the world exactly what atomic war means.

When bad weather was expected the newspapermen now reported regularly the level of radioactivity in the anticipated rain, and warned their readers in the strongest terms against drinking rain-water. Almost nobody now dared to go out into the rain without some sort of a head-covering; for there was a rumour, based on nothing beyond the memory of what had happened immediately after the *Pikadon*, that 'hot' rain caused people's hair to fall out. People only dared eat rice in small quantities, for the Japanese professors had said that the quantity of Strontium 90, which causes cancer of the bone, was especially high in rice.

When early in 1957 the British announced that they too planned to test their H-bomb in the Pacific, a new wave of protest passed through Japan. The 'pro-Americans' had refused to take part in the demonstrations against American tests; the Communists and fellow-travellers had similarly and shamefacedly kept quiet when protests were made against the Soviet Russian tests; but now there was yet another enemy against whom every voice could be raised, Great Britain.

The collection of signatures, the mass demonstrations, and the sit-down strikes outside the foreign embassies had hitherto made no impression upon the great Powers. But now a new idea was put forward. This was that a Japanese ship should be sent into the sea area sealed off for the proposed H-bomb tests. And this idea was immediately received with the greatest interest and approval.

The idea was rejected by the Government spokesmen as 'too extreme', all the more so when the British declared that they would not allow their tests to be interrupted by the presence of an

'intruder' in the forbidden zone. Japanese public opinion, however, generally approved of the scheme.

Since the moment when this idea had first been put forward
Kawamoto had been wandering around like a sleepwalker. Even
his fellow-workers on the building site had noticed how absent-
minded he was, and teased him, saying that he must be 'in love'.
For he had told them that he finally planned to be married at
Easter.

But it was quite other thoughts, not at all connected with
romance, which had produced this effect on him.

'I thought that many people had probably already volunteered
to sail in the protest ship. How could I tell Tokie-chan about what
I proposed to do? How would she react when I told her of my
intention to volunteer myself? And what would all the people
whom we had already invited to our wedding say?'

One evening Kawamoto discussed with Tokie-chan the business
of the protest ship, and told her what were the arguments being
used for and against sending it into the prohibited zone. He had
managed to get the conversation on to the subject, but even so he
dared not as yet even hint at his own plan of sailing on board the
ship.

He writes:

'I could scarcely bring myself to look Tokie-chan straight in the
face. She would now surely decide that I was a totally unreliable
fellow. First I'd said that we must postpone our wedding because
we had to look after the orphan children; then I'd raised all sorts
of "financial difficulties"; and now, when we'd decided at long
last to get married in spite of everything, there was this.'

But Tokie had apparently recognized long ago what it was that
Ichiro really wanted to say.

She laid aside the newspaper she was reading and asked:

'Ichiro-san, what would you do now, if you didn't have to take
me into account at all?'

'Well, in that case . . . to tell you the truth . . . I mean, the
whole truth. . . . Well, I've been thinking all day that maybe I'd
go with the others in that ship . . .'

'In fact you've really been thinking about this for quite a long
time, haven't you?'

'Yes. . . . Of course. . . . Naturally,' he stammered. 'But, Tokie, if I do go I want to go alone. Please forget about me. I really am a hopelessly incorrigible fool . . .'

'I see. That's why you've at last talked to me about this today. To tell me that you want to go, and go alone?'

'. . . in any case . . .'

'And what will happen to me?'

'You should marry somebody who can look after you properly.'

Tokie bowed her head.

'I could see in the poor light,' Kawamoto remembers, 'that her eyes were filling with tears. Two or three minutes passed, and then she said: "Why didn't you actually ask me if we shouldn't both go together and volunteer for the ship?"

'"That's nonsense. I'm all alone in the world. You've got a mother and sister to think about . . ."

'"You don't really love me. Mother and sister would surely understand. Please let me volunteer too."

'"No, no, that cannot, that must not be, Tokie-chan. This is different from war. You don't know what might happen to us . . ."

'"Yes I do . . . I do really. I was here in 1945. I grew up in Hiroshima, just in case you've forgotten."'

The rats were audible overhead, and the lamp cast a flickering glow across their room.

Tokie drew my attention to an item in her newspaper. The fifty-one-year-old writer, Eiichi Iwata, had volunteered for the ship. He had declared: 'I am not doing this in the *tokko seishin* [the aggressive spirit], nor am I a Communist. I am acting solely in the service of peace.'

'"You see," said Tokie, "even people who have only ever heard or read about Hiroshima are volunteering. And I, I who lost my own father through the bomb, should I just sit here and do nothing? After all, I'm the child of an atomic victim. Anyhow, as a Christian there is nothing else I can do."

'All of a sudden I gave in,' Ichiro recalls. 'I said: "Very well, we'll both fill in the form and volunteer. Give me your hand." I then pretended that I was going to bring my fist down with all my strength upon her hand, which lay on the sheet of paper. Instinctively Tokie drew her hand back.

'"You see? Every human being instinctively tries to avoid being hurt. We shall perhaps be deluged with boiling water and red-hot sand. Our ship may be sunk. . . . Do you still wish to volunteer? You are quite free to do so or not as you choose."

'Tokie fell silent. After a few minutes that seemed endless she spoke at last, and her voice was filled with determination. "Yes, I do want to go. Regardless. And not just out of stubbornness. It may seem mad, what we want to do. But – what else is there that we can do? If the people out there in the rest of the world would only understand that we are acting deliberately after we've thought it all out. Why in wartime is it taken for granted that people are prepared to sacrifice their lives – but when it's a question of doing something extraordinary to prevent a war, they're all immediately afraid of appearing ridiculous or being shouted down as fanatics? Oh, these too, too delicate souls! If only they'd be prepared to accept today one thousandth part of what threatens them for tomorrow!"'

Epilogue

OUR HIROSHIMA

1

THE windows on the second floor of the Hospital for Post Office Employees in Hiroshima, through which, on 6 August 1945, Dr Hachiya could see all the way across the flattened city to the sea coast far away, are nowadays made of double glass. Everywhere the eye sees walls, house-fronts, new buildings, more windows. Between them grow a few thin young trees. The sky is criss-crossed by wires. The scene is set, the city has been rebuilt.

In the 'Place of Suffering' the price of land is rising year by year. Speculation is rife, and in the business district they are already pulling down buildings put up 'after the bomb' in order to re-place them with new and larger ones of many storeys, for the price of land is now so high that low houses are no longer an economic proposition.

In Kamiyacho, where Professor Nagaoka had roasted his sweet potatoes in the complete solitude that prevailed in the midst of the atomic desert after 'that day', the great bus station now stands. Over eight hundred buses arrive there each day, to unload and load up again. From dawn to dusk there is the trampling of thousands of pairs of shoes and sandals as the pedestrians are shepherded through the traffic by the policeman on point duty. The seven hundred taxis drive at metropolitan speed. Since 1954 the number of motor-cars in Hiroshima has trebled.

Fourteen years after the atomic disaster the *Chugoku Shimbun* published the following balance sheet:

'There are now more houses in Hiroshima than before the *Pikadon*. At that time there were 76,300; today there are approxi-mately 90,000. Our population has already passed the highest point that it reached during the war. Since 1956 the average in-come of our citizens has exceeded the average for all Japan. It therefore goes without saying that the *per capita* possession of electric washing machines and of television sets is higher in Hiroshima than anywhere in Japan . . .'

The public buildings in the Park of Peace remained unfinished for years on end owing to a shortage of money: now they have been completed, a smooth, grey, chilly edifice. In the Atom Bomb Museum a tall thin building on stilts, consisting mostly of glass, is now the comfortable home of Professor Nagaoka, its Director; he presides over the relics of the horror, carefully preserved behind glass. Greasy scraps of clothing seared by fire are here displayed as if they were the treasures unearthed in some Egyptian King's tomb. Nearby, in the somewhat uninviting permanent exhibition staged by the Regional Board of Industry, there is a not dissimilar display of rubber goods, tinned foods, textiles, insecticides, and wood products. But now, as in the old days, three large industrial combines really mould the face of Hiroshima: the Mitsubishi shipyards, the 'Toyo Kogyo' transport works, and the Nippon Steelworks. Writing about these on 6 August 1958, the *Japan Times* reported that they had 'completely renewed their factory equipment, paying particular attention to the production of munitions. Here American artillery pieces are being remodelled, and adjusted to suit the requirements of the smaller Japanese soldiers. The monthly output of such remodelled guns in Hiroshima is the second highest for all Japan . . .'

2

Many of the inhabitants of Hiroshima can now say of themselves that their 'pockets are warm' with the money they have recently earned. Almost every evening the great flood-lamps blaze above the new baseball diamond, and almost every evening all the seats in its big stadium are sold out. Hiroshima now has fifty-one cinemas; this is the second largest number in all Japan.

Some of the keenest promoters of the 'new Hiroshima' are now asking whether the time has not come for a complete break with the past: should not an attempt be made finally to forget what happened on 'that day'? They would really like to see the very symbol of the *Pikadon*, the naked girders of the 'Atomic Dome' (which even now is not a scheduled public monument), pulled down, so that this gaunt ruin need no longer trouble the ambitious, forward-looking citizens of the new Hiroshima with sad thoughts concerning the past.

Yet in Hiroshima of all places such a 'destruction of past destruction' can hardly hope to achieve the desired end. Anywhere else in the world it may be possible to act as if the last war were now a part of history, and thus to include the possibility of a new war in calculations concerning the future. But here in Hiroshima the past has not ceased to exist: with each new victim of the radiation sickness who, after years of being spared, is struck down by the disease, the past is once again and unavoidably present.

Hiroshima does not point the way towards peace because it uses the word *Heiwa* (Peace) as a sort of trademark which it attaches to everything and anything, but because it gives a faint indication of what the world would look like after an atomic war. We may assume that what would be left after such a war would not be totally dead desert without human inhabitants, but rather a single huge hospital, a world in which everyone was sick and wounded. For decades and even for centuries after the last shot had been fired the survivors would go on dying because of a quarrel whose origins they and their descendants would have probably forgotten long ago.

The monumental municipal buildings are not Hiroshima's memorial, but the survivors whose skin, blood, and genes are branded with the memory of 'that day'. They are the first victims of an entirely new sort of war, which cannot be ended by an armistice or a peace-treaty, a 'war without end' which, reaching forward from the present, embraces the future as well in its circle of destruction.

3

A man who lives in Hiroshima for any length of time will one day fall victim to the 'vision of ruins'. Behind the white façades of the new buildings he will see the tragic, pitiful, twisted girders; the neon lights will fade and only broken glass and trailing wires will remain; the fresh green trees will be blackened and burned, the broad streets scattered with rubble and ash. In the 'new Hiroshima' a man develops an ear for the undertones of fear and morbidity that the clatter of the new buildings now going up cannot smother. For fear and horror are constantly forcing their way into the city's daily life.

Almost every day the newspapers here publish some item about an 'atomic tragedy'. Most of these, to tell the truth, are the same story that we already know so well, and arouse scarcely any conscious attention. But again and again something will happen to shock even the indifferent. For example, there was the story of the thirteen-year-old schoolboy, Kenji Kajiyama. On 7 August 1945, that is to say the day after the disaster, his mother had left her home on the Island of Toyoshima, a fantastically beautiful place famous for its oranges, and had come to Hiroshima to look for the remains of her aunt. While digging in the rubble she had probably received a dose of radioactivity which, though not of great strength, was yet enough to damage the child in her womb, for she was five months pregnant.

Four months later Kenji was born, a perfectly healthy child. Thirteen years later he had to die, the victim of a catastrophe that had taken place before his birth.

There has recently been a sharp increase in the incidence of radiation sickness among those who had only come to Hiroshima after the dropping of the bomb. These cases of very long delayed action are, however, not the only puzzle confronting the Japanese doctors as a result of the bomb. In mid June 1959 a congress of specialists took place in Hiroshima at which the consequences of total bodily exposure to radioactivity were discussed. Dr Masanori Nakaizumi of Tokyo University then announced that the Hiroshima survivors must expect to be stricken by a wave of 'hitherto unidentified sicknesses'. In particular the incidence of boils (both harmless and malignant) had increased considerably. It was only now that the secondary consequences of atomic radiation were beginning to become apparent in large numbers: these included damage to the brain mechanism, to the heart, to the pulmonary organs, and to the circulation of the blood, as well as premature senility both physical and mental. At this Congress Dr Gensaku Oho, a doctor who had been practising in Hiroshima since 1938, and who had spent almost all his personal fortune in studying the biological results of the atomic bombing, produced a great deal of statistical evidence. With the help of students he had studied all the fatal cancer cases since 1951, and had established that the number of people dying of cancer in Hiroshima was considerably higher than in the rest of Japan.*

The number of cases of sickness directly attributable to the after-effects of the atomic bomb have thus been increasing rather than diminishing. Since April 1957 anybody so afflicted has been entitled to free medical treatment, yet to everybody's surprise the number of those applying for such aid in the first year after this new law came into force was only 23,000 'victims', that is to say less than a third of those entitled to the new benefits. What is the reason for this? Dr Kubo, the psychologist at Hiroshima University, has studied this problem and has questioned many hundreds of people awaiting treatment. The conclusion he has reached is that most of the atomic sick do not go to be examined because they are convinced that nothing can be done to help them. So, according to them, there is no point in wasting their time undergoing a treatment that will prove useless. For many of them the economic motive is decisive: most of the survivors simply cannot afford to spend days on end being examined in a clinic, for who will support their families while they are away? So precisely those who need treatment most urgently are staying away from the clinic.

4

Even in these circumstances there were individuals who, prizing the laws of humanity above the letter of inadequate man-made law, gave their help and by their example forced the authorities to pay closer attention to the financial needs of the 'atomic pariahs'. At the time of writing there are more than a dozen different charitable organizations active in Hiroshima, assisting those suffering from the radiation sickness and their families. They are

---

* In Hiroshima, between 1951 and 1958, the percentage of deaths due to cancer was 10·92 for men and 8·96 for women; in the rest of Japan the corresponding figures were 9·09 and 7·72.

hindered in this work by the fear lest they be exploited by persons simply feigning sickness; the result is that it takes so long, and involves so many problems, before financial assistance can be obtained that many a would-be applicant gives up and does not bother to go ahead with his application.

Nobody has so far got to the root of the problem, which is to move the atomic sick out of the slums in which they now putrefy and to instal them in a healthy, modern housing settlement. Despite all the current 'prosperity', the large sums that would be required for this have not been forthcoming.

In one of these crumbling *barraku* districts Ichiro and Tokie now live. The ship in which they both wished to sail to the Christmas Islands in 1957, in protest against the atomic tests, never in fact put to sea, for the leaders of the Japanese Anti-Atom Bomb Movement recoiled at the last moment from sending any of their followers to an atomic death.

So Ichiro Kawamoto and Tokie Uematsu were able to get married as they had planned, on Easter Sunday 1957. It was, they told me, a beautiful wedding, and many of their friends turned up to congratulate the bridegroom, who wore his old white gym shoes for the occasion.

'When we were alone together at last,' Kawamoto has said, 'I took Tokie's hand and we repeated once again our mutual promise that we did not wish to have any children. It was hard, but it has to be.'

Helping people whom society cannot or will not help – that is still today the principal task to which Ichiro and Tokie devote themselves.

'We have reached the conclusion,' says Tokie, 'that inhumanity begins with the contempt and neglect of the individual. The atomic weapon is the end product of this indifference towards the many individual, inexchangeable, and irreplaceable human beings. We must protest against the bomb. But that is not enough. In addition we wish to try to change, quite slowly, the attitude of man to man. Had the *Pikadon* never happened I should now be an average dancing teacher and I should certainly never have understood how much we still need one another, how much each of us needs every other human being.'

A new member has recently joined that large 'family' of people whom Ichiro and Tokie regard as their 'children': Kazuo M. It was owing to my colleague, Kaoru Ogura, that Kawamoto read part of my correspondence with the murderer. Without saying anything to us, he immediately set about seeing what could be done for that most unusual 'atomic victim'. He wrote to the solitary man, visited him in his prison together with Ogura, and brought him books to read. He has done more: he has taken the whole of the M. family beneath his wing. Since Kazuo's crime they had been shunned by all their neighbours.

I recently received a letter from Kazuo, in which he says:

'I have now learned how to set Braille. Should I ever be pardoned, I should like to work as a typesetter in a Braille printing works. Kawamoto will be by my side, if I am ever allowed to live outside again.'

This was written by the same human being who in 1945 'murdered' his reading primer, because he then thought that words could only lie. But since then the written word has shown him, first, the truth about himself, then friendship, and has finally given him the courage to start a new life.

5

The work that this book has entailed has thus ended by affecting the lives of its two principal characters. But that is not all. The author must admit that his efforts to understand Hiroshima's post-war story, and to commit this to paper, have also given a new meaning to his own life.

When I first visited Hiroshima I went there simply as a reporter who wished to write the interesting history of a foreign city. But the more deeply preoccupied I became with this story the more apparent it was to me that I could not remain outside and above it. For I too was and am part of that story.

As it happens, I too am a 'survivor'. If fate had not, in its inscrutable way, ruled otherwise, I should have died in one of the mass extermination camps of the Third Reich. And so, at the other end of the world, at the farthest extremity of Eastern Asia,

I was now looking for an answer to the question that my own life had posed for me.

The question is this:

'What have we, the survivors of the Second World War, so far done to justify our survival?' Like many others I had, for years on end, thoughtlessly accepted the fact that I had been spared. But then I met the atomic victims of Hiroshima. From them I received a warning of the new evil that menaces us all. Since then I know that we, the generation of those who 'got through', must devote our entire strength to ensuring that our children do not merely survive, as fortuitously as we did.

Let every man find his own way to fight for the preservation of life.

Only: this must be his most serious and even sacred task.

ACKNOWLEDGEMENTS

WITH THE AUTHOR'S THANKS

WHEN I left Japan with my notebooks, I came to an arrangement with a private teacher, Kaoru Ogura, that he should translate into English the notes made by some of the people I had interviewed. We then assumed that our work together would last for two or three months at the most; it has been going on for almost thirty-two months, and has grown into friendship. During this period Ogura has written me 213 letters, methodically numbered, in answer to my questions, and at my request has interviewed dozens of people in Hiroshima. In some cases I had established contacts which he has known how to deepen and enlarge between the author and those he questioned, so that my interviews have frequently become expanded into confessions. Unfortunately I have only been able to make use of a fraction of these written communications; had I printed them all, this book would have been eight times its present length. It is my hope that a research institute may be interested in safeguarding this material.

My thanks are due in the first instance to this ideal colleague, with whom, when first I was in Hiroshima, the indefatigable Willie Togashi, my guide and interpreter, put me in touch. It is not possible for me to express my gratitude to all those who have helped me by giving me information.

Here, at least, are a few of those whom I should like to thank:

PRINCIPAL SOURCES: Ichiro Kawamoto (Labourer), Kazuo M. (Prisoner in Hiroshima Prison), Tokie Kawamoto née Uematsu, Shinzo Hamai (Mayor of Hiroshima), Shogo Nagaoka (Director of the Atom Bomb Museum), Tsugio Kunitani (Judge in the Family Court), William A. Togashi (Librarian), Kiyoshi Kikkawa and wife (Souvenir salesman), Rihei Numata and all the archivists on the *Chugoku Shimbun*, Professor Floyd Schmoe of Seattle, Norman Cousins of New York.

DOCTORS: Dr M. Hachiya, Dr F. Shigeto, Dr T. Harada, Dr G. Oho, Dr G. Ouchi, Dr M. Konuma, Dr R. Okabe, Dr N. Kaneko, Dr H. Kikuchi (all of Hiroshima); Dr J. Robinson (Chicago), Dr G. N. Hazlehurst* (Phoenix), Dr Robert C. Holmes (New York), Dr G.

* Contacted by post only.

Muth (Frankfurt), Dr R. Beck* (Karlsruhe), Dr H. Melching* (Karlsruhe), Dr O. Messerschmidt* (Sonthofen), Dr H. Schmidt (Offenbach).

HIROSHIMA UNIVERSITY: Dr T. Morito (Rector), Dr K. Sakuma (Physics), Dr S. Nakano (Sociology), Y. Kubo (Psychology), Y. Moritaki (Education), F. Kanazawa (Jurisprudence), H. Yamanaka (Librarian).

ATOMIC BOMB CASUALTY COMMISSION: Dr R. K. Cannan (Chairman of the National Research Council, National Academy of Sciences, Washington), Dr G. Darling (Director), Dr H. Maki (Deputy Director), Dr S. Matsumoto (Sociology), Mr M. E. Rappaport (Administration).

HIROSHIMA MUNICIPAL ADMINISTRATION: M. Nude (Public Relations Office), S. Morihiro (Municipal Historian), Y. Matsuo (Sick Chest for Atomic Victims), T. Yamamoto (Tourist Office), S. Hattori (Trade), S. Wada (Construction Office), K. Kamei (General Information).

CHURCHMEN AND MISSIONARIES: Rev. Y. Tamai, Rev. K. Tanimoto, Miss M. Macmillan, Miss M. Jones.

WRITERS: H. Agawa, Y. Ohta, Y. Matsuoka (all of Tokyo), K. Tanabe (Hiroshima), E. Toll-Morris, I. Morris (Paris), H. Strauss (New York).

MISCELLANEOUS: A. Foutohi (Director of the American Cultural Centre, Hiroshima, at present in Washington), M. Fujita, F. Kawasaki (Hiroshima Prison Administration), Professor Mrs Nakano (Head of the Atomic Orphans' Association), H. Yokoyama (Hiroshima Maidens Project), S. Kano (Actor and Theatrical Director, at present in Chicago), D. Honma (Kazuo M.'s Counsel for the Defence), K. Matsue (Communist Town Councillor), Y. Nakata (State Attorney), M. Mino (Landlord), Y. Yanagawa (The Musica Tea-room), F. Kamei (Film director), Y. Fukuii (Painter), and a great number of 'survivors'.

The following were kind enough to read my manuscript and give me valuable advice, and I should therefore particularly like to thank: Ursula Ibler, Günther Anders, Gregor von Rezzori, Walter Schneider, and William M. Treichlinger.

* Contacted by post only.

BIBLIOGRAPHY*

MANUSCRIPTS

Diary and Recollections of Kazuo M.

Diary and Recollections of Ichiro Kawamoto.

Diary and Recollections of Tokie Uematsu.

Shinzo Hamai: *Genbaku go Ju nen*, *Shisei Hiwa* (Ten Years after the A-bomb. The Unknown History of City Politics).

Shogo Nagaoka: *Haikyo ni tacni* (On the Ruins).

Stenograph of the Kazuo M. Case (in the archives of the State Attorney, Hiroshima).

NEWSPAPERS AND PERIODICALS

Chugoku Shimbun, 21 August 1945–6 August 1959 (morning and evening editions).

Ayumi No. 9 ('Radioactivity and Marriage'), 15 January 1958.

Japan Times, 6 August 1958.

Shukan Shincho, 12 August 1957.

Chuo Koron, August 1958, August 1959.

Sekai, April 1958.

Asahi Shimbun, 1 August 1958.

Asahi Graphic, Special Edition, 17 August 1952.

'*No More Hiroshimas*', Tokyo, 1956–9.

Life Magazine, 15 September 1947, 29 September 1952.

Time Magazine, 8 April 1957.

Saturday Review of Literature, September 1945–9.

REPORTS AND PAMPHLETS

Semi-annual Reports of the Atomic Bomb Casualty Commission, Hiroshima 1950–7.

Y. Scott Matsumoto: *Patient Rapport in a Foreign Country*, A.B.C.C., Hiroshima, undated.

Hiroshima shisei yoran (The Hiroshima City Almanack), 1951–7.

Hiroshima no heiwa undo (The Peace Movement in Hiroshima), 1957.

Lara – a Friend in Need (A report on the Activities in Japan of the Licensed Agencies for Relief in Asia), Tokyo, 1953.

* I have not included medical books in this bibliography, since extensive bibliographies dealing with publications about the radiation sickness in Hiroshima are available elsewhere.

BOOKS (SELECTED)

Michihiko Hachiya: *Hiroshima Nikki* (My Hiroshima Diary), German Edition, Freiburg, 1957.

Ken Doman: *Hiroshima*, with 128 pages of plates, Tokyo, 1958.

Seiji Imahori: *Gensuibaku jidai* (The Age of the A- and the H-bomb), Hiroshima, 1959.

Chugoku Shimbun 65 nenshi (The History of the *Chugoku* Press for 65 Years), Hiroshima, 1957.

Tomoe Yamashiro et al.: *Genbaku ni ikite* (We experienced the Atom Bomb), anthology, Hiroshima, 1952.

Sankichi Toge et al.: *A-bomb Anthology*, Hiroshima, 1952.

Furyo shudan no kenkyu (Studies of Neglected Youth), Hiroshima, 1950.

Genbaku hignai no jisso to higaisha no kurushimi (The Situation at this Moment of the Atomic Victims and their Sufferings), published by The Japan A- and H-bomb Council, August, 1959.

John Hersey: *Hiroshima*, New York, 1946.

Günther Anders: *Der Mann auf der Brücke* (The Man on the Bridge), Munich, 1959.

Floyd Schmoe: *Japanese Journey*, Seattle, 1952.

Fernand Gigon: *Formula for Death*, London, 1959.

Jean Stoetzel: *Without the Chrysanthemum and the Sword*, Unesco publication, London – Paris, 1955.

R. Swearingen and P. Langer: *Red Flag over Japan*, Harvard Univ. Press, Cambridge, Mass., 1952.

Hugh Borton et al.: *Japan between East and West*, New York, 1957.

Ralph E. Lapp: *The Voyage of the Lucky Dragon*, New York, 1957.

LIST OF PERSONS

KATASHIMA	Reporter with the Japanese news agency *Domei*
KAWAMOTO, ICHIRO	Fitter, later casual labourer, friend of humanity
KAWASAKI, F.	Education director, Hiroshima prison
KAZUO M.	Born 1931, a painter, follows many professions, found guilty of murder
KIHARA	Member of the Japanese Diet, first Mayor after 6 August 1945
KIKKAWA, KIYOSHI	Souvenir salesman
KITAMURA	Head of Health Department
KURIYA	Mayor before 1945, killed by bomb
KURIHARA, SADAKO	Poetess
KUSANO, DR	Doctor
KUSUNOSE	Governor of Hiroshima Province
'KUTSUHEI'	Protector of four atomic orphans, Kawamoto's first real friend
'KUTSUKEN'	Kutsuhei's fifteen-year-old brother
KYOTO	Workmate of Kazuo M.
MACMILLAN, MARY	Methodist missionary
MACNAUGHTON, GEN.	U.S. Army
MARUGUMA	Head of firm for demolishing and transporting houses
MASON, COL.	C.O. Special Unit, U.S. Army
MATSUDA, SHIGAJIRO	Director of the Toyo Kogyo Factory
MATSUMARA, MAJ.-GEN.	Chief of Staff of the Province
MATSUMOTO, TAKIZO	Member of Diet, long resident in U.S.A.
'MINDANAO'	Orphan, looked after by Kutsuhei
MINO, MOTOJI	Brothel proprietor
MIYAKE, JUI	Blood specialist
MONTGOMERY, LIEUT.	American reconstruction adviser
MORI, YOSHIAMORO	Young gymnastics instructor
MORIZAKI, TAKASHI	Counsel for the Prosecution
MOYA	Painter, portraitist of the atomic sick
MULLER, HERMANN J.	'The father of modern genetics'
NAGAOKA, PROF. SHOGO	Geologist, Hiroshima University, later Director, The Atomic Museum
NAKA, MIDORI	One of the most beautiful and famous Japanese actresses
NAKAIZUMI, DR MASANORI	Radiation specialist, Tokyo University
NAKAMURA, TOTARO	Chairman, Chamber of Commerce

TSUKUSHIMO	Language teacher
TSUZUKI, MASAO	Japan's foremost radiation specialist
UEMATSU	Smith, Tokie's father
UEMATSU, TOKIE 'Miss Woodstick'	Friend, and later wife, of Ichiro Kawamoto
WATANABE, PROF. ZAN	Hiroshima University
WILLIAMS, MR	MacArthur's liaison officer with the Japanese Diet
YAMAJI	Black-market operator, murdered by Kazuo M.
YAMAMOTO, H.	Chairman of the City Council
YASUJI	Kazuo M.'s closest friend
YOSHIDA	Prime Minister of Japan
YUKIKO	Daughter of demolition chief Maruguma

*Some other books published
by Penguins are described
on the following
pages*

HAS MAN A FUTURE?

Bertrand Russell

S 206

What spurs a famous philosopher, at the age of 89, to plunge into a political campaign of civil disobedience and to go to prison for his beliefs? The answer is an urgent concern for the continuance of the human race.

In the million years during which man has lived on this planet, he must have survived many hazards. Can he hope to survive a nuclear war? Here lies the most agonizing question of our era.

Refuting the theory that scientists have been the willing tools of governments, Bertrand Russell exposes the hypocrisy of official attitudes to nuclear weapons. The one hope for man, he proclaims, is to be found in world government. He maps out a reasoned scheme in this book, and details the practical steps we can take towards it today.

This moving pronouncement – in its admiration of man's past achievements, in the despair engendered by his present plight, in its unquenchable concern for those who follow – is no less than Bertrand Russell's living testament to mankind.

A cloth-bound edition of this work is published by
George Allen & Unwin Ltd

TORTURE: CANCER OF DEMOCRACY

Pierre Vidal-Naquet

S 215

In June 1957 Maurice Audin, a brilliant young mathematician, was seized without warrant by French paratroopers, tortured as a matter of routine, and almost certainly murdered a few days later. For in Algeria torture was employed as an instrument of intelligence.

If you feel inclined to say: 'But it can't happen here', you should read this closely documented book. In it Pierre Vidal-Naquet traces the course of an ugly regression whereby torture, once re-admitted as an instrument of policy, tended to establish itself in a general conspiracy of guilt and silence throughout the French administration, the law, and the Press.

But the shadow does not only lie on France. We, too, set a foot on the same path in Kenya and Cyprus. One must ask whether any democracy can stoop to such barbarities and survive? Or must brutality and the use of torture inescapably lead to policies of hugger-mugger and the ultimate gagging of truth?

THE A6 MURDER: Regina v. James Hanratty

Louis Blom-Cooper

S 216

In the early hours of 23 August 1960 a young car-driver was shot and killed on a lay-by on the A6: and his companion was raped, shot, and left for dead. The search for the killer led to James Hanratty who was convicted by a jury of the capital murder of Gregsten after the longest murder trial in English criminal history.

R. v. Hanratty is a classical demonstration of the strengths and weaknesses of the English criminal system: the publicity at magistrates' proceedings, the publication of Identi-kits, the prejudicial nature of the opening speech for the Crown, the total exclusion of hearsay evidence – all these and many other issues of public importance were spotlit by the prosecution of Hanratty and are here examined by the legal correspondent of the *Observer*.

Above all, the author shows that the strangest features of the case, for example that in all the twenty-one days of trial the jury heard not one word of Hanratty's mental history, stem directly from our accusatorial trial which the author compares with the continental inquisitorial system.

Mr Blom-Cooper offers a lucid, stimulating survey of just those features of English criminal justice which the man in the street will want to think about the next time an identification parade is held after the publication of an Identi-kit, the next time the magistrates' proceedings are blazoned across the front page, the next time the jury ask for the transcript of the trial, the next time the defendant is revealed to be a psychopath *after* the jury have convicted him.

COMMON SENSE ABOUT SMOKING

C. M. Fletcher, Harvey Cole, Lena Jeger, and Christopher Wood

S 213

Every twenty-five minutes somebody in Great Britain dies of lung cancer. The report of the Royal College of Physicians recently showed an unmistakeable connexion between cigarette smoking and this terrible disease.

In this book Dr Fletcher, the secretary of the Royal College of Physicians committee on smoking and air pollution which produced the report *Smoking and Health*, gives a concise account of all the available medical evidence. Mr Cole, an economist, asks and answers such questions as: how much do we spend on cigarettes? does the Government depend on tobacco tax? Mrs Lena Jeger discusses such social aspects of the problem as how our young people can be helped over the convention that the cigarette is a natural extension of the human face. Finally, some methods of fighting the habit are described by Dr Wood, who directs a non-smokers' clinic at the Central Middlesex Hospital.

In Britain four times as many people die every year of lung cancer as are killed on the roads. It is high time we applied some common sense to smoking.

PENGUIN SCIENCE SURVEY 1963 A and B

Arthur Garratt; S. A. Barnett and Anne McLaren

1924, 1925

Penguin Science Survey 1963 A contains the following papers on the physical sciences:

'The Upper Atmosphere' by Sir Harrie Massey; 'The Cosmological Problem' by R. A. Lyttleton; 'Optical Astronomy: The Present and the Future' by Patrick Moore; 'Physics of the Oceans' by G. E. R. Deacon; 'Synthetic Fibres' by J. R. Whinfield; 'Plastics in Perspective' by C. W. Welch and M. Kaufman; 'Non-Metallic Materials' by Sir Harry Melville; 'Computers: A Progress Review' by K. L. Smith; 'Optical Illusion and Scientific Measurement' by S. Tolansky; 'Science Teaching in 1962' by H. F. Boulind; 'The Behaviour of Materials at Supersonic Speeds' by John Brunton; 'Three Books on Physics and Astronomy' by Arthur Garratt; 'Some Physical Units and Constants' by P. H. Bigg.

Penguin Science Survey 1963 B contains the following papers on biology:

'Scientists and Writers: The Growing Cleavage' by N. W. Pirie; Matters of Life and Death: 1 'Radiation' by Barbara Holmes; 2 'Congenital Malformations' by J. H. Edwards; 3 'Chromosomes and Disease in Man' by D. G. Harnden, Patricia A. Jacobs, and W. M. Court Brown; 4 'World Health' by B. B. Waddy; 5 'Contraception in its Modern Context' by A. S. Parkes; 6 'Family Planning in East Asia' by Barbara Cadbury; 'Culturing Animal Cells' by John Paul; 'Warts' by Michael Stoker; 'Cell Surgery' by T. R. Elsdale; 'New Light on Tissue Transplantation' by J. G. Howard and Donald Michie; 'Biological Rhythms and Self-Regulating Mechanisms' by R. J. Goldacre; 'Food from the Sea' by C. M. Yonge; 'The World of the Chimpanzee' by Desmond Morris; 'The Present State of Consciousness' by J. Schorstein; 'Life and Mind as Physical Realities' by Professor J. B. S. Haldane.

MAN AND ENERGY

A. R. Ubbelohde

A 600

It is the control and use of 'dead' energy – whether from coal, oil, or uranium – which is the distinctive mark of modern civilization. The machine (powered by men or animals) is comparatively ancient. It was not until about A.D. 1700 that men began to move slowly forward from the employment of wind and water as prime movers towards the use of steam and atomic energy. With unlimited power now at our command, Utopia has yielded to Tektopia in human dreams. Technical perfection, however, is accompanied by such threats as dislocation of labour and total destruction in war.

The Professor of Thermodynamics at the Imperial College of Science and Technology surveys in these pages the shifting relationship between man and energy, in history and in the new era. The growth of man's power is illustrated with many woodcuts and drawings and his final chapters on the science of thermodynamics, with its two famous laws, explain very lucidly the theoretical advances which have allowed men to enslave the energy latent in matter.

THE BOUNDARIES OF SCIENCE

Magnus Pyke

A 593

Do the minds of scientists impose a definite limit on the possibilities of science? And are certain things outside the province of science?

Dr Pyke begins his inquiry by discussing the limits traditionally fixed for the different sciences, such as chemistry, physics, and biology. Then, in a wide survey of their latest findings, he shows how interdependent they are. For the tools of physics are being used in the chemistry of living matter while atomic research modifies the concepts of astronomy, and the idea of evolution is being applied to the structure of molecules.

Finally the author turns to the future. Are there, he asks, limits to our understanding of the atom? Is it likely that we shall ever be able to create living organisms? What, in fact, are the boundaries of science?

'Dr Pyke has now established a reputation, in broadcasting no less than in print, as an exact and sympathetic interpreter of the sciences, and his latest work can only enhance the reputation he has already won' – *The Times Literary Supplement*

NOT FOR SALE IN THE U.S.A.

THE COMPREHENSIVE SCHOOL

Robin Pedley

A 613

Nearly everyone interested in education today wants to abolish the '11+' examination, but few people are clear what the alternatives are.

The best alternative is the comprehensive school, and in this new appraisal the Reader in Education at the Leicester University School of Education gives a clear and critical picture of the comprehensive school as it exists in England and Wales today. Dr Pedley first describes just what the '11+' is and does. Then, after dispelling the bogey that comprehensive schools need at least two thousand pupils in order to function, he goes on to demonstrate, by statistics, that those in existence are already rivalling the grammar schools in academic achievements. Finally, and most important, he argues that a good comprehensive school can both focus and mirror a community as can no other school.

Of all our educational establishments the comprehensive school is the least understood. This book, which contains a glossary of educational terms and a list of comprehensive schools, offers to interested readers – especially parents – all the facts.

THE INSECURE OFFENDERS:
Rebellious Youth in the Welfare State

T. R. Fyvel

A 608

The term 'juvenile delinquency' scarcely describes the world-wide malaise of youth which beset the 1950s and which – although Teddy Boys are now almost period pieces – continues into this decade. What causes this rebellion of youth in a Welfare State?

T. R. Fyvel's survey is in the tradition of George Orwell. He conjures up for us a world of sharp clothes, gang life, coffee, motorbikes, juke-boxes, pin-tables, cafés, and cinemas, and adroitly relates the toe-tapping young non-conformers of today to the conditions of an affluent society which for them is little better than a dead end. This is incomparably the best study of a grave post-war phenomenon in Britain.

'An admirable book – balanced, humane, perceptive and thorough' – *New Statesman*

'A deeply sympathetic, highly informed and thoroughly positive examination of what is, along with the Bomb, the post-war world's greatest problem . . . a valuable and moving contribution' – Wolf Mankowitz in the *Sunday Times*

'As an account of all that it means to be out of step in contemporary society his book deserves to be widely read for its detachment and humanity' – *The Economist*

NOT FOR SALE IN THE U.S.A.

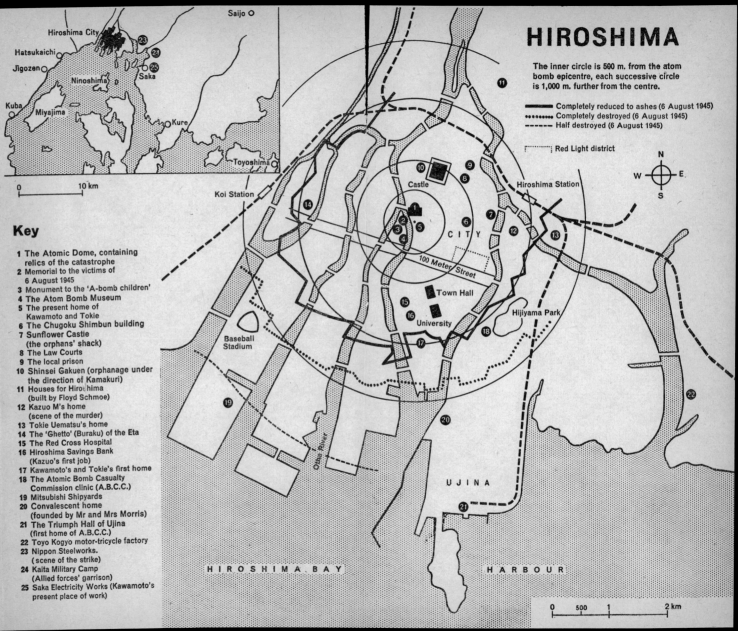

HIROSHIMA

The inner circle is 500 m. from the atom bomb epicentre, each successive circle is 1,000 m. further from the centre.

──────── Completely reduced to ashes (6 August 1945)
•••••••• Completely destroyed (6 August 1945)
- - - - - Half destroyed (6 August 1945)

┊┊┊┊ Red Light district

Key

1 The Atomic Dome, containing relics of the catastrophe
2 Memorial to the victims of 6 August 1945
3 Monument to the 'A-bomb children'
4 The Atom Bomb Museum
5 The present home of Kawamoto and Tokie
6 The Chugoku Shimbun building
7 Sunflower Castle (the orphans' shack)
8 The Law Courts
9 The local prison
10 Shinsei Gakuen (orphanage under the direction of Kamakuri)
11 Houses for Hiroshima (built by Floyd Schmoe)
12 Kazuo M's home (scene of the murder)
13 Tokie Uematsu's home
14 The 'Ghetto' (Buraku) of the Eta
15 The Red Cross Hospital
16 Hiroshima Savings Bank (Kazuo's first job)
17 Kawamoto's and Tokie's first home
18 The Atomic Bomb Casualty Commission clinic (A.B.C.C.)
19 Mitsubishi Shipyards
20 Convalescent home (founded by Mr and Mrs Morris)
21 The Triumph Hall of Ujina (first home of A.B.C.C.)
22 Toyo Kogyo motor-tricycle factory
23 Nippon Steelworks. (scene of the strike)
24 Kaita Military Camp (Allied forces' garrison)
25 Saka Electricity Works (Kawamoto's present place of work)

Saijo
Hiroshima City
Hatsukaichi
Jigozen
Ninoshima
Saka
Kuba
Miyajima
Kure
Toyoshima

0   10 km

Koi Station
Castle
Hiroshima Station
CITY
100 Meter Street
Town Hall
Hijiyama Park
Baseball Stadium
University
Ota River
UJINA
HIROSHIMA BAY
HARBOUR

0   500   1   2 km